WOMEN'S LETTERS IN WARTIME
1450 – 1945

WOMEN'S LETTERS
IN WARTIME
1450–1945

Edited and introduced by

EVA FIGES

Pandora
An Imprint of HarperCollins*Publishers*

Pandora
An Imprint of HarperCollins*Publishers*
77–85 Fulham Palace Road,
Hammersmith, London W6 8JB
1160 Battery Street,
San Francisco, California 94111–1213

First published by Pandora Press 1993
1 3 5 7 9 10 8 6 4 2

The acknowledgements on pages 5–6 constitute
an extension of this copyright page.

Eva Figes asserts the moral right to
be identified as the author of this work

A catalogue record for this book
is available from the British Library

ISBN 0 04 440755 6

Phototypeset by Harper Phototypesetters Limited,
Northampton, England
Printed and bound in Great Britain by
Hartnolls Limited, Bodmin, Cornwall

TEXT ACKNOWLEDGEMENTS

The author and the publisher would like to thank the following for their kind permission to reproduce material in this anthology:

The letters of Margaret Paston from *The Paston Letters* published by Everyman Library in 1924; the letters of Jane Lovejoy reprinted by kind permission of the Hayne and Bragg Archive in the Dorset County Record Office, ref. D/HAB: F17; the letters of Frances Nelson from *Nelson's Letters to his Wife* published by Routledge & Kegan Paul in 1958; the letters of Florence Nightingale reprinted by kind permission of the British Library Board, copyright © Henry Bonham-Carter Will Trust; the letters of Emma Hamilton from *The Life and Letters of Emma Hamilton* by Hugh Tours published by Victor Gollancz; the letters of Fanny Burney reprinted from *The Journals and Letters of Fanny Burney* vol. 8 edited by Peter Hughes with Joyce Henlow, Althea Douglas, and Patricia Hawkins (1980) by permission of Oxford University Press, copyright © Oxford University Press, 1980; the letter of Elizabeth Mackenzie reprinted by kind permission of the Trustees of the National Library of Scotland; the letter of Annie Cecilia Eld reprinted by kind permission of Staffordshire Record Office, Staffordshire County Council; the letter(s) from Queen Victoria, Charlotte Canning and from Florence Nightingale to Queen Victoria all reprinted by the gracious permission of Her Majesty The Queen; the letters of Queen Victoria are published in *Letters*, Series 2, vol III; the letters of Minnie Wood from *From Minnie with Love* by Minnie Wood and Jane Vansittart reprinted by kind permission of William Heinemann Ltd; the letters of Isabel Gore and Babbs van der Byl reprinted by kind permission of the owner and Clwyd Record Office; the letter of Mrs E Spear reprinted with the kind permission of Polly H Bargh; the letter of Nancy Isobel Buchanan reprinted with the kind permission of John Buchanan. The following have granted permission for their own letters to be reprinted: Eleonora Pemberton, Nancy Bosanquet, the Honourable Mrs Whitehead (aka Lucia Lawson) and Beatrice Carter.

CONTENTS

INTRODUCTION

In the age of the telephone we say that 'the art of letter-writing' is dead, but most letters, written by the majority of people, were not written as art but as a necessary form of communication during periods of separation. The self-consciously artful is often tiresome, and is most obvious in certain types of letter, the formal expression of regard or regret. The real art in a genuine letter, one that is not written from a sense of duty, or with half an eye on posterity, is very hard to pin down. It involves self-expression, that is, a willingness to express what one is, and does, and thinks as though ink and paper were no barrier, but as open as the atmosphere which carries our voices when we speak.

Many letters written by ordinary people, undistinguished by rank or accomplishment, and sent for mundane reasons, can be very tedious to the snooping eyes of posterity. Legal matters involving property, household accounts, or births and deaths in the locality, even the most avid appetite for the trivia of the past – and I confess to being endlessly curious about the nature and content of lost lives – would pall after a while. Perhaps only love and war can raise the temperature of life sufficiently to give real life and interest to letters written by lost generations, and the vicissitudes of war have more infinite variety than even the most consuming passion.

War not only brings separation, which is a necessary prerequisite for writing letters, but, like love, heightens our experience of life. Everything has a new urgency as people are expected to face new dangers, new challenges, and unexpected responsibilities. Life is suddenly far from ordinary, but this very fact also increases our hunger for the familiar. A mother, writing to her son in North Africa from an English village, tells him that the daffodils are out, or that the cat has given birth to kittens. A nurse, writing home of wounded and dying soldiers, mentions a clear sky full of stars or asks for news of home.

War letters are fascinating because they tell us of great historic events seen at ground level, from an individual point of view. There are many angles to every war, and no war is quite like any other. So a collection of war letters provides an infinity of glimpses into the past. But for me the most enduring fascination of my task as an anthologist was the human factor, the constant juxtaposition of the personal and the impersonal, the intertwining of the historic with the commonplace. Amidst the chaos, the carnage, the tedium of war, the search for a nice cup of tea, a dry bed to sleep in, or the sound of music when the gunfire stops.

My interest in women's wartime letters dates back several years, to when I was reading primary texts whilst researching for a novel entitled *The Seven Ages*. The novel seeks to show a thousand years of English history from women's point of view, and war is one of the predominant themes. Whilst researching the civil war period in the seventeenth century I was captivated by the letters of Brilliana Harley, written whilst her husband was far from home, engaged in the Parliamentary cause, and she was left – quite literally – holding the fort. A dutiful wife and devoted mother, Brilliana was no heroine in the obvious sense: she wanted to abandon the estate and join her husband in London, but was told to look after his interests at Brompton Castle, which was twice besieged, though she had died by the time the second siege took place.

Most of the surviving letters are written to her young son, sent to study at Oxford, and a whole family seemed to come alive under my eyes. Written in the heat of the moment, with no thought of posterity peering over her shoulder, the letters were both touching and immediate, full of the vivid details of life being lived, the usual and the unusual, which is manna from heaven for the novelist. I cannot say that any one of my characters in *The Seven Ages* is Brilliana, but an entire chapter was coloured and brought to life as a result of reading her letters.

I said that Brilliana Harley was no heroine. Perhaps it would be fairer to say she was a true heroine, in that she did not seek out danger, but faced up to it when it was forced upon her. To do your duty despite fear is braver than to act devoid of fear. I stress this because I want to make it clear from the outset that, in collecting the contents of this anthology, I did not have a crude and simplistic feminist agenda. I certainly wished to bring women to the foreground, to let them have their say, but it was no part of my purpose to present women as swashbuckling heroines on the one hand, or as saintly healers and peacemakers on the other.

War has always been seen as a male activity and, when this has been possible, men have gloried in it. They award themselves medals, put up statues in their own honour, and name city squares and railway stations in commemoration of great victories. Women are seen as cheerleaders on the sidelines, or as comforters, standing by with cups of tea and bandages. Often they are perceived as silly and frivolous, enjoying tea-parties and fashion parades whilst men are dying far away. Feminists often try to distance their own gender from the whole awful business, and remind the world of enlightened women who have attempted to put a stop to bloody conflicts. It is true that women convened a conference during the first world war to try and stop the fighting, but it is also true that other women were handing out white feathers to men not in uniform.

The human race has always been a community of two sexes, living and working together, and for the most part they see their interests in common. Women, willy-nilly, have always been involved in war; it has touched their lives in a thousand different ways, and involved hardship, deprivation and grief. They also serve who only sit at home and wait, and keeping the home fires burning, the business going, the children healthy and the house safe is not exactly an easy option at the best of times, and at the worst of times, during the London Blitz, for instance, absent men worried more about their families than they did for their own safety. But very many women have, whether by chance or choice, found themselves more directly involved, and more actively engaged, in all sorts of different ways.

These pages will show the variety of that engagement, and their thoughts on what was going on around them. For each conflict involves more than merely personal emotions, fears for those we love, and so on, but a whole bedrock of beliefs, religious and political. It would be naïve to suppose that, because they took little or no part in public affairs, women did not share the ideology which justified the conflict in which they found themselves directly or indirectly involved. For the most part they did. Brilliana Harley knew that God was on the side of Parliament. Charlotte Canning, wife of India's Governor-General during the Indian Mutiny, knew that the British were bringing civilization to backward natives. Some women, in these pages, express ideas which seem to us 'ahead of their time', enlightened, liberal, or whatever. Frances, the long-suffering wife of Lord Nelson, for instance, understood that if seamen were driven to mutiny, their officers were to blame. But such exceptional beings are to be found amongst men too.

There are heroines amongst these pages. Florence Nightingale, strong-minded and clear of purpose, a genius at organizing (not the tender lady of the lamp, the stereotypical ministering angel) is certainly one of them. Those who followed in her footsteps, to nurse the wounded and dying in conditions of great difficulty, are also heroines in my eyes, and their unknown names, a very few, are brought to light in this book, their thoughts and impressions unexpectedly revealed. For these women certainly did not regard themselves as heroines, though many realized they were living through a great adventure, and their intimate letters were hurriedly scribbled in a spare moment to reassure family or friends. The fact that war was often an exciting opportunity for a young woman to escape the tedium imposed upon her by social convention must not be forgotten, and many of the letters, particularly those written during the first world war, bear this out.

There are also a few women in this collection who are famous, and for reasons which have nothing to do with any war. Fanny Burney, for instance, found herself caught up in Napoleon's return from Elba, the frantic Hundred Days, culminating in Waterloo, because of her marriage to a general in the royalist French army, and her breathless letters reflect both her literary personality and the panic of those weeks. But, for the most part, the women represented in this book are ordinary people caught up in extraordinary situations. Wives who followed their husbands to India or South Africa, women who drove an ambulance or worked in a service canteen, or a mother anxious about her son, sending news of home. A few are famous by virtue of birth or marriage. Queen Victoria took a very active interest in any wars conducted by her people. Henrietta Maria, in her efforts to keep her husband Charles I on the English throne, sent him all the wrong advice before fleeing to her native France. Famous or unknown, women are as much creatures of their period as men, and the reader will find sentiments expressed here which are often offensive to modern sensibilities. I am not interested in doctoring the past, in censorship by selection, in order to pander to political correctness or women's self-enhancement. On the contrary, I am interested in being truthful, in showing the many-sidedness of human nature. I revel in that many-sidedness. There are silly women here, feather-brained society ladies, snobs, racists even. But all are richly human too, capable of affection, of humour and, most important of all, of writing engaging letters that involve the reader, and not merely the person for whom they were originally intended.

Wherever possible I have tried to select, not just one or two letters by a particular woman, but a whole group of them. This will enable the reader to get truly involved, to see the writer as a rounded individual and get some insight into the life she was living, her hopes and fears, her attitudes and social background, her family ties and leisure pursuits. When a large bundle of letters has survived I have tried to choose the most interesting, without exposing the reader to the tedium of repetition. For the most part I have succeeded; where I have not I hope the reader will bear with me, and agree that the policy was worthwhile. It was often very hard to choose.

For the same reason I have also followed a policy of publishing letters in their entirety or not at all. I do not think the collection is any the poorer for this, it has merely made my own task more difficult for, in the case of published letters, I have now and then had to get sight of the original manuscript. The first letter by Margaret Paston is the only exception.

I did not wish to collect high-minded sentiments on any particular conflict, or truncated extracts of description. I have to admit that a trail of dots in any published book always leaves me full of frustrated curiosity. War is not experienced in isolation. Usually it goes on for months or years, and gets inextricably bound up with our ordinary lives, one way or another. If, like me, you were a child during the second world war, which went on for six years, then it *was* ordinary life. Other wars, or series of wars which were really one and the same, have dragged on for much longer. Wives did not see their husbands for years, children did not recognize their fathers. Even on the battle-front, those directly involved have thoughts of home, often very painful. Indeed, it is often in just such situations that the values of 'normal' life are most intensely present, treasured most dearly, and this comes through in many letters. Even when a letter written from a field hospital in 1917 ends with a mundane request for woollen gloves or bars of chocolate it tells us so much. Many, many letters end with requests of this kind. The daily reality of war is so often physical discomfort, making do in alien, makeshift surroundings.

I have tried, as far as is possible, to get as representative a selection as possible in terms of social class, but here there was a difficulty. Women's literacy is fairly recent, and did not quickly percolate down to the working class. Indeed, the habit of expressing oneself naturally and easily on paper seems to be confined, until very recently, to the middle and upper ranks of society. (No doubt some would say that universal literacy is still a pipe dream.) Eleonora Pemberton, who served as a nurse in France during the first world war, put it like this in 1914:

> The longer I am here, the more sorry I am for the poor Tommies' home people. Officers have so many more means of communicating with them and setting their minds at rest; they can tip orderlies to telegraph for them – often their wives can come out or friends are asked to look them up; but Tommy is

just one of the herd; he has neither pens, ink nor paper, even if he feels well enough to write and as many of them have said when I have asked them – "I'm not much good at writing, Sister – *you* write for me". Almost every one I have asked has preferred to have it done for him and has not even been willing, or I suppose able, to dictate his own letter, but has preferred a stranger like myself to say whatever they chose! It seems strange, doesn't it? but I suppose it is a different level of education. In most cases they had hardly anything in the way of *news* to suggest and yet when one persevered one could drag quite an interesting story of personal exploits out of them.

This perceptive comment (which reminds me rather forcefully of many a creative-writing class!) highlights a problem for the anthologist. Even as late as the second world war, when primary education was universal and when all women, one way or another, were actively involved in the war, and when the government encouraged regular correspondence between the various battle-fronts and home, even for this period the archives of the Imperial War Museum, donated by the general public, contain relatively few letters written by working-class women, and the few there are tend to be sparse on content. The ability to write an informative and chatty letter which will engage the recipient and, years later, the prying eyes of posterity, seems for the most part to be an art form of the educated and more leisured classes. Such letters are indicative, not merely of education, but also of inner confidence. Having said which, I hasten to add that I have read many, many letters which are literate, informative, and deadly dull. Happily, I was able to exclude these in favour of more lively letters from the same area of conflict since, for the first and second world wars, there is a good deal of surviving material to choose from.

The choice of material which has survived is limited by yet another factor. Whether or not their lives were restricted to the domestic sphere, women have always been considered less important than men. And, despite the lip-service paid to the angel in the house, domestic duties have been looked upon with open or secret contempt. Whatever work women do, as Margaret Mead noted in another social context, it is less highly regarded than the tasks men perform. As a result, the letters written by women were often thought not worth preserving. Love letters, such as those by Dorothy Osborne, might be preserved by a doting recipient, other letters, like those written by Margaret Paston, survive as part of a family archive. The letters of reigning Queens were of course kept, as were those written by women with an established literary reputation. Henrietta Maria, Queen Victoria and Fanny Burney fall into these categories, and are all represented here. Florence Nightingale was regarded as a national heroine from the time she went to the Crimea, so her letters were preserved by their recipients. As she was also an indefatigable correspondent there is scarcely an archive in the land without a sample of her handwriting!

But the comparative paucity of women's letters reflects their standing in society. As usual, they are hidden from history. I found this very early on, when first exploring the shelves of the London Library. A volume purporting to be the correspondence of the Duchess of Marlborough was full of letters written by the Duke. I tracked down the letters written by Frances Nelson in a volume of Nelson's letters to his wife – hers were tucked in at the back as an appendix. The Imperial War Museum has many letters and diaries written by women during the first and second world wars, and they directed me to the National Army Museum in search of earlier material. The attitude at this latter institution, which presents war as a history of military campaigns, was very different. The archive staff were clearly taken aback when I told them what I was looking for. Finally a woman member of staff said to a male colleague, who was looking utterly perplexed: 'You know, women's letters to their chaps.' Not surprisingly, the visit was unfruitful.

War is a time of discomfort and upheaval, so the preservation of war letters depends on two things, the recipient's attitude to them, and his or her ability to look after them and keep them safe. It soon became clear to me that, judging by the material which had been given to the Imperial War Museum, people tended to think letters interesting and worth preserving if they were written by women away from home and doing active service of some kind, since the vast preponderance of the letters were of this kind. There were very few letters written by munition workers, bus conductresses, mothers of young children, teachers or civil servants, or by elderly women sitting anxiously at home. This bias reflects the proud perception of the recipient, usually a parent, occasionally a husband, that the person who wrote the letters is doing sterling service for her country. But is also reflects the mundane fact that the parent or husband is comfortably settled at home, able to collect the letters in the bottom drawer of the bureau. But if the woman is writing from the home front to someone sharing a barrack room with forty men, or moving forward with the fighting front, or out at sea, keeping letters from home becomes difficult or wellnigh impossible.

As I said at the outset, I am not interested in presenting women in a heroic light, and if women in uniform tend to predominate in the later pages of the book it is for the reasons outlined above. In fact I found myself looking extra hard for letters *not* by nurses or women in the ATS. The copious letters of Mrs John Buchanan, who had lost one son in the North African campaign of the second world war, and wrote so regularly to a second son, are doubly touching when we consider how much trouble Peter Buchanan must have taken to bring them safely back to England.

I have confined myself to letters written by British women during British wars. This, I think, gives some narrative continuity to the whole collection, which is arranged chronologically. The reader will get a sense of how things change with time and how, oddly enough, they do not. Working through the material certainly gave me a strong sense of how little human nature changes. Language changes, as do the formalities of letter-writing, but feelings do not. Another reason for confining myself to British conflicts is the fact that the reader is more likely to know something of the historical background, and to read such documents in a vacuum of ignorance is pointless. I have assumed a general historical knowledge on the part of the reader, but not a comprehensive one: obscure wars, events and personages are, wherever possible, explained. I decided to finish the collection with the ending of the second world war in 1945 because more recent wars tend to involve political controversy. Often the dust has not yet settled and I have no wish to stir it up. There is no hidden pacifist agenda in this volume: war is hideous but it is part of human existence and likely to remain so. It brings out the best in human beings, and the worst. It is horribly destructive but, ironically, it often heightens people's sense of being alive. To countless women it has brought tragic bereavement, to others it brought adventure, an open door, escape from an unbearable tedium imposed on women by social convention, stifling their energies and aspirations. Florence Nightingale turned her back on marriage and found a vocation. A nurse writing from the front during the first world war speaks of dreadful local conditions, but adds that living at home is worse. A girl from a privileged background, in the ATS during the second world war, views the prospect of peace in 1945 with deep misgiving: settling down in the expected fashion no longer seems enough.

Women may have been hidden from history, but they are as much part of it as men. They were there, always. One way or another, they were always part of the struggle for survival. They did not merely give birth to warriors, and bury them afterwards. They had minds, opinions, hopes. Often they followed their men to the far corners of the earth, and distant battlefields. Some tried to bring fighting to an end, others handed out white feathers. Always they were there, rolling bandages, ploughing, managing the estate, infiltrating enemy lines, filling sandbags, filling shells with explosive, bringing up baby, running canteens, doing work thought unfit for women in times of peace. History, being written by men, excludes women from its pages. When it comes to war, men have tended to portray themselves as heroes risking their lives in defence of the weak, their women. The reasons for conflict are usually a good deal less worthy and, until recently, death in childbirth was a far greater risk than death on the battlefield. But war also involves more than the immediate combatants, and so it has always involved women. Hidden in the shadows, I have brought just a very few of them into the light.

When letters have been taken from published sources, the spelling is reproduced as in the original publication. The exception is the correspondence of Brilliana Harley, where I felt the archaic spelling reproduced by the Camden Society would interfere with the reader's enjoyment. Occasional anomalies may result. In particular, I feel the educational and social gap between Frances Nelson and her rival Emma Hamilton has been unfairly exaggerated, since Lady Nelson's correspondence has had the spelling modernized and Emma Hamilton's has not. Unpublished letters have been reproduced as written. Where the calendar year was held to begin on March 25th the actual year by modern reckoning is given in brackets.

I would like to thank the staff at the Imperial War Museum for their help, also Sheila de Bellaigue, registrar in the Royal Archives at Windsor Castle, who not only provided me with material but helped to decipher some of it. Thanks are due to the many archivists throughout Great Britain who responded to letters of inquiry, and to my publisher for sending them out. As for the staff at the London Library, I simply cannot imagine life without them.

MARGARET PASTON

The Paston letters cover one of the most violent periods in English history, the civil wars which began in 1455 and continued for thirty years. Popularly known as the Wars of the Roses, and celebrated by Shakespeare to glorify the ultimate ascendancy of the Tudors, it was a power struggle between two branches of the royal line, Lancaster and York. The Lancastrian Henry VI was twice deposed by Edward IV as a result of these conflicts. His son Edward V was in turn deposed by his uncle Richard III, whereupon Henry Tudor defeated Richard at the battle of Bosworth and became Henry VII, thus ending a long and bloody chapter of English history.

The Pastons appear to have supported the Yorkists. Nevertheless John Paston, Margaret's husband, fell out of favour sufficiently to have his lands seized by Edward IV, and he was committed to the Fleet prison just before his death in 1466. The estates were then granted to his son, Sir John Paston.

The Pastons were an important family in Norfolk. John Paston was born in 1420, and studied law at the Inner Temple. He married Margaret Mauteby some time before 1440, when their son John was born.

Margaret, mother of six sons and two daughters, died in 1484. She was frequently left in charge of the house and estates whilst her husband was away on business and sometimes had to organize the defence of their home against military attack by the men of Sir John Fastolf, Lord Moleyns, and other powerful neighbours. Her letters vividly reflect the violence and lawlessness of England at that time.

To my right worshipful master, John Paston, be this   1452
delivered in haste.

Right worshipful husband, I recommend me to you, praying you to weet, &c. (*here follow some account of money received, &c.*)

19

As for tidings, the queen came into this town on Tuesday last past after noon,[1] and abode here till it was Thursday three (*o'clock*) afternoon; and she sent after my cousin Elizabeth Clere by Sharinborn to come to her; and she durst not disobey her commandment, and came to her; and when she came in the queen's presence, the queen made right much of her, and desired her to have a husband, the which ye shall know of hereafter; but as for that he is never nearer than he was before; the queen was right well pleased with her answer, and reporteth of her in the best wise, and saith, by her truth, she saw no gentlewoman since she came into Norfolk that she liked better than she doth her.

Blake, the bailey of Swaffham, was here with the king's brother, and he came to me, weening that ye had been at home; and said that the king's brother desired him that he should pray you in his name to come to him, for he would right fain that ye had come to him if ye had been at home; and he told me that he wist well that he should send for you when he came to London, both for Cossey and other things.

I pray you that ye will do your cost on me against Whitsuntide, that I may have something for my neck. When the queen was here, I borrowed my cousin Elizabeth Clere's device, for I durst not for shame go with my beads amongst so many fresh gentlewomen as here were at that time.

The blessed Trinity have you in his keeping.

Written at Norwich on the Friday next before St. George.

By yours,
Margaret Paston

Norwich, Friday
   21st of April, 1452.

To my right worshipful husband, John Paston.

Right worshipful husband, I recommend me to you, and pray you to get some crossbows and wyndacs[2] to wind them with and quarrels[3] for your houses here be so low that there may none shoot out with no long bow, though we had never so much need.

I suppose ye should have such things of Sir John Fastolf if ye would send to him; and also I would ye should get two or three short pole-axes to keep with[in] doors, and as many jackets and ye may.

Partrich and his fellowship are sore afraid that ye would enter again upon them, and they have made great ordinance within the house, and it is told me they have made bars to bar the doors crosswise, and they have made wickets on every quarter of the house to shoot out at, both with bows and with hand-guns: and the holes that be made from hand-guns they be scarce knee high from the plancher [floor], and of such holes be made five, there can none man shoot out at them with no hand-bows.

Purry fell in fellowship with William Hasard at Quarles's, and told him that he would come and drink with Partrich and with him, and he said he should be welcome, and after noon he went thither for to espy what they dedyn, and what fellowship they had with them; and when he came thither the doors were fast sperred and there were none folks with them but Maryoth, and Capron and his wife, and Quarles's wife, and another man in a black yed somewhat halting, I suppose by his words that it was Norfolk of Gimmingham; and the said Purry espied all these foresaid things.

And Maryoth and his fellowship had much great language that shall be told you when ye come home.

I pray you that ye will vouchsafe to do buy for me one lb. of almonds and one lb. of sugar, and that ye will do buy some frieze to make your children's gowns, ye shall have best cheap and best choice of Hays's wife as it is told me. And that ye will buy a yard of broad cloth of black for one hood for me of 44*d*. or four shillings a-yard, for there is neither good cloth nor good frieze in this town. As for the children's gowns and I have them, I will do them maken.

The Trinity have you in his keeping, and send you good speed in all your matters.

[No date, but before 1459]

Margaret Paston

To my right worshipful husband, John Paston,   1459
in haste.

Right worshipful husband, I recommend me unto you; pleaseth you to weet that on Thursday last was, there were brought unto this town many privy seals, and one of them was indorsed to you, and to Hastyngs, and to five or six other gentlemen; and another was sent unto your son, and indorsed to himself alone, and assigned within with the king's own hand; and so were but few that were sent as it was told me; and also there were many more special terms in his than were in others; I saw a copy of those that were sent unto other gentlemen; the intent of the writing was, that they should be with the king at Leicester the 10th day of May, with as many persons defensibly arrayed as they might according to their degree, and that they should bring with them for their expenses for two months.

As for the letter that was indorsed to you, and to others, it was delivered to William Yelverton, for there appeared no more of the remulaunt [remaining].

Hastyngs is forth into Yorkshire; I pray you that ye vouchsafe to send word in haste how ye will that your son be demeaned herein. Men think here, that be your well-willers, that ye may no less do than to send him forth.

As for his demeaning since ye departed, in good faith, it hath been right good, and lowly, and diligent, in oversight of your servants and other things, the which I hope ye would have been pleased with and ye had been at home; I hope he will be well demeaned to please you hereafterward.

He desired Arblaster to bemoan to you for him; and was right heavy of his demeaning to you, as I sent you word also by Arblaster how I did to him after that ye were gone; and I beseech you heartily that ye vouchsafe to be his good father, for I hope he is chastised, and will be the worthier hereafter.

As for all other things at home, I hope that I and others shall do our part therein as well as we may; but as for money it cometh but slowly, and God have you in his keeping, and send you good speed in all your matters.

Written in haste at Norwich on the Sunday next before the Ascension day.

Sir, I would be right glad to hear some good tidings from you.

> By yours,
> Margaret Paston.

Norwich, Sunday,
   29 April, 1459.

1460–61

Please[4] it you to weet that it is let me weet by one that oweth you good will, that there is laid a wait upon you in this country if ye come here at large, to bring you to the presence of such a lord in the north as shall not be for your ease, but to jeopardy of your life, or great and importable loss of your goods; and he that hath taken upon him this enterprise now, was under-sherriff to Giles Saintlowe; he hath great favour hereto by the means of the son of William Baxter that lieth buried in the Grey Friars; and as it is reported the said son hath given great silver to the lords in the north to bring the matter about, and now he and all his old fellowship put out their fins, and are right flygge [ripe] and merry, hoping all thing is and shall be as they will have it; also it is told me that the father of the bastard in this country said that now this shire be made sure for him and his heirs, and for the Baxters' heirs also, whereby I conceive they think that they have none enemy but you &c.

Wherefore like it you to be the more wary of your guiding for your person's safe-guard, and also that ye be not too hasty to come into this country till ye hear the world [is] more sure. I trow the bearer of this shall tell more by mouth as he shall be informed of the rule in this country. God have you in his keeping. Written in haste, the second Sunday of Lent, by candlelight at even.

By yours, &c.
Margaret Paston.

1st March, 1460–1.

To my right worshipful husband, John Paston,   1465
in haste.

Right worshipful husband I recommend me to you, praying you heartily that ye will seek a mean that your servants may be in peace, for they be daily in fear of their lives; the Duke of Suffolk's men threaten daily Daubeney, Wykes, and Richard Calle, that wheresoever they may get them they shall die; and affrays have been made on Richard Calle this week, so that he was in great jeopardy at Norwich among them; and great affrays have been made upon me and my fellowship here on Monday last past, of which Richard Calle telleth me that he hath sent you word of in writing more plainly than I may do at this time, but I shall inform you more plainly hereafter.

I suppose there shall be great labour against you and your servants at the assizes and sessions here, wherefore me seemeth, saving your better advice, it were well done that ye should speak with the justices ere they come here; and if ye will that I complain to them or to any other, if Good fortune me life and health, I will do as ye advise me to do, for in good faith I have been simply entreated among them, and what with sickness and trouble that I have had, I am brought right low and weak, but to my power I will do as I can or may in your matters.

The Duke of Suffolk and both the duchesses shall come to Claxton this day, as I am informed, and this next week he shall be at Cossey; whether he will come further hitherward or not I wot not yet; it is said that he should come hither, and yet his men said here on Monday that he claimed no title to this place. They said their coming was but to take out such riotous people as was here within this place, and such as were the king's felons, and indicted and outlawed men, nevertheless they would show no warrants whereby to take none such, though there had been such here. I suppose if they might have come in peaceably they would have made another cause of their coming.

When all was done and they should depart, Harleston and other desired me that I should come and see mine old lady, and sue to my lord, and if anything were amiss it should be amended.

I said if I should sue for any remedy that I should sue further, and let the king and all the lords of this land to have knowledge what hath been done to us, if so were that the Duke would maintain that hath been done to us by his servants, and if ye would give me leave.

I pray you send me word if ye will that I make any complaint to the Duke or the Duchess, for as it is told me they know not the plainness that hath been done in such things as hath been done in their names.

I should write much more to you but for lack of leisure.

I commanded my master Tom this day to have come again by me from Norwich when he had spoken with Richard Calle, but he came not; I would he were quit of his indictment so that he were quit of your service, for by my truth I hold the place the more ungracious that he is in for his disposition in divers things, the which ye shall be informed of hereafter.

The Trinity have you in keeping. Written the Friday next after Saint Thomas.

> By your
> Margaret Paston.

Friday, 12th July, 1465.

To my right worshipful husband, John Paston, be this delivered in haste.

Right worshipful husband, I recommend me to you; please it you to weet that I was at Heylesdon upon Thursday last past, and saw the place there, and in good faith there will no creature think how foully and horribly it is arrayed but if they saw it; there cometh much people daily to wonder thereupon, both of Norwich and of other places, and they speak shamefully thereof; the Duke had by better than a thousand pound that it had never been done, and ye have the more good will of the people that it is so foully done; and they made your tenants of Heylesdon and Drayton, with other, to help to break down the walls of the place and the lodge both, God knoweth full evil against their wills, but that they durst none other wise do for fear; I have spoken with your tenants of Heylesdon and Drayton both, and put them in comfort as well as I can: the Duke's men ransacked the church, and bare away all the good that was left there, both of ours and of the tenants, and left not so much but that they stood upon the high altar and ransacked the images, and took away such as they might find, and put away the parson out of the church till they had done; and ransacked every man's house in the town five or six times; and the chief masters of robbing was the bailiff of Eye, the bailiff of Stradbrook, Thomas Slyford, and Porter; and Slyford was the chief robber of the church, and he hath most of the robbery next the bailiff of Eye; and as for lead, brass, pewter, iron, doors, gates, and other stuff of the house, men of Cossey and Cawston have it, and that they might not carry they have hewn asunder in the most despiteous wise. If it might be I would some men of worship might be sent from the king to see how it is both there and at the Lodge, ere than any snows come, that they may make report of the truth, else it shall not mowe be seen so plainly as it may now; and at the reverence of God speed your matters now, for it is too horrible a cost and trouble that we have now daily, and must have till it be otherwise; and your men dare not go about to gather up your livelihood, and we keep here daily more than thirty persons for savation of us and the place, for in very truth and the place had not been kept strong the Duke had come hither.

Arblaster thinketh verily that Hugh a Fenn may do much in your matters, and he thinketh he will do for you faithfully if ye will, &c.

At the reverence of God, if any worshipful and profitable mean may be taken in your matters, forsake it not in eschewing of our trouble and great costs and charges that we have, and may grow hereafter; it is thought here that if my Lord of Norfolk would take upon him for you, and that he may have a commission for to inquire of such riots and robberies as hath been done to you and other in this country, that then all the country will await upon him and serve your intent, for the people loveth and dreadeth him more than any other lord, except the king and my Lord of Warwick, &c.

God have you in his keeping, and send us good tidings from you. Written in haste, upon the Sunday Saint Simon and Jude's even.

By yours,
Margaret Paston.

Sunday, 27th of October, 1465

1468   *To Sir John Paston, Knight, be this delivered*
in haste.

I greet you well, and send you God's blessing and mine; letting you weet that Blickling of Heylesdon came from London this week, and he is right merry, and maketh his boast that within this fortnight at Heylesdon should be both new lords and new officers; and also this day was brought me word from Caister, that Rysing of Fretton should have heard said in divers places there, as he was in Suffolk, that Fastolf of Conghawe maketh all the strength that he may, and proposeth him to assault Caister, and to enter there if he may, insomuch that it is said that he hath a five score men ready, and sendeth daily spies to understand what fellowship keep the place; by whose power, or favour, or supportation, that he will do this I know not, but ye wot well that I have been affrayed there before this time, when that I had other comfort than I have now; and I cannot well guide nor rule soldiers, and also they set not by a woman as they should set by a man; therefore I would ye should send home your brothers or else Daubeney to have a rule, and to take in such men as were necessary for the safeguard of the place, for if I were there, without I had the more sadder or worshipful persons about me, and there came a meny of knaves and prevailed in their intent, it should be to me but a villainy. And I have been about my livelihood to set a rule therein, as I have written to you, which is not yet all performed after mine desire, and I would not go to Caister till I had done; I will no more days make thereabout if I may, therefore in any wise send somebody home to keep the place, and when that I have done and performed that I have begun, I shall purpose me thitherward if I should do there any good, and else I had lever be thence.

I have sent to Nicholas and such as keep the place, that they should take in some fellows to assist and strength them till ye send home some other word, or some other men to govern them that be therein, &c.

I marvel greatly that ye send me no word how that ye do, for your elmyse [enemies] begin to wax right bold, and that putteth your friends both in great fear and doubt, therefore purvey that they may have some comfort that they be no more discouraged, for if we lose our friends it shall [be] hard in this troublesome world to get them again.

The blessed Trinity speed you in your matters, and send you the victory of your elmyse, to your heart's ease and their confusion.

Written at Norwich, the Saturday next before Relic Sunday, in haste.

I pray you remember well the matters that I wrote to you for in the letter that ye had by James Gresham's man, and send me an answer thereof by the next man that cometh &c.

By your mother,
Margaret Paston.

Norwich, Saturday,
   9th of July, 1468.

HONOR LISLE

Lady Lisle was the daughter of Sir Thomas Grenville, but her date of birth is unknown. She became the second wife of Sir John Basset in 1515 and bore him seven children before his death in 1528. She married Arthur Viscount Lisle, an illegitimate son of Edward IV, as his second wife in 1529. He was Lord Deputy of Calais from 1533 until 1540, when he was recalled and charged with conspiracy. He died in the Tower, immediately after receiving the King's pardon, 'through too much rejoicing', as Holinshed puts it. His widow survived until 1566.

Calais, at the time the Lisles were stationed there, was very much a frontier town, and had a permanent garrison. Anglo-French relations were uneasy and usually hostile, and although Henry VIII, who had allied himself with the Holy Roman Empire against the French, did not launch an attack on France during the period 1533 to 1540, he had done so before Arthur Lisle took office and was to do so again very shortly after his return, and the atmosphere in Calais must have been very much that of a phoney war, or phoney peace. Although Charles V and Francis I had made peace in 1529, they were fighting again between 1536 and 1537, and would resume hostilities in 1542, when Henry VIII again allied himself with the Emperor and landed a force in 1544.

The letters reprinted here and the Lisle collection as a whole show how fully Honor Lisle participated in her husband's public and private affairs. This was clearly a marriage of both heart and mind.

1538

7 November 1538

Mine own sweet heart. This shall be to advertise you that I have had a goodly and fair passage, but it was somewhat slow, and long ere I landed, for this night, at x of the clock, I arrived. I thank God I was but once sick in all the way; and after that I was merry and well, and should have been much merrier if I had been coming towards you, or if you had been with me. Your absence and my departure maketh heavy, also for that I departed at the stair at Calais so hastily without taking my leave of you accordingly, made me very sorry; but I assure you, my lord, that I thought you had been in the boat, and would have brought me to the ship, as you said ye would do.

And this letter I began yesternight at supper time, intending to have sent it to you by John Nele; and at supper time, because it was in the night late, they looked not for me, so that there was no provision here ready for me; but while the supper was in dressing I told to John Nele, Markes, John Smythe, and Lamb, whom I had at supper, merry teles; and then John Nele promised me to come again in the morning for a token and letter to your lordship; but contrary to his promise he went his way at iij of the clock in the morning, giving me no warning thereof, which I assure you have not made me a little sorry, for that I fear you should conceive any unkindness or displeasure towards me, thinking me so negligent that I would not write to you. The counsel and company of John Nele did me much ease, and caused us to win to land much sooner than we should have done; but he did me not so much pleasure that way but he have done me much more displeasure by this means. I beseech your lordship to be good lord to Asheton, the gunner, for I assure you he is an honest man and I think he loveth your lordship as well as any man in Calais.

Lamb had a very evil chance and ran his ship against the pier. I think John Nele have shewed you thereof, but I was out of the ship ere that time. The said Lamb will take no money of me for passage, not for the ship; but he have taken of me ij crowns for himself, which I gave him for the passage. He saith you shall agree with his owner. I gave him the ij crowns because he had loss by the breaking of his bowsprit and fore-part of his ship. And thus, good sweet heart, I bid you most heartily farewell, praying to Almighty God to send me good speed in my suit, that I may have a short end and return to you shortly again, for I shall think every hour x till I be with you again.

From Dover, the vij day of November.

I pray you shew Mistress Minshaw that William, her son, was not sick in all the way. Husee is not yet come. I intend to ride to Sittingbourne this night, if I may. Howbeit, it was very late ere I went to bed this night, and the morning boystews[1] and windy, which causeth it to be late ere [I] do take my journey.

By her that is both your and her own,

Signed   Honor Lyssle

Mine own sweet good lord, Even with whole heart and mind, I have me most heartily commended unto you. And yesterday I wrote you by George Browne of the Wardrobe how the King's Highness entertained me, yet forgot I to write you that his Grace at the banquet wished you there; and I answered his Highness that you would, with all your heart, have been there, and that notwithstanding your absence it shall not be a little comfort to you to hear that his Grace had you in remembrance. I assure you, my lord, his Highness asked heartily for you, and wished you as heartily to have been at this banquet, which was the best that ever I was at, and was partly made for me. For at my coming to the court I thought not upon it till Mr. Grenway, the gentleman usher, met me with a wherry, and caused me to land at the privy-stairs, where Mr. Henneage received me, and so conveyed me to my chamber appointed, and there Mr. Comptroller met me, where was a rich bed furnished, and nothing lacking for me nor my folks; where I also found his Grace most singular lord unto me in my suits; so that both the lords[2] are commanded no further to meddle with any part of my son's inheritance.

And this day I thought to have spoken with my Lord Privy Seal, but his lordship hath deferred it till to-morrow by vj of the clock, which I will not fail, and then to break unto him, amongst other matters, for the parks and lands in Devonshire, whereof I have received your letters this day by Byrcham; and with mine own servant, which I will send incontinent after I have spoken with my Lord Privy Seal, I will make you answer, particularly, to all the rest of your affairs. And this day hath Mr. Pollard been with me, whom I find very good unto me, who hath partly broken unto me concerning Painswick,[3] to whom I made such answer, that I trusted so to use me to my lord that he should have no cause to say that I have been ingrate, trusting farther that my lord would see me no loser.

I have in hope to dispatch my business ere it be long; for fain would I be with you, notwithstanding you promised me that after my departing you would dine at x of the clock every day, and keep little company, because you would mourn for mine absence. But I warrant you, I know what rule you keep and company, well enough, since my departing, and what thought you take for me, whereof you shall hear at my coming home. But now to conclude. How the King handled me, and how I was used. although I have written you part, I refer the relation of the rest till mine own coming home. And thus desiring to be heartily recommended unto my Lord Comptroller, my nephew Graynfylde and his wife, and to all others as shall please you, most heartily I bid you farewell.

From London, the xv[th] of November, by her that is more yours than her own, which had much rather die with you there, than live here.

Signed   Honor Lyssle

My recommendations may not be forgotten unto Mr. Rokewood and Mr. Fowler, Mr. Scriven, Mr. Snowden, and others at your pleasure. I pray you make no man privy to my letter; for this quarrel I make you is but my fantasy.

23 November 1538

Mine own sweet heart, Even with whole heart and mind I have me most entirely unto you recommended, not a little desirous to be with you. Howbeit, my chance hath been such to come in such time as serveth full ill for my purpose. Howbeit, I must be and am contented, and abide the time, referring all mine affairs only unto God in whom I trust.

And this is signifying you that I have been with my Lord Prince, whose life I pray God long to prosper and continue; for his Grace is the goodliest babe that ever I set mine eye upon. I pray God make him an old man, for I think I should never be weary of looking on him. Whereas I saw also my Lady Mary and my Lady Elizabeth; my Lady Mary's grace heartily asking how you did, and even so desiring to be unto you recommended. I would not for no good but that I had been there, for it was the King's pleasure I should do so. Howbeit, it was costly unto me, for there is none cometh there but they give great rewards.

And touching my Lord Privy Seal, he hath made plain answer that your annuity shall be no more but ijC^{li}, yet will I not let to do my best, notwithstanding I dare not speak to the King for his displeasure. As for Painswick, I am yet at no determinate point; howbeit, Mr. Pollard hath been in hand with me, and as far as I can perceive he doth think to have the m^l li released for the pleasures he hath done already to you and me, and specially now last concerning my son's inheritance. I shall be glad to accomplish my lord's mind, so that nor you, my good lord, nor I be no losers, which I trust, of his honour, he will not desire. You may be assured I will make as much haste as I can, that I were rid hence, for I long not a little to be with you. I have received of this bearer your sundry loving letters, with the partridges and also the bake meats you sent me along seas, for the which I most entirely thank you. Mr. Cotton, Vice-chamberlain to my Lord Prince, hath him most heartily commended unto you, and saith that all the cooks are furnished. He is right sorry that he cannot prefer the cook you wrote to him for.

The Earl of Bridgewater was this day with me at dinner, with whom I had much communication, and if he be reasonable I will do my best to make all sure ere I depart; if not, seeing the King's Highness hath been so good and gracious lord unto me, and also my Lord Privy Seal, I will let it alone; trusting in God, the King's Majesty, and him, that the said earl shall do me no wrong. Both the King and my Lord Privy Seal hath been in hand with him and the Earl of Hertford, and so shaken them up for meddling in that, that they both hath promised to meddle no farther therein; so that I can do no more to it than is done, unless the said earl would be content to make a surrender by fine, or part from the possession for some reasonable portion of money, wherein I shall know his mind within ij or iij days. Here is Mr. Windsor, which hath not yet finished his account, by reason that Acton will yet come to no reckoning. He intendeth to make clear with him ere he depart; it is sure a hard honest man.

My lord, I trust you will conceive none unkindness that I do not send you money, for as yet I have not received it of Mr. Windsor, nor you have not commanded me by any of your letters what I should send you. I would gladly have sent you some by this bearer, but I fear there are so many casualties and dangers by the way. I pray you, good mine own, let me know your mind with the first; trusting you will take no unkindness for my tarrying; for surely I lose no time, but am up every day iij hours before day; and seeing I am here I would finish that I came for gladly, ere I depart, so that I might be reasonably handled; for surely I shall never be merry till I see you. By this bearer I do send you half a doe, which my Lady Sussex sent me. I have none other goodness to send you. If Carey come, although he have put you to cost already, I will deliver him xl^s. I have put your gown to making, and it shall be sent you the next week, and Husee doth send you a cap and an under-cap. And thus, good mine own, with heart and mind most heartily I bid you once again farewell.

From London, the xxiij of November.

By her that is more than all yours,

Signed   Honor Lyssle

Good my lord, let this bearer remain still in your chamber till I come home; and Speccot goeth hence toward Calais within these ij days. I do more send you now another half doe, which my Lord Delawarr sent me this day, and I keep the other half that I sent, because it was not all of the sweetest.

3 December 1538

Mine own sweet heart, Even with my whole heart root I have me most heartily recommended unto you, and have this day received your sundry letters, the contents whereof I shall endeavour myself, as much as I may, to accomplish to the best of my power; yet the time is such (by reason of the King's weighty matters) that I could this viij days have no time to speak with my Lord Privy Seal. Howbeit, I trust on Thursday next to have my lord at some convenient leisure to open and declare unto him my whole mind concerning your sundry affairs and matters: whom if I find not something conformable unto my reasonable requests, I shall not fail to open the same at my coming unto the King's Highness' presence, whom I intend to see as soon as I have spoken with my Lord Privy Seal; yea, and I had been with his Grace ere this time, had it not been for my said lord's displeasure, which I would not gladly have. Howbeit, if I be driven to it, I must and will not fail to speak that which shall stand with reason; trusting his Grace will give me the hearing and take the same in good part. And how I speed with my lord you shall be certified within this iij days.

And where, my lord, you will me to be plain with my Lord Privy Seal for your annuity; the truth is, so have been, but how he handled me and shook me up I will not now write, nor it is not to be written. Howbeit, he made me plain answer that your annuity should be no more but ij$\mathcal{C}^{li}$. I trust the King will be better lord unto you, or else I would be sorry. And where you write that you never longed so sore for me as you now do, I assure you, my good heart root, your desire in that behalf can be no vehementer than mine is; for I know that I am here at great charge and think that small profit will rise on it, as far as I can perceive, which maketh me not a little heavy; for I can neither sleep nor eat nor drink that doth me good, my heart is so heavy and full of sorrow, which I know well will never be lightened till I be with you, which I trust shall be shortly. For after I have spoken unto the King's Majesty I hope shortly to be at a point, which is my whole desire. And so, mine own sweet heart, even as she that longeth not a little to be with you, with all my heart I bid you farewell, with long life in health.

From London, the iij day of December.

By her that is more than all yours,

Signed   Honor Lyssle

My lord, I beseech you keep my letters close or burn them; for though I have sorrows, I would no creature should be partaker, nor of knowledge with me.

BRILLIANA HARLEY

These vivid and touching letters provide a moving insight into one woman's experiences during the civil war between Parliament and Charles I, a war which began in 1641 after a dispute over the King's right to levy taxes and was to result, later in the seventeenth century, in constitutional monarchy and parliamentary government. Brilliana's name derives from the fact that she was born in Brill, in the Netherlands, in 1600, whilst her father was Lieutenant-Governor there. She was the third wife of Sir Robert Harley, marrying him in 1623. She bore seven children, and Edward, the recipient of most of the surviving letters, was the eldest of her three sons. Sir Robert was Member of Parliament for Radnor, active in the Parliamentary cause, but averse to extreme measures against the King. A moderate faction in Parliament wanted the King reinstated, not executed. But the war, instigated by the gentry and a rising middle class, had been fought by the lower orders, and an unpaid army was clamouring for much greater social change. Cromwell, military commander on behalf of Parliament, had to make a difficult choice, and chose to side with the army. During Pride's Purge in December 1648 moderate Members of Parliament, including Sir Robert Harley and his son Edward (by now MP for Hereford), were prevented from entering the House of Commons, and many were arrested, leaving a puppet parliament and a military dictatorship. The King was executed after a show trial in January 1649. Sir Robert died in 1656, but his son Edward lived to support the Restoration in 1660.

Brilliana, however, did not survive the civil war. Left in charge of Brompton Castle and her husband's estate whilst Sir Robert was away, engaged in the affairs of a nation in turmoil, Brilliana came under siege for six weeks in the summer of 1643, after which the troops moved off. She also had considerable difficulty with neighbours and tenants who either supported the royal cause, or simply exploited the situation by breaking the law or refusing to pay their dues. A year later the castle came under siege again and surrendered after three weeks, but Brilliana was no longer alive. There are frequent references to her ill health in these letters, and the 'very great cold' mentioned in her last letter caused her death in October 1643.

To my dear son Mr. Edward Harley   1639

My good Ned – The Lord in mercy bless you, and give you interest in his son Christ, and such a measure of holiness, that you may live here like his child. It is my comfort, that you enjoy your health, and I beseech the Lord, to continue that mercy to you. I persuade myself you are careful to improve your time; this is your time of harvest, and that time being over-slipped, it cannot be recalled. I am glad to hear you are cheerful. Enjoy that blessing, when God gives it you, for cheerfulness of spirit gives more freedom in the performance of any duty. I hope, as you do, that the news of so many being massacred is not true; the great God of heaven and earth look in mercy upon his poor people. It is reported, from all parts, the French have a very great army. I can not think yet, that the French would take this time to come into England, when we stand upon our guard and such preparations for wars. And the report is, that there goes 30000 foot and 10000 horse with the king to York; so that a foreign enemy could not come in a time more disadvantageous to him. But if we fight with Scotland, and are engaged in that war, then a foreign enemy may take his time of advantage. The cause is the Lords; and He will work, for his own glory. Dear Ned, you may remember I have often spoke to you about these times; and my dear Ned, would I were with you one day, to open my mind more largely than I can by writing. They call to supper, therefore I must hasten my letter, but first I must tell you, I have sent you by the carrier a box, directed to you, in which is a turkey pie and 6 pies, such as my lord, your grandfather did love. I hope to remember you again in Lent. Send me word, whether you receive them, and whether they be good. Mr. Simons is very ill and very weak. I wish his wife be not a widow again. For Mr. Walcot's sake, I will persuade them to send their son to your tutor: but Mr. Cradock is the only man that prevails with them. I thank God, your Father is well, and so is your brothers and sisters, with Ned Smith: so in haste, I rest,

Your most affectionate mother, Brilliana Harley *Feb:* 15, 1639.

I have sent your tutor a box of dried plums, the box is directed to you; tell him it is a Lenten token. Remember my service to him.

1640   *For my dear son Mr. Edward Harley,*
       in Magdalen Hall, Oxford.

Dear Ned – This morning I received your letter, which was very welcome to me and since it pleases God that you enjoy your health, I do with more ease bear my own weakness. I have not yet this week received any letter from your father, and it would much trouble me, but that your father wrote me word that he intended to send the cook down this week. I thank you for the kings prayer, and I pray God to hear all the prayers that are now put up for a happy issue of this parliament. I have heard of many bold speeches that have passed there; and that passage between the archbishop and my lord Say is diversely reported; but I believe that which I received from you. The press of soldiers is now past; so that the poor fellows may now appear, who had hid themselves for fear. I purpose and please God, to send to you sometime the next week with the money your tutor sent for. I have not been out of my bed since Wednesday, but I thank God I am but as I use to be. I long to see you, I will not say how much, lest your tutor call it fondness, and not love. I thank God your brothers and sisters with your cousin Smith are well; but your brother Robert had yesterday morning a seize of a fit, which makes me desire he should enter into a course of physic. Edward Pinner hath been very sick. I sent for doctor Wright to him, who hath been here the most part of this week, and hath given him physic which hath done him (by the blessing of God) upon that means, much good. This morning he was let blood, and bled very vile blood; and I now hope he will recover apace, but yet he keeps his bed. I pray God bless you, and give me a comfortable seeing of you, which is much desired by

Your most affectionate mother, Brilliana Harley
May 1, 1640.

I believe your cousin —— is not yet come to Oxford.
Mrs. Walcot was not long since with me. She much rejoiced that she had got so excellent a tutor for her son and nephew, and how she had contrived it, that he should have a servitor in the house, and so should not need a man to wait upon him. He now fears an ague, and his going to Oxford is put off till he be well.

For my dear son Mr. Edward Harley,
in Magdalen Hall, Oxford.

My dear Ned – I thank you for your letter by J——rth. It was welcome
to me, and I hope it will not be long before I see you, which comfort
I beg of the Lord. On Sunday morning I received a letter from your father,
by which I found the news of the dissolution of the parliament to be true.
There are many rumours in the country. The pressed soldiers in Presteign
have fought; and they say, if it had not been for the trained band they
had killed the captain that is come down for them, refusing to go with
him, because he is a papist. Mr. Harvey and his wife are now here, coming
to take their leave to go to Warwickshire. My dear Ned, the Lord bless
you, and give your father and you a happy meeting with

Your most affectionate mother, Brilliana Harley.
May 13, 1640. *Brompton Castle.*

I am glad Mr. Robert Pye's son is with your tutor.
Remember me to your worthy tutor, and tell him if he come to
Brompton, Mr. Gower expects to have him to preach for him.

To her son Edward. – Endorsed 'For your dear self.'

Dear Ned – I am glad to take the opportunity to write to you, when
your father is at dinner; for last night my cousin Vaughan and his sister
with her husband and Mr. Lawes, with others of theirs, came to
Brompton, and I believe after dinner I shall have their company. They
are come to make a full agreement with your father. Doct^r Deodate gave
your father some physic, and is confident your fathers illness only
proceeds from the spleen, and is no inclination to a palsy. Woodhouse
did as Pritchard use to do, and deceived your father, so that he would
not take this which the doctor would have had him take, while he was
with him. I thank God your father is as well as he uses to be. The doctor
let him blood under the tongue, which agreed very well with him. D^r
Deodate went away on Tuesday last. I thank you, my dear Ned, for
wishing I should take something of him; but my illness comes at certain
times, and without I should send for him just at that time, I can not have
him then to give me any thing; for he would have me take something and
be let blood two or three days before I am ill, as I use to be. If please
God, when you are with me, I will send for doctor Wright and take

37

something. It pleases my gracious God, so to dispose of it, that this illness which I have, makes me very weak, for as soon as I am pretty well I am ill again. Doctor Deodate tells me he knows many so, and he does much pity me; but my comfort is, that my God will not cast off for ever.

The soldiers from Hereford were at Leominster last Thursday on their march to their rendezvous; the captain not paying them all their pay, they would have returned into the town again, but all the town rose, and those that were come out of church, and with those arms they had, beat them back, but there being a great heap of stones out of town, the soldiers made use of them as long as they lasted, in which time the townsmen did but little good, till that powder was spent, and then the townsmen were too hard; many were hurt on both sides; the captain would have come into the town, but was kept out.

Your letter this week by the carrier was welcome. I hope, if Mr. Gower be at Oxford at the fast, that you may hear him preach that day; and I hope, we shall have him shortly at Brompton. If Dagon begin to fall, it will down. I thank you for the paper you sent me; I have not yet read it, and the book I have not yet seen; your father has it, and I have not seen him much to day.

Dear Ned, take care of your self for my sake, and do not go to be over heat in the crowd at the Act.[1] The Lord in mercy bless you and preserve you.

Your affectionate mother, Brilliana Harley.
July 3, 1640. *Brompton Castle.*

I have so scribbled that I think you will hardly read it.

By this carrier I have sent you a cape. I hope it will come well to your hand.

1642   For my dear son Mr. Edward Harley, at Mr. Cooles house, in Channel Row.

My dear Ned – I cannot let Mr. Moore go without a letter to you, though I writ to you yesterday by the post of Ludlow. I am persuaded things are now come to their ripeness, and if God be not very merciful to us, we shall be in a distressed condition; but the Lord has promised to hear His children in the day of trouble, and to deliver them, which I am persuaded He will do now.

I long every day to hear from you; I beseech the Lord to preserve you; and dear Ned, be careful of yourself. I have received a box with match and 2 bandoliers; but the box was open, before it came to me. I purpose, and please God, that your sister Brill shall begin her journey to London on Monday come sennight, and Pinner and Hackluyt shall go with her. Mr. Yeats, I believe, will go with her; your cousin Smith has not been well, though his ague was gone, so that I was fain to send for doctor Wright for him. He came when the keeper brought your letter, which was on Friday, so he met your letter, for which he returns many thanks, and would not now write to you, because he desires when he does, to write about Potters business, which he will, when he has spoken with a lawyer. He desires you would do him the favour to buy him 2 muskets and rests and bandoliers, and 15 or 16 pound of powder in a barrel, and he desires you would send them by Leominster carrier, and so directed them to Brompton, and he will give order to have them sent to Hereford, and will send you what they cost.

I am not yet very well, and yesterday I was something ill. I pray God bless you and preserve you in all safety; so I rest,

Your most affectionate mother, Brilliana Harley.
Apr: 23, 1642: *Brompton Castle.*

Doctor Wright tells me that Mr. Weaver is still sick, and for his part he would have done his utmost, that you might have had that place.

For my dear son, Mr. Edward Harley.

My dear Ned – Your letter by the post and by the carrier are both very welcome to me; for besides the knowledge you give me of the public affairs, the assurance of your health is very dear to me. We all are engaged deeply to pray earnestly to our God, that He will give both wisdom and courage to the parliament, and I hope the Lord will so guide them that the mouths of those that would speak evil of them shall be stopped. I thank you for desiring me not to believe rumours. I do not; because I assure myself I shall hear the truth of things from your pen. It is the Lords great work, that is now a framing, and I am confident, it will be finished with much beauty, so that the very enemies shall be enforced to acknowledge it has been the Lord that has wrought for His cause and children; against whom they will find that there is no divination nor enchantment.

We heard that the Kentish petition was brought by 3000 men, and that 3000 Londoners met them upon Blackheath and there fought, and many were killed. And now we hear that Sr Francis Wortley drew his sword and asked who was for the king, and so 18 followed him. I think this latter may be true; but for the fight upon Blackheath, I know it is not true.

I am glad our Hereford petition is come to London, and I hope delivered before this: your sister, I hope, met you at Wycombe on Wednesday last. Dear Ned, send me word how my lady Vere uses her, and how she carries herself.

I pray God bless you with a large measure of grace and with all the comforts of this life.

Your most affectionate mother, Brilliana Harley.
May 6, 1642.

For my dear son Mr. Edward Harley.

My dear Ned – A short letter will serve to let you know how Herefordshire stands, when Mr. Broughton is the bearer of it: therefore I will say nothing of what is done abroad, only tell you of your friends at Brompton, where I long to see you.

This day I heard out of Lincolnshire: I thank God they are all well: but I see my brother Pelham is not of my mind. I think now, my dear sister was taken away that she might not see that which would have grieved her heart.

Sr William Pelham writes me word he has given up his lieutenancy and his going to York, to the king;[2] being his servant, as he writes me word, and so bound by his oath.

Dear Ned, send me word whether your sister looks as pale as she did. I have not been well these 3 days, but it is as I use to be. Your sister Dorothy has been exceeding ill: she fell ill about 10 days since. I was very unwilling to send for any doctor, till she grew very ill, and so ill, that I much feared her; and I sent for doctor Wright, who went away this morning. I hope now she will recover, though I still fear her: she looks most lamentable, and is grown weak; but I hope God will be merciful to her.

I hope to send you your shirts shortly. I pray God bless you and preserve you in all safety: and dear Ned, let me hear the truth of things, though it be bad. We hear that the king will summon all that will be for him, to come to him.

I pray God compose things to His glory, and His church's advantage.

Your most affectionate mother, Brilliana Harley.
I have received doctor Wright's arms you sent down.
May 17, 1642. *Brompton Castle.*

For my dear son Mr. Edward Harley.

My dear Ned – Now I thank you for your letter by Mr. Broughton, who brought it this day something late, so that I am shortened in time to write to you.

I think we must all acknowledge Gods great mercy that the plot for the taking of Hull was discovered. I pray God direct the parliament what they ought to do, for they have enemies enough to look with an evil eye at what their actions.

At Ludlow they set up a May pole, and a thing like a head upon it, and so they did at Croft, and gathered a great many about it, and shot at it in derision of roundheads. At Ludlow they abused Mr. Burgess son very much, and are so insolent that they durst not leave their house to come to the fast. I acknowledge I do not think myself safe where I am. I lose the comfort of your fathers company, and am in but little safety, but that my trust is in God; and what is done in your fathers estate pleases him not, so that I wish myself, with all my heart, at London, and then your father might be a witness of what is spent; but if your father think it best for me to be in the country, I am every well pleased with what he shall think best. I have sent you by this carrier, in a box, 3 shirts; there is another, but it was not quite made; one of them is not washed; I will, and please God, send you another the next week, and some handkerchers. I writ yesterday to you by the post of Ludlow, how my thanks was taken at Hereford.

I pray God bless you and keep you from sin, and from all other evils, and give you a joyful meeting with

Your most affectionate mother, Brilliana Harley.

Your sister Doll is not well, she has a great weakness upon her; yet I thank God this day she is something better than she was.
June 4, 1642: *Brompton Castle.*

For my dear son Mr. Edward Harley.

My dear Ned – I thank you for your letter by the carrier. I hope your physic has done you good, and I pray God it may. We must all join our sorrows together that the king yet holds off. I doubt not but that the Lord will perfect His great work, He has begun.

I purpose, and please God, to send Martin with the horses your father sent for, on Monday next. I doubt not but that your father will give to his utmost for the raising these horse, and in my opinion it were better to borrow money, if your father will give any, than to give his plate; for we do not know what straits we may be put to, and therefore I think it better to borrow whilst one may, and keep the plate for a time of need, without your father had so much plate, that he could part with some, and keep some to serve himself another time.[3] This I do not say, that I am unwilling to part with the plate or any thing else in this case; if your father cannot borrow money, I think I might find out some in the country to lend him some. Dear Ned, tell your father this, for I have not writ to him about it. I have not been very well this day, but it is as I use to be, and I thank God so much better, as I keep not my chamber. Your sister Dorothy is much better than she was, and I hope she will do well, though I was much afraid of her.

I pray God bless you and give you a comfortable meeting with

Your most affectionate mother, Brilliana Harley.
June 17, 1642. *Brompton Castle.*

To her son Edward.

My dear Ned – If you believe how glad I am to have this paper discourse with you, you will read it as willingly as I write it. Since your father thinks Herefordshire as safe as any other country, I will think so too; but when I considered how long I had been from him, and how this country was affected, my desire to see your father, and my care to be in a place of safety, made me earnestly desire to come up to London; but since it is not your father's will, I will lay aside that desire. But, dear Ned, as you have promised me, so let me desire you to let me know how things go. This night I heard that my lord Savile was dead. I desire to know whether it be so or no; and whether my lord Paget be gone to York. I hear that one Mr Mason carried a letter from the justices of this country to the king at York, to let him know that they would serve him with their lives and estates. I thought it had been with the petition they made for the bishops, but they say, it was with a letter. When d^r Wright was with Mr James, he told me you had writ to him about Petters bill, and that it was well if some lords were spoken to: he desires me to make some means to speak to my lord Brooke, which I promised him I would; therefore, good Ned, either speak yourself to my lord Brooke, or get somebody to speak to him, that when the bill comes into the lords he may further it. This day Mr. Davis came from Hereford, where he went to preach, by the entreaty of some in the town, and this befell him: when he had ended his prayer before the sermon, which he was short in, because he was loth to tire them, 2 men went out of the church and cried "pray God bless the king; this man does not pray for the king;" upon which, before he read his text, he told them that m^{isters} had that liberty, to pray before or after the sermon for the church and state; for all that, they went to the bells and rang, and a great many went into the church-yard and cried "roundheads," and some said, "let us cast stones at him!" and he could not look out of doors nor Mr Lane but they cried "roundhead." In the afternoon they would not let him preach; so he went to the cath-edral. Those that had any goodness were much troubled and weep much.

Mr Yates does much lament doctor Wrights being there, and says, if he can prevail with him, he will persuade him to go to Shrewsbury; which I should be very glad of, because he has gained him enemies in standing to get voices for you.[4] You may see by this how wicked they are grown. I think it best to let doctor Rogers alone till it please God to give a fairer correspondency between the king and parliament, and then I wish he may be soundly punished.

I thank God I have been very well, and so well, that I am able to go abroad, when I am not as well as I used to be.

I have sent you a shirt and half a dozen handkerchers and some powder for your hair.

I have written so miserable that I fear you will hardly read it, but I hope, this will be legible to you, that I desire the Lord to bless you, as I desire my own soul should be blessed: so I rest,

Your most affectionate mother, Brilliana Harley.

I hope I shall see you this summer; I long for it. I thank God your brothers and sisters are well. Dear Ned, send me word whether my cousin Davis has lost Bucknell or no; he says he has not, and Mr Edwards says he has.

June 20, 1642. *Brompton.*

To her son Edward.

My dear Ned – By the enclosed paper to your father, you will know how poor Herefordshire is affected; but, dear Ned, I hope you and myself will remember for whose cause your father and we are hated. It is the cause of our God, and I hope we shall be so far from being ashamed of it or troubled, that we bear the reproach of it, that we shall bind it as a crown upon us; and I am confident the Lord will rescue His children from reproach.

I sent Samuel to Hereford to observe their ways. He had come home last night, but that he had a fall from his horse and put out his shoulder.

He tells me that they all at Hereford cried out against your father, and not one said any thing for him, but one man, Mr. Phillips of Ledbury said, when he heard them speak so against your father, "well," said he, "though Sir Robert Harley be low here, yet he is above, where he is." My dear Ned, I can not think I am safe at Brompton, and by no means I would have you come down. I should be very glad if your father could get some religious and discreet gentlemen to come for a time to Brompton, that he might see sometimes what they do in the country. I trust the Lord will direct your father what way is best, and I doubt not that we shall pray, one for another.

I could wish that my cousin Adams were out of the house, for I am persuaded he will give the other side what assistance he can. If you think good, tell your father so: your father does not know what counsels they have in Herefordshire, and what way they go.

The captain of the volunteers is one Barroll, he was a tradesman, and once mayor of Hereford.

It is so late I will but wish you a good night, and I pray God bless you, and in His good time give you a comfortable meeting with

Your most affectionate mother, Brilliana Harley.
July 17, 1642. *Brompton Castle.*

For my dear son Mr. Edward Harley.

My dear Ned – I long to see you, but would not have you come down, for I cannot think this country very safe; by the papers I have sent to your father, you will know the temper of it. I hope your father will give me full directions how I may best have my house guarded, if need be; if he will give the directions, I hope, I shall follow it.

My dear Ned, I thank God I am not afraid. It is the Lords cause that we have stood for, and I trust, though our iniquities testify against us, yet the Lord will work for His own name sake, and that He will now show the men of the world that it is hard fighting against heaven. And for our comforts, I think never any laid plots to rout out all Gods children at once, but that the Lord did show Himself mighty in saving His servants and confounding His enemies, as He did Pharaoh, when he thought to have destroyed all Israel, and so Haman. Now, the intention is, to rout out all that fear God, and surely the Lord will arise to help us: and in your God let your confidence be, and I am assured it is so. One meet Samuel and not knowing where he dwelt, Samuel told him he was a Derbyshire man, and that he came lately from thence, and so he did in discourse; the papist told him, that there was but a few puritans in this country, and 40 men would cut them all off.

Had I not had this occasion to send to your father, yet I had sent this boy up to London; he is such a roguish boy that I dare not keep him in my house, and as little do I dare to let him go in this country, lest he join with the company of volunteers, or some other such crew. I have given him no more money than will serve to bear his charges up; and because I would have him make haste and be sure to go to London, I have told him, that you will give him something for his pains, if he come to you in good time and do not loiter; and here enclosed I have sent you half a crown. Give him what you think fit, and I desire he may not come down any more, but that he may be persuaded to go to sea, or some other employment. He thinks he shall come down again. Good Ned, do not tell Martin that I send him up with such an intention. I have directed these letters to you, and I send him to you, because I would not have the country take notice, that I send to your father so often; but when such occasions come, I must needs send to him, for I can rely upon nobodys counsel but his. I pray God bless you and preserve you in safety, and the Lord in mercy give you a comfortable meeting with

Your most affectionate mother, Brilliana Harley.
July 19, 1642. *Brompton Castle.*

My cousin Davis tells me that none can make shot but those whose trade it is, so I have made the plumber write to Worcester for 50 weight of shot. I sent to Worcester, because I would not have it known. If your father think that is not enough, I will send for more. I pray you tell your father that my cousin Robert Croft is in the country. My cousin Tomkins is as violent as ever, and many think that her very words, is in the Hereford resolutions. I believe it was M^r. Masons penning. He is gone to York, for when he carried the letter from the gentlemen in this country, he was made the kings chaplain.

To her son Edward.

My dear Ned – My heart has been in no rest since you went. I confess I was never so full of sorrow. I fear the provision of corn and malt will not hold out, if this continue; and they say they will burn my barns; and my fear is that they will place soldiers so near me that there will be no going out. My comfort is that you are not with me, lest they should take you; but I do most dearly miss you. I wish, if it pleased God, that I were with your father. I would have writ to him, but I durst not write upon paper. Dear Ned, write to me, though you write upon a piece of cloth, as this is.⁵ I pray God bless you, as I desire my own soul should be blessed. Theres a 1000 dragooners came into Hereford 5 hours after my lord Hertford.

Your mother, Brill: Har.
Decem: 13, 1642.

To her son Edward.

My dear Ned – I thank you for your letter by Prosser; he is a trusty messenger. I must now tell you how gracious our God has been to us: on the Sabbath day after I received the letter from the marquis, we set that day apart to seek to our God, and then on Monday we prepared for a siege; but our good God called them another way; and the marquis⁶ sent me word he remembered him to me, and that I need not fear him, for he was going away, but bid me fear him that came after him.

Mr Congsby is the governor of Hereford, and he sent to me a letter by Mr Wigmore. I did not let him come into my house, but I went into the garden to him. Your father will show you the letter; they are in a mighty violence against me; they revenge all that was done upon me, so that I shall fear any more parliament forces coming into this country: and dear Ned, when it is in your power show kindness to them, for they must be overcome so. Bardlam has played the very traitor to me, and Richard Bytheway never comes at me: Mr Phillips takes much care and pains. Dear Ned, write him thanks though it be but in a little scrip of paper. My dear Ned, I pray you advise with your father whether he thinks it best that I should put away most of the men that are in my house, and whether it be best for me to go from Brompton, or by Gods help to stand it out. I will be willing to do what he would have me do. I never was in such sorrows, as I have been since you left me; but I hope the Lord will deliver me; but they are most cruelly bent against me. I thank you for your counsel, not to take their words; the Lord in mercy preserve you, and if it be His holy will, give me the comfort of seeing you, in whom is much of the comfort of

Your affectionate mother, Brilliana Harley.
Decem: 25, 1642.

To her son Edward.   1643

My dear Ned – Your welcome letter I received on Monday last, but Hopkis was taken at Rickards Castle, but sent me your fathers letter and yours. But I hear he had 6 other letters, and they were carried to Mr Coningsby. He is still at Hereford. How he will be used I know not; for poor Griffiths was cruelly used, but he is now set at liberty. But the poor drummer is still in the dungeon, and Griffiths says he fears he will die. I cannot send to release him.

My dear Ned, I know it will grieve you to know how I am used. It is with all the malice that can be. Mr Wigmore will not let the fowler bring me any fowl, nor will not suffer any of my servants pass. They have forbid my rents to be paid. They drave away the young horses at Wigmore, and none of my servants dare go scarce as far as the town. And dear Ned, if God were not merciful to me, I should be in a very miserable condition. I am threatened every day to be beset with soldiers. My hope is, the Lord will not deliver me nor mine into their hands; for surely they would use all cruelty towards me, for I am told that they desire not to leave your father neither root nor branch. You and I must forgive them. Dear Ned, desire the prayers of the godly for us at Brompton. I desire to . . . as it is possible that I may keep the possession of your fathers house for him.

I know not whether this will come to your hand or no, but this I know,

47

that I long to hear from you, and I pray God bless you, as I desire the soul should be blessed, of your

Most affectionate mother, Brilliana Harley.
Jany. 28, 1642. [1643]

For my dear son Mr. Edward Harley.

My dear Ned – I am confident you long to hear from me, and I hope this will come to your hand, though it may be it will be long first. We are threatened and injured as much as my enemies can possible. There is none that bears part with me but Mr James, who has showed himself very honest; none will look towards Brompton, but such as truly fears God; but our God still takes care of us, and has exceedingly showed His power in preserving us. Nine days past my lord Herbert was at Hereford, where he stayed a week; there was held a council of war, what was the best way to take Brompton; it was concluded to blow it up, and which council pleased them all. The sheriff of Radnorshire, with the trained bands of that county and some of Herefordshire soldiers, were to come against me. My lord Herbert had appointed a day to come to Presteign, that so his presence might persuade them to go out of their county. He had commanded them to bring pay for vitals for 10 days. The soldiers came to Presteign, but it pleased God to call my lord Herbert another way, for those in the forest of Dean, grew so strong, that they were afraid of them.

Now they say, they will starve me out of my house; they have taken away all your fathers rents, and they say they will drive away the cattle, and then I shall have nothing to live upon; for all their aim is to enforce me to let those men I have go, that then they might seize upon my house and cut our throats by a few rogues, and then say, they knew not who did it; for so they say, they knew not who drave away the 6 colts, but Mr Coningsby keeps them, though I have writ to him for them. They have used all means to leave me have no man in my house, and tell me, that then I shall be safe; but I have no cause to trust them. I thank God we are all well. I long to see my cousin Hackluyt. I pray God bless you.

Your most affectionate mother, Brilliana Harley.
Feb. 14, 1642. [1643]

For my dear son Mr. Edward Harley.

My dear Ned – I should have been very glad to have received a letter from you by Mr. Taylor; and dear Ned, find some way or other to write to me that I may know how the world goes, and how it is with your father and yourself; for it is a death to be amongst my enemies, and not to hear from those I love so dearly.

Here I have sent you a copy of the summons was sent me; I wish with all my heart that every one would take notice what way they take: that if I do not give them my house, and what they would have, I shall be proceeded against as a traitor. It may be every ones case to be made traitors; for I believe every one will be as unwilling to part with their house as I am. I desire your father would seriously think what I had best do; whether stay at Brompton, or remove to some other place. I hear there are 600 soldiers appointed to come against me. I know not whether this cessation of arms will stay them.[7] I cannot tell what to think, that I hear nothing of your sister Brills son, nor that you did not write me word, that he was come to you. I hear captain Jeffreys is drowned. I am very much beholding to doctor Wright, for he will not go from Brompton till he sees me out of my trouble.

Mr. Phillips carries himself very well, and Mr. H as he was used to do. Good Mr Baughly is fain to come to Brompton. Mr Legg is still at Brompton, and Mathes and the Welshmen and Staney and 2 of Knights brothers, who were fain to fly out of their own country. My dear Ned, I will promise myself a letter from you by this bearer, who has carried himself very well to me; therefore I pray you give him thanks for it. I pray God bless you, and in His good time give us a joyful meeting, which I believe you think is longed for, by

Your most affectionate mother, Brilliana Harley.

I hear they have put up proclamations in this country, that there shall be no cessation of arms.

Doctor Wright and Mrs. Wright remember service to you.
Mar: 8, 1642. [1643]

To her son Edward.

O! my dear Ned – that I could but see you! I live in hope that the Lord will give me that comfort, which I confess, I am not worthy of. I hear from a good hand that you are ready to come out of London. The Lord in much mercy go with you and make you to do worthily; and dear Ned, believe my heart and soul is with you.

I heard from Gloucester on Thursday last, by one sent a purpose. Sr William Waller went on Tuesday towards the west. Lieut. colonel Massey is commanded to be governor of Gloucester by my lord general. I have and am exceedingly beholding to colonel Massey, as much as I was ever to one, I did not know; and I pray you tell your father so, and pray him to give him thanks. I sent to him to desire him to send me an able soldier, that might regulate the men I have, and he has sent me one that was a sergeant, an honest man, and I think an able soldier; he was in the German wars. He came to me on Thursday last, but your brother has the name of the command. I writ to you the last week, that the Welshmen were gone from me; this bearer will tell you the reason. Honest Petter is come out of prison. He was grievously used in Ludlow. Turks could have used him no worse; a lieutenant colonel Marrow would come every day and kick him up and down, and they laid him in a dungeon upon foul straw. Mr. Goodwin showed him kindness. In Shrewsbury he was used well for a prisoner; but he is very glad he is come home again, and so am I. The Lord in mercy bless you, and give you a comfortable meeting with

Your most affectionate mother, Brilliana Harley.

Mr Phillips is very careful, and longs to see you.
June 11, 1643.
I shall be full of doubts till the fair be past. Some soldiers are come to Knighton; my old friends that were there before.

To her son Edward.

My dear Ned – I cannot but venture these lines, but whether you are at London or no, I know not. Now, my dear Ned, the gentlemen of this country have affected their desires in bringing an army against me. What spoils has been done, this bearer will tell you. Sir William Vavasour has left Mr Lingen with the soldiers. The Lord in mercy preserve me, that I fall not unto their hands. My dear Ned, I believe you wish yourself with me; and I long to hear of you, who are my great comfort in this life. The Lord in mercy bless you and give me the comfort of seeing you and your brother.

Your most affectionate mother, Brilliana Harley.
August 25, 1643.

Mr Phillips has taken a great deal of pains and is full of courage, and so is all my house, with honest Mr Petter and good Doctor Wright and Mr Moore, who is much comfort to me. The Lord direct me what to do; and, dear Ned, pray for me that the Lord in mercy may preserve me from my cruel and blood thirsty enemies.

For my dear son Mr. Edward Harley.

My dear Ned – I received your most welcome letter by Mr Greens man, but I had none by Fisher, which did trouble me. I hope before this, you are assured of the Lords mercy to us in delivering us from our enemies.

My dear Ned, a thousand times I wish you with me, and then I should hope, by Gods assistance, to keep what is left your father with comfort. It is true, my affection makes me long to see you, and my reason tells me it would be good for you to employ yourself for the good of your country, and that which I hope shall be yours. My dear Ned, if the Lord should be so merciful, it would be such a comfort, that it would revive my sad heart and refresh my dried up spirits.

The Lord in mercy direct you and preserve you, and give you a comfortable meeting with

Your most affectionate mother, Brilliana Harley.

My dear Ned, let me know your mind whether I had best stay or remove.

Remember me to your brother.
Sep. 24, 1643. *Brompton Castle.*

For my dear son Colonel Harley.

My dear Ned – your short but welcome letter I received by Prosser, and as it has pleased God to intrust you with a greater charge, as to change your troop into a regiment, so the Lord in mercy bless you with a double measure of abilities, and the Lord of Hosts be your protector and make you victorious. My dear Ned, how much I long to see you I cannot express, and if it be possible, in part meet my desires in desiring, in some measure as I do, to see me; and if pleased the Lord, I wish you were at Brompton. I am now again threatened; there are some soldiers come to Leominster and 3 troops of horse to Hereford with Sr William Vavasour, and they say they mean to visit Brompton again; but I hope the Lord will deliver me. My trust is only in my God, who never yet failed me.

I pray you ask Mr King what I prayed him to tell you concerning Wigmore.

I have taken a very great cold, which has made me very ill these 2 or 3 days, but I hope the Lord will be merciful to me, in giving me my health, for it is an ill time to be sick in.

My dear Ned, I pray God bless you and give me the comfort of seeing you, for you are the comfort of

Your most affectionate mother, Brilliana Harley.
Oct: 9, 1643.

QUEEN HENRIETTA MARIA

Henrietta Maria (1609–69) was the daughter of Henri IV and Marie de Medecis. She married Charles I in 1625, the year of his accession, and bore him nine children, three of whom died in infancy. Her last child was born in 1644, after their final separation and shortly before her return to France, where she would remain until the Restoration.

The letters Henrietta Maria wrote to her husband during the civil war began in the spring of 1642, when the Queen left for Holland, ostensibly to convey her daughter Mary to her bridegroom, the Prince of Orange, but really to sell or pawn the royal jewels to help pay for the cost of the war, and to try and muster foreign support for the Royalist cause. She returned to England in the spring of 1643, was reunited with Charles for the last time, and left for France in the summer of 1644, from where she continued to write to him. The letters were written in French, and the royal couple also employed a cipher, which accounts for the occasional doubt about proper names.

The fact that Henrietta Maria was a Roman Catholic made her unpopular. The Parliamentarians regarded her as a danger to their cause, and with good reason. Throughout the conflict she was constantly involved in intrigues designed to help her husband's cause and, as these letters show, she was adamantly opposed to any form of compromise.

After the shattering blow of Charles's execution in 1649, her influence on her eldest son was resisted by his advisers. Charles II was restored in 1660, but Henrietta Maria remained in France until 1662, and spent only three years in England before returning to her native France.

My dear heart,   1642

It was with no small joy that I received your letters, for you were arrived at York a fortnight before I received tidings from you, but all at once I have had two newspapers. Sir William Baladin having been driven back by the tempest three times, the other at last overtook him, and they came together. I am extremely glad to hear that you have been so well received at York, and that you find the country so well affected. Take advantage of it, and lose no time; you know that the affection of the people changes like the wind, therefore you should make good use of it whilst it lasts; you have a precedent before you, for the parliament will make use of it.

As to what you write me, that everybody dissuades you concerning Hull from taking it by force, unless the parliament begins, – is it not beginning to put persons into it against your orders? If you wait for it to be done publicly otherwise than that, you will be ruined altogether, and as for the assurance that you have of Scotland, I have many doubts about it, for I hear that Argyle and the others, who I believe are rather for the Parliament, have regiments on foot to go to Ireland. Believing that you are going to Scotland, they design to have their people on foot, in order to make them now do what they wish. Take good care about it, and try to dispatch them to Ireland before going, if it be possible. If you have the people of Yorkshire, as assured to you as you found, take advantage of it, whilst they are in good temper: at the beginning, people can do things, about which, in the end, they grow cool, and then they can no longer be done. There is no more room for repentance. For my part, I think that the Parliament believes that you are constantly expecting an accommodation, in fact, that they draw back themselves perhaps to what they would desire, if they saw you in action, and that else, perhaps they would speak after another fashion. For you having Hull is not beginning any thing violent, for it is only against the rascal who refuses it to you.

As to money, I am at work: I must send into Denmark, for in the mean time, they will lend nothing upon your rubies. Nevertheless, I will put all my jewels in pledge; but as to you, when that is done, and you have expended that money, still waiting till the Parliament declares war against you, there will be no further means of getting other monies, and thus you will be reduced to do what the Parliament shall please, and I shall be constrained to retire into a convent, or to beg alms. Also it is to be feared that the Parliament will take a path more moderate in appearance, but in effect, worse for you; wherefore, that ought to be well considered. A report is current here, that you will grant the militia for one year, but your letter relieves me from that fear, for you assure me of the contrary. Continue in your resolutions; and pardon me if I have written a little too much on this subject by Ringfield. My whole hope lies only in your firmness and constancy, and when I hear anything to the contrary, I am mad. Pardon once again my folly and weakness: I confess it. The letter of which you speak to me, and which you sent me concerning an accommodation, is so insupportable, that I have burnt it with joy. Such a thing is not to be thought of; it is only trifling and losing time. Think that if you had not stopped so prematurely, our affairs would perhaps be in a better state than they are, and you would at this moment have Hull. This is only an example of what I say, and not to reproach you, for that is over. As to your having passed tonnage and poundage, I confess that it is against my opinion, for it is only for them and not for you – but I submit.

As to what has been told you that Cognet has sent word to her husband concerning Digby, it is a very great lie, for I can assure you that she only wrote about her private affairs, and about her mother, all whose goods the Parliament has arrested, their only ground being that she carried away all my jewels. As to Digby, I assure you that he has no intention of returning to England; he finds himself very comfortable where he is. It is true I have heard him say that if the Parliament wished to accuse him, and that he could defend himself without being sent to prison, he was so innocent that he would venture to go to defend himself; but it was with the intention that in case he went to see you, and were taken at sea, he might say that he was going to justify himself to the Parliament; but now, since you do not think it proper, he will not venture it. As to the ambassador who is to go from this country, I had a long conversation with him yesterday. I think he is a very honest man: you have seen him before; he is a tall man, who kissed the hands of Jeffry, taking him for my son. As to Isabelle [1] she cannot go with him; for she is too much suspected to be of your party.

I hear no news of the commission which I wrote to you to send, concerning my daughter and the rest. Please do not forget. I have received the addition of the cipher. I have nothing more to say except ever to urge upon you constancy and resolution: for it must be by these that we emerge from our miseries. I expect many lords have come to you. Beware of the persecutions of some: I name no one, but assuredly you will understand me. It is not only for Hamilton [?] that I speak, but for others yet, who you know are addicted to the commission, and who are come to join you. Since you are there, you must above all try to have a safe sea-port, for without that, you can have no correspondence with me, nor can I send you money. If you are forced to get Hull by force, assuredly you will need some powerful aid for besieging places. The Prince of Orange will send some if you wish it. As fast as I write, something always comes into my head; but adieu, I have such a bad tooth-ache that I scarcely know what I am doing.

The Hague, this 16th April.
The letter, on which there is no direction, is for Will Murray [?].

My dear heart,

After much trouble, we have at least procured some money, but only a little as yet, for the fears of the merchants are not yet entirely passed away. It was written from London, that I had carried off my jewels secretly, and against your wish, and that if money was lent me upon them, that would be no safety for them; so that all this time, when we were ready to conclude anything, our merchants always drew back. At last, it was necessary to show your power, signed under your own hand, about which I have written to you before, and immediately we concluded our business. I thought it better and safer to send it you as I do without noise, than for you to send different persons to fetch the money, for it will not be known that it will be for you, and as much, and as little at once, as you please. I thought this way more assured than to send it in specie, for were you to change your place, the money of this country would not pass, and in money of England we could not get it. I have given up your pearl buttons, and my little chain has done you [good]. You cannot imagine how handsome the buttons were, when they were out of the gold, and strung into a chain, and many as large as my great chain. I assure you, that I gave them up with no small regret. Nobody would take them in pledge, but only buy them. You may judge, now, when they know that we want money, how they keep their foot on our throat. I could not get for them more than half of what they are worth. I have six weeks' time in which to redeem them, at the same price. My great chain, and that cross which I had bought from the queen my mother is only pledged. With all these, I could not get any more money than what I send you. I will send to-morrow to Antwerp, to pawn your ruby collar, for as to [that], in Holland, they will not have it. For the largest collar, I am waiting a reply from Denmark. Every day, hopes are given me that those of Amsterdam will lend me money.

This is all that concerns money: but if we put all our jewels in pledge, and consume them without doing anything, they would be lost, and we too; for we should have nothing left to help ourselves with, when we should need it. For this reason, lose no time; you have lost enough already. Take a good resolution and pursue it. Remember your own maxims, that it is better to follow out a bad resolution, than to change it so often. I have received your letters by the man already named – they have made me very sad, for you do not speak of giving up your magazine as lost. I must tell you again, that you see that if at first you had acted as you had resolved, it might have been gained at this time, and also, since you had once tried to get it, it was needful to go on; for to begin, and then to stop, is your ruin – experience shows it you. It is not enough to declare yourself in writing;

action must afterwards be seen. It is true that your game is yet fair enough, but if you do not play it well, it will not be gained. You must dare, and as to Hull, if your magazine is not yet out of it, you must play Hotham[1] some skilful trick, for otherwise, there is nothing to hope. As long as you do not declare yourself, you cannot judge of your power, for no one will dare to declare himself. And think too, that I am risking all we have left in the world to get money, and that, when that money fails, there is no more, and that when it will be needful to pay persons for fighting, there will be no more; wherefore, time is precious. I am very glad that you have commanded . . .

[The rest of this letter, written in May, is missing.]

My dear heart,

I have received your letter by the post, with the message that the Parliament has sent you, which I think is pretty fair, since they believe they can have every thing by speaking high words. As to your journey into Ireland, I say nothing about it, having written on that subject before; but as to the discourse you have had with Culpeper [?] about Hull, I must say in truth, that to me it is a strange thing, that there is any one who can argue against that, and that you have not attempted to get it already; for the longer you wait, the worse it will be: and [can you] believe, that if there come a fleet to fetch away the arms, you will be able to hinder it? If, before that, you do not get the place, the folly is so great, that I do not understand it. Delays have always ruined you. As to your answer on the militia, I would believe that you will not consent to pass it for two years, as I understand you will be pressed to do, and that you will refuse it. But perhaps, it is already done; you are beginning again your old game of yielding everything. For my own consolation, however, I will hope the contrary, till I hear the decision; for I confess that if you do it, you ruin me in the ruining yourself; and that, could I have believed it, I should never have quitted England; for my journey is rendered ridiculous by what you do, having broken all the resolutions that you and I had taken, except of going where you are, and that to do nothing. If you had been willing to cede the militia when I was in England, I could have satisfied the Parliament, as I said; but you have done in this, I am afraid, as you did in the affair of the bishops; for at one time, you could have entered into an accommodation about that, and you were obstinate that you would not, and after all, you yielded it. Meanwhile, I went out of England, contrary to every body's opinion, in the confidence I had of what you would do, and I have made myself ridiculous; whereas, if you had done as you had resolved, it would have been seen that what you yielded all that time, was only out of fear of danger to my person, and from your affection to me, and not for want of resolution, and that I had been in the right to go away: whereas, hitherto there is ground for believing that it is a vagary or a folly; for as for staying in York, without doing anything, I might have done that.

Forgive me for writing all this to you: the truth is, that I see I shall be constrained by my misfortunes, to retire to some place where I can pray to God for you. I understand they are willing to give you tonnage and poundage for three years. I repeat to you, that if you cannot have it as you ought, that is to say, in your own power to dispose of it, you pass a thing against yourself: you see it by experience, for all that has been hitherto done with it, has been against you. As to what you write me, concerning the 7000 pieces, I will not fail to send them.

As to the esquire of James, the man to whom you have promised it is Mr. ——. He was a cornet of Henry Percy's company, a gentleman of worth. I think, that for the present, one in that place is enough. I send you this man express, hoping that you will not have passed the militia bill. If you have, I must think about retiring for the present, into a convent, for you are no longer capable of protecting any one, not even yourself.

Adieu, my dear heart.
The Hague, this 11th May.

My dear heart,

Since the wind has detained Barclay, I will write you again that I hope in three or four days to send you six pieces of cannon, with one hundred barrels of powder, and two hundred pairs of pistols and carabines; the rest soon after. I shall also send for the present ten thousand pieces. I assure you that I lose no time; do you the same. I have thought of one thing, now that you have the great seal. Something should be done to show that Warwick is not legally in his place, for as long as he is placed there by the admiral, he has some pretext of right.[3] This is all I have to say.

Send me word whether you wish the ambassadors from here to set off or not, for I shall delay them as long as I can, till I receive tidings from you; since I confess that, as affairs stand, I think it would be better for them not to go: I shall wait your reply. I will send you in a very few days, an excellent petarder, an engineer, and two others whom he desires to take with him.

Believe, my dear heart, that I have no joy but when I can serve you, and shew you that I am,

Entirely yours.

This 4th June.

I wish that you would send and fetch away the children who are at London; for, if affairs get to an extremity, they are not well to be there.

My dear heart,

I had written you a letter by Prince Rupert, when he was at Helvoet Sluys, waiting for a wind, in answer to the other; but my letter having arrived too late, it was brought back to me, Prince Rupert having set off, which makes me dispatch this man to you at Dunkirk, the wind being contrary by the other routes, to bring you the letter, which ought to have gone sooner, and also to know if Prince Rupert has arrived, being extremely uneasy about him, on account of the great tempest which has been on the sea; and, since Dunning has returned to Helvoet Sluys, on account of the force of the tempest, I stop him, not knowing whether Prince Rupert has arrived where he expected, and not thinking it fit for him to go before I know where the other ships are. You must therefore send me word, and quickly, what you wish him to do.

I must tell you, in reply to your letter by the post, that you have no reason to complain of not having received my letters for a long time. The winds have been so contrary, over which I have as little power as you have over the Parliament, since they would not obey me when I commanded them; and, as to the post, I have no inclination to send by that way. You tell me, that you have been advised to send and ask the advice of the judges. Without any jealousy whatever, I advise you not to do it; it is a thing than which nothing could be more ridiculous, and assuredly it were a folly to do it. As to the signature of the lords, I will send it you; Goring [?] is at Antwerp, the rest are away from here, but I will do it as soon as possible. I am astonished that you have not yet made another admiral. I would have you make James, and under him Pennington, as Warwick is under Northumberland. I think that should be done quickly.

I cannot refrain from alluding again to two things in your demand for reparation. The first touching the judges, upon which I dare not enlarge, as this letter passes through London; but I will only say, that I fear by that, you have lost a considerable sum of money – I think you will understand from whence. As to the other about the pardon, keep to the rule of my

59

grandfather. You pardon your enemies, but not your friends, and it is a strange thing that those who have offended you should be pardoned, and those who have obeyed you, excluded. I hope the Parliament, in their refusal to give up Sir John Hotham, who has been in actual rebellion, will set you an example; and the others have only spoken of serving you, and beg your orders, and are abandoned, even after you assured me of the contrary, in parting from me at Dover.

It might shake these persons, if they had not a great affection for your service; but I know they have too much generosity for that. I have no interest in this but yours, although I esteemed the unfortunates who have been ruined for us, which, I fear, is not the case with those who have advised you to do what you have done thereupon, and that their interest is to remove some, if not all, of those persons from you. I have nothing more to say, except that Lanark [?] will give you some papers, and will tell you what it is which, if you think proper to do it, will cause you to have some money. Keep the matter very secret, for Will Murray [?][4] even does not know it. As to the gifts, I have signed warrants here just as in England.

Excuse my letter being so badly written; I am troubled about my loss of the queen my mother, who died a week ago, but I only heard the news this morning. You must put on mourning, and all your suite also, and all the children.

Adieu my dear heart, I cannot write more.

This $\frac{\text{9th}}{\text{19th}}$ July.

My dear heart,

I think you do not yet know that the rebels, under the name of Parliament, have sent here to the States an ambassador or envoy, with letters of credence which I send you, just as they have similarly sent Augier into France. The man who is come here, is called Strickland. As soon as I knew it, I sent to tell the prince, and Sir William Boswell[5] went to see the States, to prevent his public reception, which has been done: but still they have sent to the rogue in private, to know what his commission was. He has brought a declaration which is not yet public, but there are persons here in whom the gallant has confided, who have not kept the secret, although being of the elect: and by them, I understand that they desire the assistance of these States to free them from their present slavery, and render them free men, as the kingdom of England helped them to do the same against their king. [6] They complain also, that the Prince of Orange assists you, and desire the States not to permit any arms, money, or men, to leave these States to order to go against them: and upon that, they say that the same arms might easily be turned against them one day. In three quarters of it, they preach upon religion, how you are wanting to change it. This is all that I have been able to learn; as soon as I can get that declaration, I will send it you. If I think fitting, I will make a reply quickly, in order to show their malice, and try to undeceive Holland; simply a relation of the things which the Parliament has done against you, and that you have done for the Parliament. I hope you will avow me when you hear it spoken of, or else that you will not say a word about it.

The elector [7] has proposed to me to go to Denmark himself for your service. I do not know whether you think it fitting for your service, and also whether those who are with him are persons to whom one may trust: for you know what the man is of himself. He has formed some propositions – namely, whether you wish to have men or money, ships, and so on. If you think the elector is a person fit to go, send instructions. I do not however forbear sending Cochrane at once into Denmark. Consider well what you wish to do about what I write to you; I am so weary, having been talking all day, and been in a passion about the envoy, that I am afraid my letter is no sense. Please to get some one to help you to decipher it, for I have written in such a fashion that I fear you will have trouble. If I do not turn mad, I shall be a great miracle; but, provided it be in your service, I shall be content – only if it be when I am with you, for I can no longer live as I am without you.

Adieu, my dear heart.
The Hague

This $\dfrac{\text{21st August}}{\text{8th September}}$.

My dear heart,

I had sent off a person to come to you, but the wind has not permitted. I am in extreme anxiety, hearing no tidings from you, and those from London are not advantageous to you. Perhaps by this they think to frighten me into an accommodation; but they are deceived. I never in my life did anything from fear, and I hope I shall not begin by the loss of a crown; as to you, you know well that there have been persons who have said that you were of that temper; if that be true, I have never recognised it in you, but I still hope, even if it has been true, that you will shew the contrary, and that no fear will make you submit to your own ruin and that of your posterity. For my own part, I do not see the wisdom of these Messieurs rebels, in being able to imagine that they will make you come by force to their object, and to an accommodation: for as long as you are in the world, assuredly England can have no rest nor peace, unless you consent to it, and assuredly that cannot be unless you are restored to your just prerogatives: and if even in the beginning you should meet with misfortunes, you will still have friends enough who will assist you to replace yourself. I have never yet seen nor read an example which can make me doubt of it by any means. Resolution and constancy are two things very necessary to it, assisted by the justice of our cause. Neither God nor men of honour will abandon you, provided you do not abandon yourself.

You see that I do not even fear lest this should be opened. I will venture to say that although it be not thought good, it will not be printed; that would be just the contrary of what is now done, for what they find just and good they hide, and what is thought bad is printed. That shews that JUSTICE suffers with us. Always take care that we have her on our side: she is a good army, and one which will at last conquer all the world, and which has no fear. Although perhaps for a time she hides herself, it is only to strengthen herself to return with greater force. She is with you, and therefore you should not fear: you will both come out together, and will appear more glorious than ever. I am very sure of it. See the effects of a melancholy solitude, but not at all of vexation, for, when I reflect well on all these things that I have been writing to you, I find myself so satisfied that no ill-humour can have any power over me, not even the ordinances of Parliament, which are the effects of one of the worst humours in the world. Considering the style of this letter, if I knew any Latin, I ought to finish with a word of it; but as I do not, I will finish with a French one, which may be translated into all sorts of languages, that I am yours after death, if it be possible.

This ___31st August___ .
          11th September

1643   My dear heart,
        As soon as I am returned to the Hague, I am anxious to let you know of it, believing you will be in trouble on my account, because of the terrible

storm there has been, which by God's grace we have escaped; after having been nine days at sea, in constant danger of perishing, we were at last compelled to return to Holland, whence I hope to set out again as soon as the wind is good, although a storm of nine days is a very frightful thing: nevertheless, when your service is concerned, nothing frightens me. I was but twenty hours distant from Newcastle, when we were obliged to return. God be praised that he has still spared me to serve you, but I confess that I never expected to see you again. The only regret I felt about dying was that this accident might encourage your enemies, and discourage your friends, and this consideration I confess troubled me; for, but for your sake, life is not a thing of which I fear the loss. I am so stupified that I cannot easily write more, for I have not slept during nine nights.

Adieu, my dear heart.

This 27th $\dfrac{\text{January}}{\text{February}}$.

My dear heart,

As soon as I landed in England, I sent Progers to you, but having learned to day that he was taken by the enemy, I send you again this man to give you an account of my arrival, which has been very fortunate, thanks to God; for just as stormy as the sea was the first time I set sail, just so calm was it this time, till I was within some fifteen hours of Newcastle, and on the coast, when the wind changed to the north-west, which forced us to make for Burlington Bay, and after two hours waiting at sea, your cavalry arrived. I landed instantly, and the next day the rest of the army came to join me.

God, who took care of me at sea, was pleased to continue his protection by land, for that night, four of the Parliament ships arrived at Burlington without our knowledge, and in the morning about 4 o'clock, the alarm was given that we should send down to the harbour to secure our ammunition-boats, which had not yet been able to be unloaded; but, about an hour after, these four ships began to fire so briskly, that we were all obliged to rise in haste, and leave the village to them: at least the women, for the soldiers remained very resolutely to defend the ammunition. In case of a descent, I must act the captain, though a little low in stature, myself.

One of these ships had done me the favour to flank my house, which fronted the pier, and before I could get out of bed, the balls were whistling upon me in such style that you may easily believe I loved not such music. Everybody came to force me to go out, the balls beating so on all the houses, that, dressed just as it happened, I went on foot to some distance from the village, to the shelter of a ditch, like those at Newmarket; but before we could reach it, the balls were singing round us in fine style, and a serjeant was killed twenty paces from me. We placed ourselves then under this shelter, during two hours that they were firing upon us, and the balls passing always over our heads, and sometimes covering us with dust. At last, the Admiral of Holland sent to tell them, that if they did not cease, he would fire upon them as enemies; that was done a little late, but he excuses himself on account of a fog which he says there was. On this they stopped, and the tide went down, so that there was not water enough for them to stay where they were.

As soon as they were retired, I returned to my house, not choosing that they should have the vanity to say that they had made me quit the village. At noon, I set out again to come to the town of Burlington, as I had previously resolved. All to day, they have unloaded our ammunition in face of the enemy. I am told that one of the captains of the Parliament ships had been beforehand to reconnoitre where my lodging was, and I assure you that it was well marked, for they always shot upon it. I may truly say, that by sea and by land, I have been in some danger, but God by his favour has saved me, and I have such confidence in his goodness as to believe that he will not leave me in other things, since in this he has protected me; and I protest to you, that in this confidence, I should dare to go to the very cannon's mouth, only that we should not tempt Him. This bearer is witness of all that has passed; nevertheless, I would not refrain from giving you this relation. It is very exact, and after this, I am going to eat a little, having taken nothing to-day but three eggs, and slept very little.

Adieu, my dear heart.

As soon as I have arrived at York, I will send to you to ascertain how I can come and join you; but I beg you not to take any resolution till you have had tidings from me.

Burlington, this $\dfrac{15\text{th}}{25\text{th}}$ February.

My dear heart,

I need not tell you from whence this bearer comes, only I will tell you that the propositions which he brings you are good, but I believe that it is not yet time to put them into execution; therefore find some means to send them back, which may not discontent them, (and do not tell who gave you this advice).

Sir Hugh Cholmley is come with a troop of horse to kiss my hand; the rest of his people he left at Scarborough,[8] with a ship laden with arms, which the ships of the Parliament had taken and brought thither; so she is ours. The rebels have quitted Tadcaster, upon our sending forces to Wetherby, but they are returned with twelve hundred men; we send more forces to drive them out, though those we have already at Wetherby are sufficient; but we fear lest they have all their forces thereabouts, and lest they have some design, for they have quitted Selby and Cawood, the last of which they have burnt: between this and to-morrow night, we shall know the issue of this business; and I will send you an express. I am more careful to advertise you of what we do, that you and we may find means to have passports to send; and I wonder that, upon the cessation, you have not demanded that you might send in safety: this shows my love. I understand to-day from London, that they will have no cessation, and that they treat at the beginning of the two articles, which is of the forts, ships, and ammunition, and afterwards of the disbanding of the army. Certainly I wish a peace more than any, and that with greater reason; but I would the disbanding of the perpetual parliament first: and certainly, the rest will be easy afterwards. I do not say this of my own head alone, for generally, both those who are for you and against you in this country, wish an end of it; and I am certain that if you do demand it at the first, in case it be not granted, Hull is ours, and all Yorkshire, which is a thing to consider of; and for my particular, if you make a peace, and disband your army, before there is an end of this perpetual parliament, I am absolutely resolved to go into France, not being willing to fall again into the hands of those people, being well assured, that if the power remain with them, that it will not be well for me in England. Remember what I have written to you in three precedent letters, and be more careful of me than you have been, or at the least dissemble it, to the end that no notice be taken of it.

Adieu, the man hastens me, so that I can say no more.

York, this 30th of March.

This letter should have gone by a man of Master Dimsdale, who is gone, and all the beginning of this letter was upon this subject; and therefore by this man it signifies nothing; but the end was so pleasing, that I do not forbear to send it to you. You now know by Elliot, the issue of the business of Tadcaster; since, we had almost lost Scarborough. Whilst Cholmley was here, Brown Bushell would have rendered it up to the Parliament, but

Cholmley having had notice of it, is gone with our forces, and hath retaken it, and hath desired to have a lieutenant and forces of ours to put within it, for which we should take his; he hath also taken two pinnaces from Hotham, which brought forty-four men to put within Scarborough, ten pieces of cannon, four barrels of powder, four of bullet. This is all our news; our army marches to-morrow to put an end to Fairfax's excellency, and I will make an end of this letter: the third of April. I have had no news of you since Parsons.

30th March, 3rd April.

My dear heart,

I received just now your letter by my Lord Saville, who found me ready to go away, staying but for one thing, for which you will pardon two days' stop, it is to have Hull and Lincoln. Young Hotham having been put in prison by order of Parliament, is escaped, and hath sent to me that he would cast himself into my arms, and that Hull and Lincoln shall be rendered. He is gone to his father, and I wait for your answer, so that I think I shall go hence Friday or Saturday, and shall go lie at Whatton, and from thence to Ashby, where we will resolve what way to take; and I will stay there a day, because that the march of the day before will have been somewhat great, and also to know how the enemy marches, – all their forces of Nottingham at present being gone to Leicester and Derby, – which makes us believe that it is to intercept our passage. As soon as we have resolved, I will send you word. At this present, I think it fit to let you know the state in which we march, and what I leave behind me for the safety of Lincolnshire and Nottinghamshire: I leave two thousand foot, and wherewithal to arm five hundred more, and twenty companies of horse; all this to be under Charles Cavendish, whom the gentlemen of the county have desired me not to carry with me – against his will, for he desired extremely to go. The enemies have left within Nottingham one thousand. I carry with me three thousand foot, thirty companies of horse and dragoons, six pieces of cannon, and two mortars. Harry Jermyn commands the forces which go with me, as colonel of my guards, and Sir Alexander Lesley the foot under him, and Gerard the horse, and Robin Legg the artillery, and her she-majesty, generalissima, and extremely diligent, with one hundred and fifty waggons of baggage to govern, in case of battle. Have a care that no troop of Essex's army incommodate us, for I hope that for the rest, we shall be strong enough; for at Nottingham we have had the experience, one of our troops having beaten six of theirs, and made them fly.

66

I have received your proclamation, or declaration,[9] which I wish had not been made, being extremely disadvantageous for you, for you show too much fear, and do not what you had resolved upon.

Farewell, my dear heart.

Newark, 27th June.

My dear heart,   1644

I have so few opportunities of writing, that I will not lose this, which will I believe, be the last before I am brought to bed, (since I am now more than fifteen days in my ninth month,) and perhaps it will be the last letter you will ever receive from me. The weak state in which I am, caused by the cruel pains I have suffered since I left you, which have been too severe to be experienced or understood by any but those who have suffered them, makes me believe that it is time for me to think of another world. If it be so, the will of God be done! He has already done so much for us, and has assisted us so visibly in all our affairs, that certainly whatever way He may be pleased to dispose of me will be for your good and mine. I should have many things to say to you, but the roads are so little sure, that I should not dare to trust this letter, only I will beg you to believe what Lord Jermyn and father Philip will say to you from me. If that should happen to me, it is a great comfort to me to have written this letter to you. Let it not trouble you, I beg. You know well that from my last confinement, I have reason to fear, and also to hope. By preparing for the worst, we are never taken by surprise, and good fortune appears so much the greater. Adieu, my dear heart. I hope before I leave you, to see you once again in the position in which you ought to be. God grant it! I confess that I earnestly desire this, and also that I may be able to render you some service.

Exeter, this 18th June.

My dear heart,

Up to this time, I was unwilling to trouble you with my complaints, having always hoped that time would remove my reasons for so doing, and because that would only grieve you: but when there is a probability of an increase of misery, it is well to prepare those whom we love to bear it. This then is what induces me to write you this letter about my condition, which compels me to it by the violence of more ailments, all at once, than either the state of my body, or that of my mind, depressed by the body, can support.

Since I left you at Oxford, that disease which I began to feel there has constantly increased, but with attacks so violent as no one ever felt before. I bore it patiently, in hopes of being cured by my accouchement; but instead of finding relief, my disease has increased, and is so insupportable, that if it were not that we ought not to wish for death, it would be too much longed for, by the most wretched creature in the world. And to render my condition complete, from three days before my confinement to this present time, Essex has been threatening us with a siege, to which I cannot make up my mind, and would rather set out on the road towards Falmouth, to pass from thence into France, if I can do it, even at the hazard of my life, than stay here. I shall show you by this last action, that nothing is so much in my thoughts as what concerns your preservation, and that my own life is of very little consequence compared with that; for as your affairs stand, they would be in danger, if you come to help me, and I know that your affection would make you risk everything for that. This makes me hazard my miserable life, a thing which in itself is of very little consequence, excepting in so far as you value it.

You will perhaps wish to know the particulars of my disease; it is always a seizure of paralysis in the legs and all over the body, but it seems to me as though my bowels and stomach weighed more than a hundred pounds, and as though I was so tightly squeezed in the region of my heart, that I was suffocating; and at times I am like a person poisoned. I can scarcely stir, and am doubled up. This same weight is also upon my back; one of my arms has no feeling, and my legs and knees are colder than ice. This disease has risen to my head, I can not see with one eye. It has pleased God to prove me, both in body and mind. I trust in His goodness that He will not abandon me, and that He will give me patience.

Adieu, my dear heart.

The most miserable creature in the world, who can write no more.

From my bed, this 28th June, Exeter.

My dear heart,

This letter is to bid you adieu. If the wind is favourable, I shall set off to-morrow. Henry Seymour will tell you many things from me, which the miserable condition in which I am does not permit me to write. I beg you to send him to me again to France, where, if God grant me grace to recover my health, I hope yet to serve you. I am giving you the strongest proof of love that I can give; I am hazarding my life, that I may not incommode your affairs. Adieu, my dear heart. If I die, believe that you will lose a person who

68

has never been other than entirely yours, and who by her affection has deserved that you should not forget her.

I send you back my company, to be with you, and beg that it may remain undissolved, as long as I live, if I do not die during these troubles; and if you would give Brett a pension of two hundred pieces, you would oblige me extremely. You are assured that during these times, he will never ask you for anything, and after the peace, he deserves a reward. I beg you also to please to give the commission of Cansfield's brother-in-law, to that Colonel Tilsley; Cansfield cannot ask for it on account of his religion, and the other is the nearest relation the young man has, and one against whom there can be no objection; and Cansfield has served you so well, and will do so yet, that you should not refuse so small a thing. Also my lord marquis[10] has begged me to write to you for him, and to recommend him to you. It is a miserable condition in which he is. Well, adieu.

Truro, this 9th July.

JANE LOVEJOY

These letters were addressed to Joanna Hayne, whose son Joseph died after losing a leg in the War of the Spanish Succession (1701–14). In 1707 there was heavy fighting between French troops and an army under Marlborough near Oudenaarde. Marlborough's generalship decided the battle, and 6,000 French were killed or wounded, whilst Marlborough's losses were 3,000.

1708

From the Duke of Marlboroughs
Quarters at Verveck [Werwik]
July the 26th 1708.

Honored Maddam

This is to lett you understand that Your Son Mr Joseph Hayne att the flight neer Audiner [Oudenaarde] was Shott in the right Legg; very dangerously and the Docters the next day following were oblidged to Cutt his Legg off; and since He is dangerously ill and every body that comes from that Place sayes he will not live Long; He hath sent me his Last will from his owne hand writeing; which if he Dies I will give Your Ladyshipp an Account; the Reason of givein me his Will was; I being a Souldiers Wife in the same Company and his Countrey woeman and Kin to Esq; Wiseman; he came always to Dyett and Drink in my Tent; Therefore I hope Madam you will Excuse me in giveing you the Trouble of these, lines being a Stranger to you; butt ready to serve you in any thing that Lyes in my Power; is all at present from M . . .

Your Ladyshipps humble . . .

[Letter torn.]

from the Grand Camp Neer Lille
Aug^st the 30th 1708

Honored Maddam

yours I Recived dated the Ninth Instant; Butt before itt came to my hands Your Son Departed this Life being very sensible to the last Minnitt; And before his Death desired me to give You a Letter with my own hand; He knowing I should come for England in the Winter; And upon my word Madam there was nothing wanting in the Assisting him of all matters that was nessasary for him; dureing his Life; And by the help of God I doe designe to see your Ladyshipp sometime next Winter and give a firsthand Account how he behaved himselfe and with what Vallior and Curridge; he haveing the Love of all Officers; And if itt had pleased God to spare his Life; my Ld: Duke would have preferr^d: him; which Coll: Gorsuch will give You an Account of when You see Him; Maddam before He Dyed there was some money due to me from him; but not very much; However he was pleased to give my Daughter Something in a Will he made some dayos before the fight; Which Will: Madd: I make bold to send You a Coppy of; being his Last Will he made; and after this will was compleated; what he had in the World Overplus; he desired may be giveing to his Sisters perticularly; Mad^m. I have no more att present butt rest Your Ladyshipps most Humble servant

Jane Lovejoye

To Madam Joanna Hayne living at Wallington in the Parish of Kintbury   1714
near Hungerford in the County of Bucks

Honoured Madam

'Tis some time since I gave your Ladyship the trouble of a letter on the account of a small Legacy left me by Your poor unfortunate Son by his last Will and Testament out of his Annuity Taxes being paid, Twenty three pounds, (which is the express Words of his Will). which Summe is but a very inconsiderate trifle to one of your birth and Honour; But wou'd be of the greatest consequence to such a poor Soul as me in my low Station. And sure I am, when he did me that Honour to grant it me, 'twas with an intent and design of doing me a signal favour and kindness, which I hope good Madam you will not frustrate the good and Charitable intent of the Deceas'd. If your Lady pleases I will send you an other Copy of the Will taken by a Notery publice and the witness's affidavids of the

Signing Sealing & cᵃ. and what farther proofs is requisite to testifie the verity of my pretentions, and that i'm the person, tho' since I have chang'd my name. There also remainds a small Sume due to Jane Lovejoy for necessarys that she furnish'd him with during the time he lay ill. All which we most humbly recommend to your goodness, charity, and clemency – hoping that you will be pleas'd to grant us a favourable answer and order the payment of both; and you will forever oblidge

>   Your Ladyships
>   most Humble and most
>   obedient Servant
>   Christ: Hartwell

be pleas'd to direct for me at Colonel Blakeneys in Dartmouth Street Westminster – London July 27th 1714

FRANCES NELSON

Nelson met his wife Fanny on Nevis, one of the Leeward Islands. At the time of his arrival in 1784 she was Mrs Nisbet, a widow with a young son, and acted as housekeeper to her uncle, President Herbert of Nevis. Nelson was very zealous in trying to get the Navigation Act enforced, currently being flouted by the newly independent Americans, and was helped by President Herbert.

Nelson and Frances were married in March 1787. He sailed for home in June, whilst his wife, with her uncle and family, took passage in a merchant ship. Her son, Josiah Nisbet, joined the Navy under his stepfather at the age of 12, the same age as Nelson had been when he first went to sea.

Frances Nelson spent much of her life preparing a home for her absent husband, and caring for her father-in-law. Her letters give a very good picture of social life at the time, as well as reflecting the anxieties of a naval wife during war time. She passes on naval news and gossip, rejoices in Nelson's increasing fame as a national hero, but her hopes for his return are rarely rewarded and, in 1801, Nelson enforced a final separation, due to his infatuation with Lady Hamilton. Frances died in 1831.

Kentish Town, 1794
September 30, 1794

MY DEAREST HUSBAND, – Yesterday was your birthday. Mr. Suckling drank it with no small pleasure, gave some of his best wines and a Norfolk man deserved two geese. We were cheerful. Mr. Rumsey and family were of the party. Mr. Mentz as usual intreated his best respects to you and said many handsome things which I received with pleasure knowing how deserving you were of them. A happy birthday for me, the next I hope we shall be together.

Your letter and my son's of the 5th September I have received and look every day for one telling me you are coming. Everybody that Mr. S. and

Maurice has asked if they know who are the captains that are coming home seems to say, you of course, that the ship must want much rest. Maurice came here last Sunday. He is much wanted at the Navy Office, but I do not know that they have offered him what would make it worth his while to quit his present station, for his half pay is £130 yearly and profitable one now. He is grown stout.

Your assurances of health and I hope the prospect of soon seeing my dear husband and child has made me happy beyond expression. It has given health for before you wrote me you were well and Calvi was taken, I was fallen into the same way I was last year, now I am quite well. Mr. Suckling behaves in kindest manner. Miss Suckling I shall always have a sincere regard for. Mrs. S. is equally kind. My dear son's letter did contain news. I thank him for it and hope he is quite right in what he says.

Lord Southampton is gone to demand the Princess of Brunswick for a wife for the Prince of Wales, everybody congratulates themselves on the change he is going to make; Mrs. Fitzherbert has been long dismissed. Her violence of temper and some improprieties gave disgust. Everybody are full of the wicked design that a French watchmaker had to take away the life of our king. They were three concerned, the French man, who had made a tube, which upon blowing with his mouth a poisoned arrow was to have struck our King, a saddler and a chemist in Fleet Street. The saddler's conscience tormented him. He went and disclosed it. They are all taken up. The Playhouse was to have been the scene of wickedness, the signal for the watchmaker a call of 'riot'. I wish these French away I never liked them.

The West Indies is now a scene of mortality. Never was such a fever there before. An officer who was tried for not knowing his own things has seen most of the Court Martial dead before the trial was over. The hurricane they have had I hope will be of service to them. Guadeloupe is not yet retaken. Capt. Roberts is a prisoner, recovered his wound. [I am] glad Maurice Suckling is well. Pray [take] care of yourself. How I shall rejoice to see you. You must save yourself as much as you possibly can.

Sir Andrew Hammond[1] has a house at Hampstead. I shall call on Lady H. and the first time I can on Lady Hood. Lord H.[2] has had leave to come by land or in his ship. The French have ships cruising.

Mrs. Matcham[3] I have not heard from since I came to town, but Maurice tells me they went to Tunbridge. Surely there never was such an unsettled man. The journey I hope will be of service to her. You may depend upon it, it is a violent cold she has caught. Capt. Suckling embarks again for the continent. They are all well. Suckling Nelson and the two clergymen of Aylsham are very good friends. Mr. S. says he liked to have my letters sent to him for then he knew you were well. He is very much interested about you. Our father is well. Mr. and Mrs. and Miss Suckling send their love to you. If any little thing falls in your way bring it for Miss S. as a keepsake. I feel for her. An attachment between her and Captain Whigley: he is on the continent. Her father knows it. He is to sell out. Don't take notice of it, it is not known. How is Frank?[4] I have seen his beautiful china.

Bless you my dearest husband, your affectionate wife, Frances Nelson.

To Captain Nelson, *Agamemnon*. To the care of J. Udney Esq., His Britannic Majesty's Consul, Leghorn. Post paid 1.5.

Bath,
December 17, 1794

MY DEAREST HUSBAND, – I have been particularly fortunate in receiving your letters of October 31st and November 21st the latter came last Sunday. I am thankful to hear your health is good. Lord Hood says you never looked better. They pay me particular attention. Nothing *now* is like you. Lord Hood once asked me if I knew who had bought Petersham, answer no. I know nothing of his Royal Highness. I went to the play with them, dined and taken a long ride but as to a word of news that is never to be heard there, of all the silent men surely he is the most so, not a word of the contents of your letter. I was determined to make him smile. He had hold of both my hands, and said he hoped I heard from you. I told him yes and as his lordship's letter was dated two days after mine I had an inclination to be jealous and that I should write you so.

Mrs. Holwell is here but not very well. She is a good woman. The Court of Enquiry sits on Capt. Molloy[5] the 31st of this month, parties run high. The contributions that has been raised on the inhabitants are all to be refunded, therefore I suppose estates and carriages must be done without and what is worse than all, it is said that the young men who have been made there are not to be confirmed. The love of wealth ruins many. Mr. John has been to see us. Many enquiries after you. He begged our good father to go and see him.

Charles Mills called yesterday says the West Indies is worse than ever. Mrs. Hamilton[6] never stirs out, has thirty *cats*. His uncle a good man but he must say deserves all he meets with. Stanley[7] a great man, but is lost to all sense of kindness. The Forbes are going to the West Indies in a very great hurry, how could it be otherwise they lived quite in style.

You will be surprised to find most articles in life much increased. Our father desires me to say your bill he had given orders how it should be disposed of to the best of his judgement. I must tell you he won't let me pay a part of the housekeeping, only of the house rent. He says he will spend his money first and if that won't hold out he shall attack your purse whether you have the bag or himself it matters not. I shall make Mr. Pinny who is coming here tell me how I am to draw upon Baily for the money.

I read the Norfolk news to our father. A pretty estate of 300 acres to be sold near Cromer. Suppose said Mr. N. you buy it that will just do. The Rector we seldom hear from. Maurice is very busy preparing for a secret expedition so he writes us. My child I figure to myself good obedient to you and I hope tells you all the secrets of his heart. If he does you will keep him good. At his time of life much is to be feared, thank you for having a French master. Do make him clean his teeth not cross ways but upwards and downwards. When I expected you I went and had my teeth put in order and wish I had done it some years back they look much better than you ever saw them.

I don't know that you will approve of what I am going to say but it is human nature. The French I wish may keep their fleet in Toulon. My dear I rejoice not to have seen any such wicked report of your being taken nor do I think it has reached England, but thank you a thousand times for every tenderness you show me. Last night was at the concert a very good one. Learning of music that is an expense to you. I practise a great deal but am not satisfied with myself. Have seen Mrs. Southerland seems highly delighted with her husband's situation she hopes he will never go to sea again.[8] Love to my child, your affectionate wife, Frances H. Nelson.

Keep all the little things which you tell me you have got, till we meet. I hear of great delays in some departments. Capt. Troubridge has had terrible mutiny on board *Culloden*, 10 will be hanged. Obliged to order a line of battle ship to sink her before they would hear reason.

Captain Nelson, *Agamemnon,* Leghorn. Care of Consul.

1797   Bath,
                                                                         February 15, 1979

MY DEAREST HUSBAND, – No letter from you since you left Gibraltar.

I have written to you generally once a week and sent my letter to Admiral Young. Now I will try the patience of a friend General Trigge, who it seems has written his wife a very cheerful witty letter, upon your telling him 'He looked too old to have a mother living', he says you are a most excellent commander but no courtier. 'Now indeed' said Captain Trigge to me 'My brother is really a good looking man.'

I supped last night at Admiral Dickson's the first time of my doing such a thing since we came to Bath. Our good father promised to go to bed. I was at home earlier than I expected, it was curiosity, for I heard much of the style etc. of the night entertainments. However this was truly a few acquaintances. Two card tables and all stayed to supper. Admiral Mason is very ill, a stroke of the palsy. Admiral D. seems to think we shall never see him again, it has affected Adm. D. spirits very much. I asked Capt. Trigge for some news of you. He assured me there was not any stirring worthy of telling you.

Everybody are full of the talk of an invasion, that the French are desperate enough to attempt it, but all hands agree in being assured that they will be unsuccessful. While the French were off Ireland, the bank in that country would not discount. The Irish I hear are very much dissatisfied with the conduct of the Fleet. The disposition of the defenders and White Boys were strongly marked in favour of the English government, they showed a determined resolution that they should not land, that they were oppressed and wanted to be relieved but not by French masters.

Norfolk and Suffolk have taken the alarm, a camp is to be formed early in the spring in that part of the Kingdom, such a commotion in this country is attended with great and serious consequences. The miseries it has brought on private families can never be done away. Estates are every day offering for sale. Where this general calamity will end the wisest are quite at a loss. The surrender of Mantua some think may bring forward a general peace. 'They say if the Emperor deserts us we are gone.'

I pray most sincerely Sir. J. Jervis has joined you long before this time. Not a syllable do we hear from or of him, only that he was to be made an Irish Lord; that has not taken place. We see Lord Keith Elphinstone and Lord Hotham have kissed hands. I hope Maurice writes you all the news. The accounts from all parts of the West Indies are truly afflicting. The deaths of the unfortunate men who are sent out there are not noticed. Government suppresses the accounts reaching the public as much as possible.

I think the contractors for medicines have much to answer. Mr. Searle called on our father and said he was intimately acquainted with one of the Directors of Apothecaries Hall, and that day the directors had received an order to pack up fourteen thousand pounds worth of medecine for the West Indies. The bark which had been sent out had grown in this country, and even the James' powders were so adulterated that no quantity remained I think their act is truly wicked. I am sure the contractors were French people for they do not allow there is a Supreme Being.

I have now on a pair of bracelets made of the chain you sent me. They are beautiful. The Italian flowers I have worn, they have been much noticed. I had occasion to enquire the character of a woman servant of Mrs. Dillon. She speaks very little English however she told me the Col. [her husband] had charged her to tell Mrs. Nelson the truth for he had heard of Com. Nelson. It was fortunate the Col. had charged her to tell the truth which was three gentlemen were trying to get her and that she had not character enough for *you*. I have a very nice young woman, she comes from Torbay and does not care where she lives.

Our father is better than when I last wrote to you. He seems to have quite unloaded his mind to me about the Matchams. He has again written to them, begging they would consider what they were about, as to his part he did not think they had income enough to live in the neighbourhood of Bath. He says he is sure Mr. M. will never be a settled man. Mrs. Suckling has written me. The sunshine I want must come from the Mediterranean. A feeling temper was certainly a great inconvenience but what will be the pleasure when I see my dear husband. We were speaking of the chance of your coming home which people think very probable. And then your good father says you must not go to the West Indies. The idea of it I verily believe would end his days. He certainly gets very infirm and this fever and cold have shook him very much, but I assure you he is better than when I wrote to you.

He desires me to give you his blessing. I pray God to bless and protect my dearest continuing his great successes. Believe me your affectionate wife, Frances N. Nelson.

I long to hear Josiah is with you. Mrs. Napier is very well. Compliments to General Trigge.

Commodore Nelson, *La Minerve*. To the care of General Trigge, Gibraltar.

Bath,
March 11, 1797

MY DEAREST HUSBAND, – Yesterday I received your letter of February 16th, thank God you are well and Josiah. My anxiety was far beyond my powers of expression, M. Nelson and Capt. Locker behaved humanely and attentive to me. They wrote immediate. Capt. Locker assuring me you were perfectly well, Maurice begging me not to believe idle reports, the Gazette saying you were slightly wounded. Altogether my dearest husband, my sufferings were great.

Lady Saumarez came running to tell me she had letters from her husband all this was on the day week. He speaks generously and manly about you and concluded by saying 'Com. Nelson's conduct was above praise.' You were universally the subject of conversation. Lord, Lady and Lady Mary Howe amongst others sent to know how you were, and if I had heard from you. The letters that I have had from common acquaintances will take me at least a week to answer them. But not one from my cousin Kelly. Mr. Sutherland's letter was very handsome. 'I have this instant heard of Sir. J. Jervis's battle in which Adm. Nelson bore a most conspicuous part, as he has in every service he was engaged in. The naval officers I heard speak on the subject in the course of yesterday and today all declare that 'he has displayed more professional skill more zeal and more intrepidity than any officer who served this war', and I think it impossible that he can escape being made a lord or at least a K.B. for such honours are sometimes bestowed on men who really deserve them. Be this as it may happen, yet it is the general *wish*!'

Lord Hood wrote that he was astonished to hear that you were there, that he congratulated us on the glorious share Adm. Nelson had in the late action with the Spanish fleet. Lady is very ill and from what his Lordship says, I don't think she will rally again, and begs I will write him all you say about the action. Yesterday after I received your letter I went to Colonel Glover's morning concert, you had I think his regiment on board *Agamemnon*. The colonel or his wife told me something about it. I thought Baron Dillon would have kissed me he said 'Madam, I have seen you at Mr. Glass's therefore I will speak and sincerely do I wish you joy.' In short he announced who I was, they all made their bow, enquired if I had heard from you, hoped you were well. 'What does Adm. Nelson say about the battle, does he not give you the particulars?' The Baron who is very much respected, indeed beloved by everybody, said you had something else to do. I was very glad when they had taken their seats and

79

the misses taken their seats at the pianoforte. This concert consists entirely of gentlemen and lady performers. All the Glovers are musical.

I had a letter from poor Mrs. Bolton expressing her joy in your being well and their concern at not hearing from Wm. Bolton. I have received (yesterday) your letter off Cape St. Vincent Febry. 13th. Mile End House is not yet disposed of, 38 acres of land may be had with it. I will make further enquiries about it. The distance is a great one from London. Our father thinks it too small, the eating room may be, but if it answers in all other respects but that a window may be thrown out. I wish you would say something more positive about it.

Our good father has bore his great joy of your being well and the many congratulations very well: but he attempted to walk out, but was obliged to return, however he is pretty well. I shall not be myself till I hear from you again. What can I attempt to say to you about boarding. You have been most wonderfully protected. You have done desperate actions enough. Now may I, indeed I do beg, that you never board again. *Leave* it for the *Captains*.

How rejoiced Jo. must have been to have seen you, although it was but an absence of two months.

Tomorrow is our wedding day, when it gave me a dear husband, and my child the best of fathers. I hope he will deserve all the blessings Providence has bestowed on him. Maurice Suckling has written me his very best production, they are the sentiments of an affectionate heart. He would like to be employed with you but won't stir till he hears what command you are to have, in the Channel or North Seas. Now I shall tell M.S. your flag is sent you 3 days back. Do come home this summer or in the autumn. It is said a change in the administration would certainly have taken place had not this wonderful and fortunate victory taken place. Admiral Parker it seems had written the *Captain* and *Culloden* bore the brunt of action. This instant have I received a letter from Lord Hood telling me Sir Robert Calder was gone to Portsmouth.

Thank you my dearest husband a thousand times for your letter of February 22nd. God bless and protect you and my Jos. crown all your endeavours with success and grant us a happy meeting. I can bear all my extreme good fortune. Your affectionate wife, Frances H. Nelson.

Our father sends his blessing to you and offers up his prayers for your protection. God bless you.

To Rear-Admiral Nelson, *Captain*. By favour of Sir Robert Calder.

Bath,
March 26th, 1797

MY DEAREST HUSBAND, –I have had no letter from you since the one dated March 1st. therefore I have very little to say, excepting I hope in God you are well and Josiah. The newspapers have told the world that Admiral Nelson has sailed with a squadron on purpose to take the Spanish flotilla. I sincerely hope to hear Sir. R. Calder has joined Sir J. Jervis with the reinforcements. Lady Northesk[9] called on me on Saturday. Her mother has been confined to the house or would have called on me. This day I shall return the visit. She told me Lady J. had received letters of a very late date from Lisbon.

I had a letter from Maurice yesterday he tells me 'The Navy Board yesterday informed me that they had replaced me in my former rank in the office and had ordered me a salary of three hundred a year. I am perfectly satisfied.' I rejoice at it most sincerely, he tells me he has many letters to send you by Capt. Hollowell, one from Sir R. Hughes who is going on in the same old way. Our father has at last received a letter from old Crow I thought he was afraid of saying too much. 'Although he was desired by a numerous set of respectable people to express their admiration of your extraordinary gallant conduct and hoped it would not be long before he was blessed with the sight of such a son that few had to boast.'

The Rector wrote us a very affectionate letter: he is determined to make you a visit, he will set off as soon as you arrive, he is *determined* on it. They have invited me to spend the summer with them. Our father has talked of going into Norfolk. He sometimes expresses his anxiety about Suckling, but any movements of his must be regulated by Mrs. Bolton,[10] as he has offered to accommodate her and girls for 6 months. Mrs. Bolton's girls go to the Matchams in May, therefore everything will soon be determined upon. I shall send you a barren letter but indeed one hears of nothing but banks stopping. The Bury bank has stopped payment. Lord Cornwallis has lost thousands, Sir Charles Davis is a very great sufferer. Mr. Maynard who is here from Suffolk has lost five hundred, which he says is a serious inconvenience. The Cambridge bank is broke. Bridport bank totters, Bristol bank is not thought to stand very firm. Mr. Baillie gave me two bank notes of Bristol, each twenty pounds, I got rid of one as soon as I received it, the other stuck fast, I sent it to Mr. Tobin last week and requested him to get a Bank of England note for me. I hope he will succeed, scarcity of money is very great. The times are very unpleasant. Our father tells me the old women get hold of me and make me quite melancholy. It is not the old women that make me look grave. I leave you to guess where my thoughts are. They will fly across the sea and settle on board ship. Mr. Tarleton and his wife are here. Mr. T. tells me the Duke of Clarence begins to be a favourite of his Majesty's. Many who thought him wanting in common sense find they are deceived. We have been blessed with fine rain. It was seriously wanted. Bread begins to be raised.

One of the handsomest letters I have received was from Scotland. Miss Nisbet hopes government intends the Admiral a title and something better, sends her love to Josiah, 'and desires me to tell him I hope he will tread in such steps of honour and glory and one day equally be the pride and boast of his country.' If you go to Gibraltar do notice G. Tobin. Mr. Tobin is sure you will like him, 'for he would take a *lion* by the beard, as to Harry he likes a good dinner and minds the counting house.' Our good father has answered old Crow's letter very charmingly, says envy itself dare not show its head. He will write to you next Monday. He is grown young. These blessings in his declining days cheer him. He desires his love to you and prays God to bless you. My love to Josiah, God bless you both and continue your great success. Believe me your affectionate wife, Frances H. Nelson.

Compliments to Capt. Collingwood. I hope the Portuguese make much of you. I long to hear from you.

To Rear-Admiral Nelson, *Irresistible*, Lisbon. Post paid 1/8d.

Bath,
April 3, 1797

MY DEAREST HUSBAND, – I have wrote to you by the *Lively*, at least I directed a letter from our father. Lord Hood writes me he can send another letter, therefore it gives me an opportunity of enquiring after you and Josiah, not but I think the packet is as good a conveyance as any. As to news we have none not even a little chat, excepting meeting last night Mr. Lucas from Norfolk he says Admiral Duncan speaking of your engagement nothing could ever be done to equal it, therefore he hoped never to meet an enemy, everything must fall short of such an action. The Norfolk man wanted to know what title they were to give you for they must give you what you please. They don't like their present member for

Yarmouth Mr. Joddrill, he has never been near the place since his election. A navy man was absolutely necessary for them. I said Sir. J. Jervis had offered his services, it was very true but they wanted a man that the ministers would recommend else they would not get anything done. Mr. Lucas mentioned a house and twenty acres of land that would soon be offered for sale eight miles from Norwich either in the Bury or Bungay road, which I am not certain. The house is not large, two very good parlours and a study, the house was Sir Barney Bargraves; he mentioned several large overgrown houses. No bidders for Lyndford. I wrote you about the house near Norwich, the roof was fallen in and otherwise very much out of repair. Land is increasing in value. Sir Frank Laforey called on us yesterday, he is going to London, has asked for a frigate, is to have one. His accounts from the West Indies are very alarming. The French have seized all the American vessels going to the islands and sent them to St. Martins. The want of corn and flour is very great, they are fearful of being in extreme distress. The West Indian seas swarm with privateers from Guadeloupe.

Captain Stanhope's business is accommodated: Lord Keith had nothing to say against him, excepting he thought him not quite so respectful as he might have been and the Admiralty lawyers could not find that a court martial could be granted, upon which Capt. Stanhope asked for the *Neptune* and he has her. He came down on Saturday. Mrs. Stanhope tells me all this, she says she and her children were to return with him to Woolwich as it would be some time before the ship would be ready for sea.

Our father's cough is better, he is writing to Mrs. Bolton to enquire how she intends disposing of herself and her children after her visit to the Matchams, therefore I shall tell you in my next how matters are going on. I would fain go into Norfolk but our father seems to say a great many inconveniences would attend it, plenty of time yet to talk about it for much depends upon Mrs. B. I long to hear from you, some say you are gone to the Western Islands, other off Cadiz. God grant you are well and that I may soon hear from you.

Did I write you I had Lady Northesk's visit. I like Mrs. Rickets,[11] she is a pleasant well bred woman. The ladies of quality have fashion in their mode of speaking, laughing, or smiling, at every word they say which I don't like. Such revolutions in our dress since you left me. Now our waists are lengthened, heads dressed *flat* at the *sides*, very high in front and low upon the forehead, short sleeves, some ladies show their elbows, short petticoats, nay above the ankle with the fashionable, and little or no heels to the shoes. Gloves almost beyond the pocket of anyone, none but the long ones are of use. None less than 3/–, a pair. Coloured and white the same price. I have just heard that Admiral Kingsmill's secretary has absconded and joined the French fleet, the same of Lord Corhampton's secretary changing all the signals. I think more of this on account of you not hearing it. When shall we meet and have rest? I hope before long. God Almighty bless and protect you and Josiah continuing to you your great success. Believe me my dearest husband your affectionate wife, Frances H. Nelson.

To Rear-Admiral Nelson.

Bath,
May 15, 1797

MY DEAREST HUSBAND, – Although you did not mention where you were going in your letter of April 12th, I heard it from Admiral Barrington who first asked me if you had told me. My answer No, then said the Admiral <u>I will tell</u> and so he did, had it from good authority, General Rainsford.

Captain Shank thinks you will proceed to Elba. I hope soon to hear of your return to the fleet, indeed you fag too much. October is always uppermost in my mind. I pray God we may meet not to part again. I had a kind letter from Maurice, telling me all he had heard which was the same as the Admiral's. He had seen Captain Woodhouse, Spicer and Noble who all assured him you were well, congratulates me on Josiah's promotion and seems very sanguine in his further rise. I suppose you will hear from Mrs. Bolton who writes me Mr. B. has hired Mr. R.'s farm, for 15 years and of her kind reception at Shepherd's Spring. Our father talks of inviting her and the girls in September to spend a few weeks before she returns into Norfolk.

We have had a letter from the Rector of Hilborough telling of one hundred acres of land to be purchased near Pickenham. It has a very poor farm house and old out buildings, thinks that you may like to build and that you could let the land that you did not want. However I have said nay: that will never do these times. Building is so very expensive and besides our father says the situation is a very bad one. Mr. Hoste was here on Thursday he thinks Mr. Hogge's house at Aylsham will soon be to dispose of, as Mr. H's female attachment lives in London, and has promised that he will request a friend of his who lives in that neighbourhood and is acquainted with Mr. H. to let him know whenever it is to be offered for sale, but he thinks it has not much land. He describes the house as being very good, few rooms but those are large and well fitted up.

You will see by the papers the unhappy situation this country has been from the seamen, wishing for an increase of pay and their dislike for some particular officers. Sir Bickerton, Mrs. Shaw tells me she hears from her husband, although the sailors have suffered him to return to his ship, still threaten his life. After they had once driven him on shore and allowed him to return he addressed them on the impropriety of their conduct, the great lenity of his Majesty etc. (it would have been well had he stopped there) but he said he knew he had a set of rascals to deal with, that expression has made them more inveterate than ever. However he is still on board his ship. Mrs. Athill who has been very kind to me I feel most sincerely for. Lady B.[12] is at Portsmouth her sister is gone there to her. What a lesson it is to those entering life to use the power which certain situations give them with moderation and great evenness of temper.

I have bought the narrative of the action of the 14th of February.[13] I like it because it has done my dear husband justice. It was written by a land officer on board the *Lively*. The late Viceroy's wife of Corsica[14] I hear was not liked. She would not mix with the inhabitants. I readily believe her to be very proud. The day I returned her visit I thought she received me as if I was honoured. I told our father on my return that Lady E. had forgot she was not the person she was at Corsica, however she is mistaken, it is not in her power by her acquaintance to honour your wife, and so little do I covet the acquaintance of the fashionable that I would rather shun it. Not that I think the air of London particularly infectious. The late poor Lady Derby. No one would perform the charitable office of burying her. Lord D. refused, and the D. of H.[15] likewise did the same, there she lay for a considerable time. At last the D. of H. feelings were roused, a spark of natural feeling being left, and he buried his sister. She was still his sister, let her conduct been ever so bad. Her unfortunate daughter whom Lord D. disputed, but the laws of his country not, has married a subaltern in the Dragoons, and is in great distress.

I have taken up much of my paper relating this history so that I can only make short enquiries after the Lieutenant who I do hope is well. Give my love to him and tell me if he adds a little gravity to the change.

God bless you my dear husband, your affectionate wife, Frances H. Nelson.

Lady Saumarez and her party has left Bath. Mr. W. Hoste leaves Bath next week. Mr. Coke it is said has some thoughts of living at Worham as he cannot afford to live at Holkham.

To Rear-Admiral Nelson, *Captain,* Lisbon.

Our father's blessing and love to you. Will write on Thursday or Monday next.

1798   Thursday [5 April] 1798

MY DEAREST HUSBAND, – I had written to you yesterday before I had received your kind and affectionate letter. Indeed I have always felt your sincere attachment and at no one period could I feel it more strongly than I do at this moment and I hope as some few years are past, time enough to know our dispositions, we may flatter ourselves it will last. You will I hope find all your things I am much mortified at their being displaced. Have the small paper parcels opened. I yesterday wrote you what Kitty said, that she had put into the box of sundries 3 velvet stocks and Ryson is quite sure the stock buckle and velvet stocks are in the trunk. Do say if they are found. Have you stockings enough? I wish very much you would examine the parcels and box yourself. The great bundle of papers which was tied up in a common coloured handkerchief in that I put several things myself. I have nothing here which would be of the smallest service. The Matchams arrived yesterday. They are gone to unpack and put their house to rights. Kitty went to them after breakfast. Your sister is delighted at leaving the Heath.

Mr. Matcham last week fell from his horse at 3 o'clock in the morning in liquor, however she knew nothing of it, and he was not hurt. The horse went home, and Tom seeing it sent it back by a careful person and Mr. M. rode home.

The news is melancholy today from Ireland, so Capt. Welsford says, who is ordered upon a recruiting party. How cruel it is for men of great wealth to be swearing off the taxes. Conceive of Mr. Braithwaite keeping 16 horses and says he uses but four, 9 men servants and enters four. Mr. Sherston it seems told him it was a shame that everybody was throwing the load off their shoulders. His opinion of the times are the same as my dear husband's and he means to do exactly what you have desired me to the cottage.

The wind is very contrary how it blew all last night. God grant you his protection and that we may meet again. As to peace I most ardently wish for it particularly as you will then be satisfied to live quietly at home. I can't help feeling quite unsettled and a little hurried for when my spirits are not quiet you know I am but a poor creature.

Our good father's love and blessing to you. He will take a little money I have offered him just what he pleases. God bless you my dearest husband, your affectionate wife, Frances H. Nelson.

To Rear-Admiral Nelson, K.B., *Vanguard*, Portsmouth.

If the *Vanguard* is sailed to be returned.

London,
May 15, 1798

MY DEAREST HUSBAND, – I have just had the pleasure of hearing from Maurice Nelson that he has seen a letter dated Lisbon April 28th which mentions you are well, thank God for it, and may the Almighty continue his goodness to me in the preservation of your life. I long to hear of my Josiah, I hope you will find him a good man. Our father will be in town this afternoon. He stays with old Mrs. Matcham, dines at Kentish Town on Thursday, and on Friday or Saturday we set off for Round Wood. Had our father stayed a few days longer at Bath, it would have suited me better. I called on Lady St. Vincent, she has had no letters from her Lord lately. She seems a good woman, spoke very humanely and tenderly of the unfortunate Lady Elizabeth Rickets. She is generally pitied. If Lord St. Vincent should ever say anything on the subject do lean on the poor woman's side; Lady E. has written to him begging that he would intercede with her husband to grant her one interview. I could write a great deal.

Captain Peard is determined to be divorced. Mrs. Thomas tells me poor Mrs. Peard won't live long. He won't see her. Mrs. Thomas will go on another message not to prevent my writing, therefore my letter in spite of my inclination will be short. Cooke and Holford has paid me, promised to send me £40 soon. I have had £100 from Marsh. When I have paid every bill I send you exactly the expenses of the furniture. I have collected a few little things for you. Two very good silver plates, bought them second hand, had them cleaned and your crest engraved upon them. Find it very inconvenient to be at Kentish Town. Shopping takes much time.

Mrs. Wigley makes kind enquiries after you. Mr. W. seems a very softly man was quite offended that he should be thought like you. The little woman will chat –

My love to my child. God bless you my dear husband and believe me, your affectionate wife, Frances H. Nelson.

Mr. and Mrs. Suckling, Mr. and Mrs. Wigley beg to send kind love. Mr. Nelson will send this letter for me. Gave him one last week – Monday.

Rear-Admiral Sir Horatio Nelson, K.B., *Vanguard*, Lisbon. 1/8d.

Round Wood,
May 28, 1798

MY DEAREST HUSBAND, – On Sunday the 20th of May we arrived at Round Wood, the satisfaction I felt was very great in being under your own roof. No thanks to any earthly being. Our father was for staying, although the house had little or no accommodation. He viewed everything attentively and I never saw him so thoroughly satisfied as he was and says the more he examines everything the better he is pleased. The house is quite large enough and the walls are of a good thickness. The trees thriven well, they have been planted five years, and your tenant Mr. Fuller thinks from their present height in five years more the house will be quite sheltered. A little more ground planted in trees will still add to its beauty.

We were obliged to take up our quarters at Ipswich that day. However on the Monday, our father's patience could not hold out, till I called on Mrs. Bolton to thank her for her civilities and a chaise to be ordered, but he set off with the footman I hired at Bath and walked up a high Suffolk hill and we are very comfortably settled. But before I proceed with my narrative I must tell you how very much he has been distressed by the sevant he hired at Bath leaving him, in a fit of insanity as he supposes. Your father and Miss Martin had just walked into Mrs. Martin's parlour, Kensington, Mr. N. says to deliver his fellow traveller, to her mother, safe when the servant set off running in the most extraordinary manner ever seen, and has never to our knowledge been heard of. Since we arrived here Mr. N. had his clothes examined that they might be packed up, when they were found in so disgraceful a state that he gave orders to the footman to burn them, and he thinks violent medecines has been improperly taken. He was the completest servant I had ever seen: so that we have but one footman, quite enough.

The pump upon examination and some money laid upon it, will do, the water is particularly good, it has been dug several feet deeper, it must have new works, the wise ones of this part of the country agreeing that Round Wood stood so exceedingly high that the uncertainty of finding water was great therefore it was worth the great expense of cleaning the old well, which has turned out well. A closet taken down in the eating parlour to admit a sideboard and a window in the damp dressing room, thrown out to the east (the little one which is in it now to be stopped up to the north) are the only expenses which are necessary besides the fixtures until I have the happiness of seeing you. Our father thinks you must throw out a good dining room next to the present eating room and a bedroom over it, then you will have a good room to yourself and a very good house good enough for anybody. Our father's dislike to Mr. W.B. [16] is great, I begged him not to show it. Mr. B. was looking at the pump he did not exactly approve of what one of the workmen said, but concluded his speech with saying: 'There must be a court martial held and I will sit upon it,' – besides he is an officious man. He nearly made a mischief between the workmen, however I will make use of him when it suits my convenience. He is to pay me next week the balance of your account. Mr. Hoste has taken no further notice. Mr. Cooper is an infamous character, you will never get your money. You had better send that knowing young lawyer home. The papers relative to the Round Wood farm Mr. Ryder gave me. Tomorrow I take them to Mr. Norcutt with a written desire of Mr. Ryder for a paper which Mr. N. has omitted sending. Mr. Norcutt is an old infirm man with a good character. Mr. Ryder's charges five guineas which I paid and he gave me a receipt. I have received my dear husband your letter No. 3 *Vanguard* Gibraltar May the 4th. I thank you for it and rejoice you have seen my Josiah and that the lady of the Admiralty[17] promises not to forget him. Captain Berry mentions him in a flattering manner to his wife. I sincerely hope he will deserve every thing you have done for him and indeed I think he will.

On Friday 25th Mr. Bolton and Susanna[18] came to dinner (Mrs. Bolton is well) they dined Mr. Bolton left Susanna and the next day she went to Ipswich. Mrs. Bolton is to come as soon as I have got a bed fitted up. Mr. Nelson said: 'I don't make use of a dressing room, therefore I think you had better have a bed put in it at once for one of the girls,' so I did it. The boys have dined here they are fine boys, but from their age quite children. I shall exactly follow your directions about the £175 had I not been so exceedingly hurried down I should have seen Capt. Cockburn for he was in London. Capt. C. will not allow me to pay him the expenses of the wine, he writes me you and him will settle it. The little trunk I was obliged to send to Mrs. Godfrey, who writes me she will take it to your brother Maurice, who I shall write to and beg he will deliver it to Capt. C.

Mrs. Norcutt has sent me word that he will call on Wednesday on his way to Woodbridge. Then I shall be able to give you a full account of your affairs here. I gave Mr. Marsh your account up to the 23rd March to copy that it might be sent to you by Capt. C. I can't tell you yet the expense of furniture. God bless you my dearest husband believe me your faithful and affectionate wife, Frances H. Nelson.

My love to Josiah. Our father's blessing to you, 'tis an excellent way to number letters. This is I think my sixth letter. No. 1 and 3 received from you. 2 silver plated plates, knife, seal, prayer book, and a hussey, 2 pr. of buckles, tape and bobbins, Italian paste.

Rear-Admiral Nelson, K.B., *Vanguard*, Lisbon.

Round Wood,
July 16, 1798
(No. 13)

MY DEAREST HUSBAND, – I only write to tell you of my extreme anxiety to hear from you, no one period of the war have I felt more than I do at this moment. I really am so affected that it has enervated me beyond description still I think all will turn out to your most sanguine wishes. I hope in God it will. The papers tell us you have been to Naples, but was not satisfied and immediately sailed for Malta. I wish I knew that Josiah was with you. A line from him would do me good. I can only hope his duty to his profession and his love for you employ his time. I am one of the old fashion mothers and think there is a something called natural affection. I am sure I feel it for him. Mrs. Berry is still with me. I find her a very pleasant young woman. Not in the least gay. We go to Capt. Boucher's just when we like.

Yesterday we called upon them after church and brought them up to dinner which cheered us all, for I assure you we all talked of the situation you are placed in till we are almost stupified. Our father was glad to have somebody to talk to. How any creature could possibly tell us this was a good neighbourhood. We talked of it to Capt. Boucher, he said by no means. The Berners never mixed with anybody. Sir W. Rowley was full

17 miles from us. Sir R. Harland was a very gay young man and no gentlewoman ever went to his house, once a year at the races he either gave a breakfast or a dinner. General Dalrimple, Sir Robert Harland's brother-in-law lives with him. The world thinks Sir R.H. is fond of gaming and has lost very much at play that he will soon be fleeced by his relation. We have been to see his beautiful seat Wherstead, the house not finished. A want of money they say is the cause. A well behaved man shewed us the house and when he came to the bedrooms he threw the doors open for us, he remaining outside. Mrs. B. Mrs. Berry and myself were not at all gratified by the indecent ornaments of a gay young man, fine, naked figures and very handsome looking glasses at the bottoms of the bedstead, so we left this handsome house and on one of the most beautiful prospects I ever beheld, not much impressed with favourable sentiments of the owner.

The Queen of a certain town that you called upon who made handsome promises about introduction and such civilities, I find as arrant a courtier as ever lived, a tongue well dipped in oil and fashioned early in life by a gay disposition and I am happy to say I am not at all of her clan therefore the communication there will be very little. She is likewise reckoned to play a steady game. Her house is opened to all card players even her old acquaintance, who have from prudence given up card playing, she never invites saying: 'Capt. you and your wife seldom play which is the reason I never send you a card, but any time you like to come I shall be glad to see you.' Even the Admiral does not escape her.

The window shutters are not all made, but this week I think will nearly finish the carpenter's work. Our father thinks it best only to patch up the rails and fences which to be sure are very bad. It will cost you a good deal to put the house in good repair but everything that can be done shall, excepting the two parlour window shutters, if it is possible the shutters shall remain as they are while we are in the house, altho' they admit wind enough when they are done up to make it a matter of some moment, where to place the candlesticks.

John Thompson[19] called here this morning. He has been a prisoner in France made his escape with five others that were confined in a church, they took everything from him. Mrs. Berry recollected his face, we had a long dish of chat. He wished himself often enough with you. Can't stoop nor go aloft poor fellow. He looked very thin could hardly eat. He took care that he had money enough to carry him to London. He told us the common people in France they were told wished for peace, they heard little. I asked him how he knew where you had a house. He said he was asked if he knew you. He said monstrous well for he sailed with you five years, all this at an ale house in the neighbourhood. Give Mrs. Berry's love to her husband and she will write to him on Thursday.

I have had a letter saying he is in hopes of having all your business settled at the Custom House to your satisfaction. Thomas Allen's money is quite safe. Our father's blessing attend you. God bless and preserve my dearest husband. Believe me your affectionate wife, Frances H. Nelson.

Rear-Admiral Nelson, K.B., *Vanguard*, Lisbon.

Post Paid 1/8d.

Round Wood,
October 1, 1798

MY DEAREST HUSBAND, – The 20th July is the date of your letter which I received the middle of last month. The newspapers let me rest a week, then began again with their conjectures and this last week have positively asserted you have gained some advantages over the French fleet assuring the public you arrived safe with your prizes at Naples. Government has sent some part of the above to Lloyds. I long to hear from you. A letter of one line will rejoice my heart, and I think I shall soon be gratified, God grant I may.

The cottage is in good repair. The window shutters are all finished, which makes it very comfortable. Our good father finds the air particularly clear and sharp. He told me it was the keenest air I had breathed he was sure for years. It is all true but I have taken less colds here than anywhere for years. However I have promised to go to Bath with him whenever he wishes. My own plan was to have left Round Wood in January but from all that has passed I think it will be the middle of November, provided Mrs. Bolton and her two children leave us. I expect her in ten days.

Every bill will be paid, the expense of drawing off the wine, bottles etc., came to £30 all very carefully put away against your coming home, in all 150 doz. I believe I mentioned to you the house was to be painted, and a part papered, I am almost afraid of papering all, the expense will be very great. Mention what you wish me to do. I feel very much your kindness in desiring I would indulge my self in everything you can afford. I go on in the same careful way I began. Six constantly in family, besides one of the Boltons and for six weeks back George, I assure you makes my weekly bills high.

Miss Patty Berry is spending a few days with me. Her brother John and his wife are gone to Trosendon to shoot for a week, from thence to Norwich to show himself after his voyage. Miss P. Berry is going to Norwich to Mrs. Berry in hopes of persuading her to go to the gay town. What will Capt. Berry say to all this? Capt. Charles Rowley has been obliged to give up his ship and is ordered to Cheltenham. Capt. B. Rowley is stationed in Ireland. Lady Harland told me yesterday that his friends were rather uneasy about him. Those who were in the same ship were not perfectly in good humour. I think that is all the news I picked up there. I met the Admiral just as I was going out of the house, who very politely begged I would dine with him, the Bouchers were to be there. So we all (three in number) went and spent a cheerful day. Very little variety here and when you make your appearance in the town you see plenty of soldiers and that is all. No kind of trade, or the least bustle.

Capt. Cockburn writes me he expects to leave England and will take charge of anything for you. I have by this day's waggon sent a box containing 9 small stone jars of cherries in brandy, five of currant jelly and five of apricot. The season was particularly unfavourable for preserving. The torrents of rain bruised the fruit very much. Sugar has raised in price beyond belief. We now drink sugar at 1/6 per pound.

We lately heard from Mrs. Matcham who is all anxiety to see her father. Miss Martin is returned from India. She and old Mr. M. are there. Tell Capt. Berry his old flirt that he often escorted to Kensington is fashion mad, exhibits without powder which makes her look particularly amiable. Miss Patty begs you will tell her brother that her mother is going to Dover St. Their house is to be painted. I trust I may say all the family are well.

Our good father will write next. I shall send my letter to Admiral Young. You can't think how very good Lord Hood has been to me. Writes very often tells me what he hears, and what he believes. I wish I could hear of my dear child. God bless and protect you my dearest husband and believe me to be your affectionate wife, Frances H. Nelson.

Rear-Admiral Nelson, K.B., *Vanguard*, Mediterranean.

April 15, 1799[20]   **1799**

MY DEAR JOSIAH, – I have written of late very frequently to you and as I generally take my letters to the foreign post office, I hope you may have received them.

I received a letter from my Lord Nelson dated January 25th where he mentions your improvements with tenderness and kindness. His love for you is very great. He flatters himself he shall see you a good and great man. It is in your power to be both. Therefore God bless you, disappoint us not. You are very young and cannot know the world, be satisfied of this truth, and implicitly follow the directions of my husband, who is truly a good man and his military achievements has stamped his character great all over the world.

You are more conspicuous than you imagine. Be assured you are much envied from having such a father to bring you forward, who has every desire to do it. To convince you I have very good reason to write you on this subject, I will in confidence repeat to you a conversation a captain of the Navy had with an intimate acquaintance of mine, not knowing I was in the least acquainted. 'I am trying all I can to remove Mr. —— first lieutenant of the *Thalia*, for her captain is no great things.' Then vented his ill-natured disposition, never once allowing himself to think he had been young. This acquaintance of mine is rather what is called passionate. He immediately said 'Do you know you are speaking of the son of a friend of my wife's, and the son-in-law of Lord Nelson's?' 'Yes' was the answer, and immediately this captain turned and left this gentleman, but in a minute returned saying 'For God sake don't mention what I have said.' And the *very next morning* he returned and intreated as a particular favour that the conversation might not be repeated. All this happened a year and a half back.

My dear Josiah take yourself to account every day. Don't excuse any foibles. I do assure you your first lieutenant has always wrote of you in a handsome manner. I have seen his letters to his mother. Silence on this subject.

There is an admiral who has got himself laughed at in wishing to defame my Lord's understanding. He wishes to be acquainted with me of all things. I suppose to speak well of my husband.

God bless you and believe me your affectionate mother, Frances H. Nelson.

Capt. Hardy's compliments to you and my Lord Nelson. He has written several times.

Have you received the medal I sent you? I will enclose this letter to my Lord fearing it might fall into other hands. I have never had a secret from him. Berry writes his wife 'you are much improved in manners and person.'

To Captain Nisbet, *Thalia*.

Round Wood,
September 23, 1799

MY DEAREST HUSBAND, – Mr. Walpole called on Saturday he tells me his son is afloat and hopes you will see him before long. He embarked in the same ship with Lord Elgin. Sir E. Berry I hope you have seen and George Bolton, how does he like the sea? We have very little chat worth your reading.

The papers give an account of the public news, and indeed when we see an acquaintance all our conversation is on the melancholy weather. You can form no idea of the vast quantity of rain that falls daily. Harvest very backward. I have one piece of news to tell you which causes a few 'is it possible?' Admiral Dickson is going to marry a girl of 18 years, surely he has lost his senses. All true, the Admiral saw Miss Willings (a daughter of one of the minor canons at Norwich) not quite three weeks at Yarmouth. He fell desperately in love, gave balls on board ship, then on shore, in short was quite desperate. The friend of Miss W. saw how matters were going on took the young damsel home which caused the Admiral to send an express that arrived at General and Mrs. White's at 12 o'clock at night. The terms were very liberal and handsome. 'The young lady was to do as she pleased.' Mrs. White says she acted with great prudence and the Admiral will soon be married to Miss W. I have seen her, she looks a gentlewoman, and is very much liked.

I hear Admiral and Mrs. Nugent have separated, a difference of temper she says is the cause. I think it will hurt Lady Parker particularly as Mrs. Nugent had a daughter not long ago which I heard had given much happiness to the Admiral. These affairs make little noise for a day. Mrs. Pearson and her daughter are doing very well. She was brought to bed last Friday.

Miss Susanna I took to the concert last Thursday. We were entertained by seeing an old nabob make love to a very rich porter brewer's daughter. The world says her father can give her £20,000 and still she must marry one of the most unpleasant looking men in the world for the sake of driving four horses. I gratified your good father very much in bringing Miss Susanna home with me. I did it I own with some little fear, her temper they say is not very good, she will meet with no contradiction from me, therefore I hope she will be able to conceal it.

We have just heard from Mr. Matcham, Mrs. Matcham is well and she has a daughter. God bless my dear husband.

Believe me your affectionate wife, Frances H. Nelson.

95

Miss Su[sanna] love to you.

Our good father sends his blessing to you. Love to Captain Nisbet.

Right Honourable Lord Nelson, *Foudroyant*, Mediterranean.

Round Wood,
October 14, 1799

MY DEAREST HUSBAND, – The public news you have by the papers, and truly my chit chat is hardly worth your reading, but such as it is you must accept.

Major Dundas Saunders is quartered at Ipswich. Mrs. Godfrey requested me to visit his wife, which I did and conclude it was acceptable from Mrs. D's returning the visit the next day. Our good father is pretty well, the garden affords him great amusement and now and then some of our acquaintance gives him a nosegay.

Lady St. Vincent writes me her Lord recovers very fast. Sir J. Orde has again made himself the subject of conversation.[21] Matters are very properly set to rights by binding him over 'to keep the peace'. Every man who refuses a challenge exalts himself in my opinion. From all this you may suppose the Earl is a first rate favourite. I long to hear from you. My latest date was August 4th. I wonder Lady Hamilton never acknowledges all the prints I requested Mr. Davison to send her. I packed them up myself and Mr. D told me he would send them by the first good opportunity. This is 10 or 11 months back. Make my best regards to her and ask if they are received.

Mr. W. Bolton came bowing to congratulate me on your being created Duke de Bronte and was surprised I had not heard it. It seems all the papers have mentioned it, excepting the *Sun* and *Star*. I hope this news is true if you have money given to support the rank. I assure you I am frightened at the money I spend, every article of life is so dear. Beef 9/4 a stone. Coals very dear. Since Sir E. Berry and his wife dined with us, I have never had any dinner company.

My love to my Josiah God bless you both believe me my dearest husband your affectionate wife, Frances H. Nelson.

Our father's love and blessing attend you.

Right Honourable Lord Nelson, *Foudroyant*, Mediterranean.

Round Wood,
October 21

MY DEAREST HUSBAND, – Lieutenant Parker[22] called last night at ten o'clock just to tell me you were well on the 8th September. Thank God for it and may you enjoy health and every other blessing this world affords. The young man's extreme gratitude and modesty will never be obliterated from your good father's and my memory. He stayed a very few minutes as the express from Vienna was in the chaise at the door. I was so glad to see anyone who could give me such late accounts of my dear husband and my son, that it had such an effect on me that I could not hear or see and was obliged to call in our good father, who made many enquiries and amongst the rest, if you were Duke of Bronte, not but we were well satisfied you were from a letter I received from my Josiah who gave us a very good account where the place was situated and from whence you took your title. Sicily may be a desirable island to have property in probably better than near Naples.

Captain Oswald[23] called last week, he came from Yarmouth and returned immediately as he was going to the Texel. I long to hear of the arrival of Sir William and Lady Hamilton. The carriage the coachmaker let me have during the building of yours is just worn out, at least the coachman says the wheels will not last long, therefore I intend to deliver the old carriage and take the new one down, and any little alterations can be made immediately. Besides all this I should have such a good opportunity of acknowledging and thanking Sir W. and Lady Hamilton for their attention and kindness to you and my son.

Our good father stays at home and Miss S. Bolton is to accompany me. What a sad thing it is those girls cannot or will not conceal these unpleasant tempers. They are, I tell our good father, very young, he says 'True Boltons, I pity the men that marry them but no man will venture.' You will find George Bolton a very affectionate temper. He speaks of Lady Nelson as a very superior creature only six weeks attention to him. The dampness occasioned by the constant rain is beyond description – However we stand high, therefore under no fear of suffering from it, which is no bad thing I assure you.

Mr. and Mrs. Hamilton are arrived in England. I congratulated her on the occasion and received a letter of thanks and full handsome expressions of you and speaks highly of your goodness to my Josiah. She concludes by saying with economy and good crops she hopes to remain in England.

I shall send this letter to Admiral Young. Our good father sends his love and blessing to you. Believe me my dear husband your affectionate wife. Frances H. Nelson.

George Tobin and his little dasher are home. Mr. T. wishes as well as G.T. he could be sent to you, if I could give him any information of your movements which I could not.

Right Honourable Lord Nelson, *Foudroyant*, Mediterranean.

1800   February 23, 1800

MY DEAR HUSBAND, – Sir Andrew Hammond called this morning not only to give me notice of his son's going to the Mediterranean but to offer me every accommodation the *Champion* could afford if I had a wish to go out to you. I told Sir A. I had the desire, but without your leave I could not think of undertaking the voyage. You may be assured I felt much obliged to them for thinking of me.

I hope our good father is generally free from pain, he is grown much thinner, at times cheerful. He has tried twice to take an airing but thinks it irritates his bowels and causes him much pain. In a day or two I shall persuade him to try a sedan chair. He rises when he can, about 9 o'clock, dines by himself at 4 and sits up till 7 if he can. I think I have given you an exact diary of his movements, with all his years and infirmities he thinks he shall last some time unless a sudden change takes place. He told me yesterday he did not think he could ever leave London. The country surgeons were not to be compared to the London ones and he should be afraid of being butchered like poor Mr. Rolfe, therefore I cannot say anything of my returning to the cottage at present. I have never left him since this severe illness, but once, that was at his own desire to dine at Mr. Davison's who had a cheerful dinner company.

I have been sadly tormented with coughs and by no means very stout yet. However a little hot sea bathing I am told is to make me quite well. The Matchams are anxious to see our father, who seems at times to consent to their coming in my absence. I shall leave him quite easy if I think he is well enough to be left provided one of his daughters are staying in the house.

How sadly tormenting the Rector has been in consequence of the Bishop of Bangor's death, such a long letter he had written to our dear father, telling him of your letters to him, extracts of my letters in '97, which only tend to shew your anxiety to get him some dignitary in the church. He now wishes your good father or myself would make some stir, by reminding Mr. Windham or the Chancellor of his promise to you. He wants to tie down the Chancellor to provide for him, so soon as Mr. Methold has a stall. Our good father wrote him a very handsome letter 'telling him if a stall at Norwich was the ultimatum of his ambition he had better at once say so to you, when you had an opportunity of saying so you would and as to my taking any steps to accomplish his wishes it was impossible', therefore he hoped he would rest quiet.

I have got the flower seeds you sent me, a gardener who works for Round Wood will raise a few for us. Lady Berry is at Kensington. They tell me she is six months gone with child. She is not in the least increased in size. She is to spend a few days with me and to take half Susanna's bed. It will be coming to London, that is the only variety I can offer her. Now it is quite out of the question any person dining with me but Maurice, and I have not been to one public place since I came to London, altho' the Parkers have once kindly offered me two tickets for the opera.

I had some difficulty to prevail on myself to go to the Queen's birthday, I am glad I did it. Admiral Christopher Parker has been dangerously ill. Lady P. tells me he is better. Our good father made me promise to dine with them next Tuesday. God bless and protect my dear husband, believe me your affectionate wife, Frances H. Nelson.

I beg my love to my dear Josiah who I hope is with you. Capt. Locker desired me to send a copy of a note.

> 'Mr. Evined's compliments to the Lieut. Governor and thanks him very kindly for his attention, his wishes are that the Lieut. Governor will be so good as to intercede with Lord Nelson to appoint Mr. James Browne Boyd now a mid. in the *Northumberland* to be a lieutenant.' 3 February 1800.

Have you ever seen the lad Miss Nisbet asked you to notice on board Captain Ball?

Right Honourable Lord Nelson, *Foudroyant,* Mediterranean. By favour of Capt. Hammond.

St. James's Street,
March 15, 1800
No. 11.

MY DEAR HUSBAND, – Admiral Young has called to tell me of this conveyance and have just time to say our good father continues to mend, and he sometimes talks of returning to Round Wood when I return from the hot sea bathing which I sometimes flatter myself will be of service to me.

I shall make you smile at my economy. My birthday suit could not be worn after Easter therefore I took the first tolerable Thursday to pay my respects at St. James's which was last Thursday. Our gracious King thought it was a long time since I heard from you, and told me the wind was changed therefore he hoped I should hear from you very soon. The Queen always speaks to me, with so much condescension that I like her very much. And Lady Harrington endeavoured to persuade me to make you a visit. Spoke of the climate how necessary it was to me who had so bad a cough. She little knew how much virtue I had in not going out.

Is my dear son with you? I hope he is. The neutral vessels that were taken by Captain Foley and himself are to be considered as prizes, therefore tell him how to send his money home. Mr. Marsh tells me private bills are very dangerous. With your affectionate advice he will do all things right. A little independence he will find a great comfort.

Aunt Mary is very ill. Mr. Nelson from the letters from Hilbro' does not think she [can] last long. To give you an idea of the extreme danger our father was in, when he was able to sit up the physician called to see him, and when he found him in the parlour, he told me he had seen a prodigy! Mr. Nelson in the parlour. Our good father wrote to you during his illness. His love and best love attend you.

God bless you is the sincere wish of your affectionate wife, Frances H. Nelson.

My love to my dear Josiah. The Berrys, the world says, are grown very great indeed. How could they give out Lady B. was with child?

Right Honourable Lord Nelson, *Foudroyant,* Mediterranean.

16 Somerset Street,   **1801**
December 18, 1801

MY DEAR HUSBAND, – It is some time since I have written to you. The silence you have imposed is more than my affections will allow me and in this instance I hope you will forgive me in not obeying you. One thing I omitted in my letter of July which I now have to offer you for your accomodation, a comfortable warm house. Do, my dear husband, let us live together. I can never be happy till such an event takes place. I assure you again I have but one wish in the world, to please you. Let every thing be buried in oblivion, it will pass away like a dream. I can now only intreat you to believe I am most sincerely and affectionately your wife, Frances H. Nelson.

To Viscount Nelson and Duke of Bronte, St. James's Square, London.[24]

EMMA HAMILTON

Born in 1765 plain Emy Lyon, she called herself Emma Hart on coming to London at the age of 14. Emma was briefly the mistress of Sir Harry Fetherstonaugh of Up Park, then from 1781 the mistress of Charles Greville, who taught her singing, dancing and acting. In 1786 he passed her on to his uncle, Sir William Hamilton, who also cleared his nephew's debts. Emma was shipped off to Naples, where Sir William was ambassador to the court, and she was not unnaturally hurt by Charles's behaviour. No longer able to afford her, the latter seems to have regarded his uncle's protection as in Emma's interest.

He turned out to be right, for Emma found herself unexpectedly in an upwardly mobile situation, and was to reach dizzy social heights. Sir William married her in 1791, and she became the friend and confidante of royalty. Nelson, having found his wife in one port, now found his mistress in another. The couple met in 1793, and he fell in love with her eventually, stimulated as much by her flattery of a national hero as by her charms. The elderly Sir William was either a blind or complaisant husband, and all three returned to England as friends, where Nelson refused to have anything to do with his wife, and where Emma bore him a daughter, Horatia, in 1801. Sir William died in 1803 and Nelson in 1805. Both provided generously for her in their wills, but she lived extravagantly, to die at Calais in 1815, destitute and hounded by creditors.

Beautiful when young, she was often painted by English and Italian artists. Romney, in particular, was fascinated by her. Later, when she was fat and famous, she was cruelly caricatured by James Gillray.

1798   Naples, September 8, 1798.

My dear, dear Sir,

How shall I begin, what shall I say to you, 'tis impossible I can write, for since last Monday (when she first heard the news) I am delerious with joy, and assure you I have a fevour caused by agitation and pleasure. God, what a victory! Never, never has there been anything half so glorious, so compleat. I fainted when I heard the joyfull news, and fell on my side and am hurt, but well of that. I shou'd feil it a glory to die in such a cause. No, I wou'd not like to die till I see and embrace the Victor of the Nile. How shall I describe to you the transports of Maria Carolina, 'tis not possible. She fainted and kissed her husband, her children, walked about the room, cried, kissed, and embraced every person near her, exclaiming, Oh, brave Nelson, oh, God bless and protect our brave deliverer, oh Nelson, Nelson, what do we not owe to you, oh Victor, Savour of Itali, oh, that my swolen heart cou'd now tell him personally what we owe to him!

You may judge, my dear Sir, of the rest, but my head will not permit me to tell you half the rejoicing. The Neapolitans are mad with joy, and if you wos here now, you would be killed with kindness. Sonets on sonets, illuminations, rejoicings; not a French dog dare shew his face. How I glory in the honner of my Country and my Countryman! I walk and tread in the air with pride, feiling I was born in the same land with the victor Nelson and his gallant band. But no more, I cannot, dare not, trust myself, for I am not well. Little dear Captain Hoste will tell you the rest. He dines with us in the day, for he will not sleep out of his ship, and we Love him dearly. He is a fine, good lad. Sir William is delighted with him, and I say he will be a second Nelson. If he is onely half a Nelson, he will be superior to all others.

I send you two letters from my adorable queen. One was written to me the day we received the glorious news, the other yesterday. Keep them, as they are in her own handwriting. I have kept copies only, but I feil that you ought to have them. If you had seen our meeting after the battle, but I will keep it all for your arrival. I coo'd not do justice to her feiling nor to my own, with writing it; and we are preparing your appartment against you come. I hope it will not be long, for Sir William and I are impatient to embrace you. I wish you cou'd have seen our house the 3 nights of illumination. 'Tis, 'twas covered with your glorious name. Their were 3 thousand lamps, and their shou'd have been 3 millions if we had had time. All the English vie with each other in celebrating this most gallant and ever memorable victory. Sir William is ten years younger since the happy news, and he now only wishes to see his friend to be completely happy. How he glories in you when your name is mentioned. He cannot contain his joy. For God's sake come to Naples soon. We receive so many Sonets and Letters of congratulation. I send you some of them to shew you how much your success is felt here. How I felt for

poor Troubridge. He must have been so angry on the sandbank, so brave
an officer! In short I pity those who were not in the battle. I wou'd have
been rather an English powder-monkey, or a swab in that great victory,
than an Emperor out of it, but you will be so tired of all this. Write or
come soon to Naples, and rejoin your ever sincere and oblidged friend,

Emma Hamilton.

The Queen as this moment sent a Dymond Ring to Captain Hoste, six
buts of wine, 2 casks, for the officers, and every man on board a guinea
each. Her letter is in English and comes as from an unknown person, but
a well-wisher to our country, and an admirer of our gallant Nelson. As
war is not yet declared with France, she cou'd not shew herself so openly
as she wished, but she as done so much, and rejoiced so very publickly,
that all the world sees it. She bids me to say that she longs more to see
you than any woman with child can long for anything she may take a fancy
to, and she shall be for ever unhappy if you do not come. God bless you
my dear, dear friend.

My dress from head to foot is alla Nelson. Ask Hoste. Even my shawl
is in Blue with gold anchors all over. My earrings are Nelson's anchors;
in short, we are be-Nelsoned all over. I send you some Sonets, but I must
have taken a ship on purpose to send you all written on you. Once more,
God bless you. My mother desires her love to you. I am so sorry to write
in such a hurry. I am affraid you will not be able to read this scrawl.

FANNY BURNEY

Fanny Burney (1752–1840) married General Alexandre-Jean Baptiste Piochard d'Arblay (1754–1818) in 1793, when she was already famous as the author of *Evelina* (1778) and *Cecilia* (1782). Their son Alexander was born in 1794. M. d'Arblay was a royalist emigré and in 1802 the d'Arblays returned to France. Fanny was vigorously opposed to her husband resuming his military career, and d'Arblay's opposition to Napoleon also made this virtually impossible. He had, however, accepted a posting to the French colony of San Domingo from Bonaparte in return for the reinstatement of his military pension, but did so upon the condition that he would never be required to bear arms against England, *'le pays qui pendant 9 ans nous a nourris',* and the authorization for him to join the expeditionary force to San Domingo was cancelled.

The d'Arblays lived in or near Paris for the next ten years, and in 1812 Fanny Burney returned to England with her son, to be reunited with her beloved father, Dr. Charles Burney, now in his 87th year. He died in April 1814, and by the end of the year Fanny Burney was back in Paris, whilst her son Alexander started his desultory studies at Cambridge. She was therefore directly involved in the dramatic events following Napoleon's return from Elba and the Hundred Days. On 19 March 1815, she parted from her husband and fled to Brussels. Meanwhile General d'Arblay, who had joined Louis XVIII's household troops in June 1814, was posted to Treves, where his task was to process deserters from Napoleon's army.

Fanny Burney's letters provide a unique insight into the actions and reactions amongst upper-class supporters of the Bourbon regime during these hectic days. Since she fled to Brussels she was very close to the Battle of Waterloo itself, and her letters give graphic details of the run up to, and aftermath of this famous battle. She observes the general atmosphere but, on account of her connections, also has access to rumour and counter-rumour at higher levels, which she passes on to her beloved husband, though fear of interception often prompted her to veil her information or merely hint at what she had heard.

But apart from the voice of the woman interested in the outcome of great public events, we have in these letters the voice of an anxious wife and also mother. A doting but by now somewhat censorious mother, she worried about the shortcomings of her son Alexander, who was largely wasting his time at Caius College, Cambridge. In the many letters to her husband we find loving concern for her husband's health and safety, expressed in the somewhat breathless, effusive style readers of her novels will readily recognize.

1815   320, rue de la Montagne,
                                                       Brussels, 23–26 March 1815

To Alexander d'Arblay
Addressed: Angleterre/Alexander d'Arblay Esqr/Caius College/Cambridge.
Re-addressed: Mrs Broome/Richmond/Surrey.
Re-addressed: Wm Locks Eqr/Norbury Park/Dorking.

Oh Alexander! – will not even this calamitous moment excite you to write? – Your noble Father – turned of 60 – is *at his post* in the Army – with the Maison du Roi – – but *how* employed, or *where,* I am yet ignorant; – & y^r wandering emigrant Mother has been forced to fly even her adopted Country?

 We parted last Sunday, March 19th – in the Rue de Mirominil, without even being able to say to each other where we might mutually write! – – – I am just arrived at Tournay – where I shall wait events – If you will let me see your hand again direct to me – by your beloved Father's honoured name – Mme d'Arblay –
                    Chez Thibaut,
               Hotel de l'Imperatrice,
             à Tournay – près Lille –
                dans la Belgique.

Ce Jeudi au soir,
23 Mars 1815,
Tournay.

 If a Letter here arrives too late to meet it will certainly follow me. *Ce 26. Mars* – Fresh alarms drove me from Tournay before I could send off my Letter, which I now finish at Brusselles – It is a week this Day since I parted from my – mine & your's – tenderest Friend – Heaven – Heaven preserve him, & grant our re-union! –

 Adieu my poor Alexander! I feel for your penitence & hope only it will lead you to more consideration for the future! amen! – the first line I receive shall seal forgiveness for your cruel negligence, if I may hope that your concern – which I cannot doubt – will lead not simply to remorse, but amendment. Amen! – Heaven bless my always dear Alex.

Direct à Madame de Burney,
Chez Madame de Maurville,
Nº 320, Rue de la Montagne, a Bruxelles.

I would not write to you during this dreadful suspence, but that I know not how long it may last, & feel sure – with all his omissions – my Poor Alex will be thankful to Heaven to find that ONE parent at least is safe. God Almighty spare the OTHER! – I fled Paris with such disturbance I was forced to aband[on] every thing! Books – Cloaths Trinkets – Linnen – arg[enterie] Goods – MSS!!! All! –
Last words
Direct to Mᵉ d'Arblay Chez Mᵉ de Maurville, Bruxelles.

Brussels, 27 March 1815,

To James Burney
Addressed: Angleterre/Captain Burney/James Street/26/Westminster/ London.

March 27 1815

Give the enclosed – my dear Brother – to Martin[1] – beg him to receive it the moment it is due, & to pay it, like the former £500, to Messrs. Hoare, desiring them to give me immediate notice of its receipt, & the name of the Banker by whom they can transmit it to me, on my demand, at Brussells – I entreat Martin also to have the kindness to let me know whether a similar receipt will suffice for the 500 of the 2ᵈ Edition.

Oh James – I know not what is become of my best & dearest half! – eternally varying accounts kill & revive me in turn – we parted THIS DAY WEEK! – how dreadfully! – neither of us able to devine the destination of the other! – He left me for the Champs de Mars – a last Review! – & he has followed, or preceded, the unhappy King. – or – horrible doubt – he is a prisoner – – In the latter case, I shall re-enter the fatal Country I have just fled, the instant I receive a power to draw here for money. I have left & lost every thing I possessed! – Goods – Cloathes – Trinkets – Books – billets – MSS!. &c but if HE arrive safe in England – I shall be RICH with NOTHING – for I shall have a[ga]in the power of happiness –

Adieu dear James – my love to all –

I have not had a line from any one – though I have written to All – except from my two kind Charlottes – & ONE Letter only from my inconceivable Alexander – unless – which I hope, his other Letters have miscarried. I shall write to him – I mean I *have* just written – & to Charlotte – speak to my dear sister Esther – Charles & Sarah – I can write no more – but

God bless you!

remember me most kindly to Mrs. B & Sally & Martin.

All the English have run away from Paris – & such is their terrour of the conqueror, that they are now flying hence! Yet I trust & believe that We are safe here. A large body of English troops passed before my window yesterday, for the Frontieres commanded by Gen Clinton. They huzza'd the whole way, & the Inhabitants huzza'd them from<the> windows.

My address is

À Madame Burney –
Chez Madame de Maurville
N° 320, Rue de la Montagne,
À Brusselles.

The good Mad^{e} de Maurville, who has received me in this distress with the most cordial hospitality, sends her best comp^{ts} to Mrs. Burney –

Last notes – Direct to M^{e} d'Arblay – Chez Me de Maurville, Bruxelles.

[286, rue de la Montagne],
Brussels, 29 March

To M. d'Arblay

Addressed: À Monseiur/Le Chevalier d'Arblay/Marechal de Camp/offi^{r} de la Garde du Corps/du Roi de France/Gand/also/à Ostende/post Restante/Bruxelles

chez Me de Maurville, Bruxelles
ce 29, Mars

Oh mon ami! mon ami! – Je viens de lire votre Lettre à Mme de Maurville – la vue de votre écriture m'a absolument renouvellé l'existence – J'étois abatue à la mort – Oh comme je vais me soigner!

Vous joindrai-je tout de suite à Ostende?

Que je vous dise Instamment tout ce qu'il y a de pire – hèlas – Je n'ai rien avec moi! excepté ce que je n'ai pas encore depensé d'argent!

All our effects remain – I have even no cloathes, but in a Napkin! –

All my MSS – my family papers – my dear Father's Memoirs – all our

Argenterie – your billets – my watch, my numerous little trinkets! – all our linnen – our BOOKS – your various curiosities – my shawls – all our meubles – all, all left in Paris, from my hurry of flight.

My new purchases at so chere an amount of pence! A Flannel shawl – 7^{fr} It amazes – nay awes – But as to money, I can write James again as is <needed>.

Je sais, à présent, que j'aurais pu avoir apporter mes trinkets – & small affairs, but the suddenness of our departure – utterly unexpected – with the deeply terrific state of my mind & Nerves from our awful separation, robbed me of all thought upon these subjects. I merely locked up every thing I saw, sealed the keys, in a bag, & told Mme Deprez[2] to carry them to M. Le Noir – with a note entreating him to keep them in his custody.

I knew not, at that time, but you might yet return at night, & have occasion for them: I can explain all when we meet – I merely state the result & great misfortune at once, so that if you can ever see any manner of reclaiming anything you may know what there is to claim. – but oh mon ami! mon ami! – I feel too *rich* in being again so blessed as to see your hand – to know you so near me – & *safe,* to be sensible of this evil: – however it has often afflicted me – & the more, as much of it I might have prevented by a happier or abler foresight. Grief-stricken & confounded, *YOUR* departure occupied all my heart – head & faculties –

I paid the Rent to the Ist of April – – all therefore is ours till then. And Me Deprez to the end of March & gave her 20 francs.

I am truly sorry I did not do better – & I beseech you to spare me all reflections &c – for I have had no practice of this melancholy nature – though *now* – I hope to Heaven I shall never again be tried! but I should certainly emigrate more skilfully!

Sometimes I think of how you could perhaps, even ask for M. de Saulnier should he be in <town>? – but every body says we must try at nothing immediately, not to excite any notice. Think it all over, & decide whether I shall join you instantly & I shall enquire about conveyances, for I shall come by the Diligence, & you will tell me where to expect you. My Journey hither has cost me 6 pieces of 20 francs & without our expenses at Bruxelles – I am fixed with M^e D'henin, &c at an equal part – 1/3 in all expences of house & house-keeping: but now I know *YOU* safe, & both are poor, I am eager to find a cheaper establishment. I have merely – alas – 2 mourning gowns,[3] & a small change of linnen! – but oh mon ami! mon plus que JAMAIS cher ami – what now can affect me? I *supplicate* that our meeting may be without Witnesses! – I *ENTREAT* you to contrive That. – I shall BURST if I must constrain my

gratitude to Heaven & my joy & tenderness – Midy – now (think of me)
– I am quite ready to come to you directly –

The Frontiers are all blocked with troops – all communication with
France – *legitime* is broken up – but we must endeavour to get a Letter
to Me Deprez – If we set sail without any precaution, all will necessarily
be confiscated – at all events, write immediately – mon ami! mon ami! –

Je viens d'écrire a *Gand*[4] –

P.S. Pray in your answer say if you know anything of M. d'Auch, or,
of Humbert La tour du Pin.

I have just heard that the soldiers are quartered in the houses at Paris
& that all is alarm for the war.

The Guard Nationale waxed at first, but is now disarmed to its great
discontent, & the people's disatisfaction.[5]

My apartment here is unhappily taken for a *month by the p*^{ss}[6] – it would
do perfectly <for both, & at rather less,> if all else were not too dear –

Is there no nearer embarkation for us than Ostende?

If you can come hither to make our arrangements – representations
to Md. Deprez & our goods, &c, come soon. If not let me hasten to you
– only name how, when. –

If you think we had best stay on the continent till we can take some
measures for our affairs, let it be in some cheap port & oh let us be
together! – mon ami! mon ami!

I will write at once to James for word which <bank> is best & to
forward or draw our funds.

F.d'A.

I will write à Ostende as to this – consider it further.

Tournay and Brussels,
23–31 March 1815

To H.R.H. the Princess Elizabeth
A ELIZA. 1

Tournay 23 Mars
1815

Madam –

What dreadful & afflicting scenes & vicissitudes have I witnessed & experienced since my receipt of those valued & condescending lines wh^{ch} gave me the last sensation of pleasure to which my heart was open in Paris![7] they came to me on the 15th from which period every hour was filled with new disorder, though all was so vague, that till the 19th March I had conceived no idea of the real danger of the state. Even then, nothing was known of the ultimate purposes of Le Roi, nor consequently of the destination *de sa Maison*, to which M. d'A. had the honour to belong. But the histories daily recorded to me of the calm dignity of his Majesty's mind[8] though exposed to every species of conflict, & of the imperturbable serenity of his manners, while suffering the most excruciating injuries, & most wounding disappointments, reflect equal honour upon his fortitude, his Temper, & his religious principles. No impatience ever escaped him; but a consoling, however modest consciousness of his worth, with a deep though never vindictive sense of his wrongs, kept him firm to his dreadful post. The poor D^{ss} d'Ang[oulême] continued at Bordeaux[9] – Oh how do I pity that most undeservedly unfortunate of Princesses!

Sunday the 19. M. d'A. left me at Noon, fully equipped for a military expedition, & expecting to march forward to the army opposed to Buonaparte, after a general muster & review of all the troops of *la Maison du Roi* on le *champs de Mars*. Alas – I have never seen nor heard from him since, except on that same Sunday night, about 9 o'clock, when M. Ch[arles] de Maubourg, an officer of la Garde du Corps, delivered me a Note from him, saying

> *Tout est perdu – Je ne puis entrer dans aucun detail*
> *– mais de grace partir! la plutot sera le mieux –* &c.

The P^{ss} d'Henin had already offered me a place in her Carriage. We set off at 10 o'clock at night. All at Paris then was quiet, – sad, dejected, & astonished. Every body had expected some great blow w^d be struck, though nobody knew by whom, nor when, nor how. Never but in the

Eastern Empires, has a great Revolution been brought to bear with a rapidity so frightful; & never before were Art, Skill & Activity so feebly opposed by disgraceful neglect, & languid, unmeaning mismanagement. The Usurper has only the Army & the Populace; the Army, of which he has corrupted the very essence by permission of pillage, & disdain of all the arts of peace; & the Populace, because, conceiving themselves already the most debased, the[y] believe any change must be to their advantage: but all proprietors, all thinking people, all superiour Officers, all Men of learning, all Gentlemen, & all women whatsoever, gentle or simple, are for the King. When I say ALL, I mean not, of course, to disclaim that there are exceptions; &, alas, many! but I speak of the mass of this classification. 'Tis a Great, firm, high-principled & dauntless *Political chief* that has been wanting, to spurn all jarring interests, be insensible to all personal attacks, & content to leave Posterity for his Judge. SUCH a one here, – as erst in my dear native land, by firmly holding in single view the one great object of ultimate General Good, might have steered the whole to anchor at an equally prosperous port. – but there was no such Pilot, alas, to *Weather the storm!*

Believing, when I quitted my home, that I deserted it only for the neighbourhood of Paris, there to wait news of an impending battle, the affright & distress of my mind allowed me no combinations by which I might have secured some part of my property; I left ALL, save what I could convey in a napkin, ie a small change of linen, & 2 mour[n]ing Gowns! I have learnt – too late – that in emigrating we sh^d carry *with us* whatever we most value. But I have nothing, absolutely NOTHING! Yet my anguish in my uncertainty of the destination & situation of M. d'A., from the fluctuating accounts that have broken in upon me *just now* relative to *La Maison du Roi*, makes all else immaterial. We arrived without molestation to this place, Tournay. At Amiens & at Arras, the 2 Prefects, acquaintances of M^e d'Henin, treated us with distinction, renewed our passports & spoke warmly *pour le Roi.* and –

BRUXELLES. I could not finish my Letter at Tournay from excess of disturbance – We were so near Lille, that varying news reached us incessantly. The Prince de Condé came to the same Inn; fear was excited of pursuit, & we came on hither; & I have been too ill, & too wretched to hold my pen again till to day, March 31st when I have just had a Letter from la D^{ss} d'Hurst, with an account that M. d'A. nearly demolished with the harrass of guarding the Artillery, & full of severe rheumatism from constant rains, while on Horse back night & day, in covering the retreat of the Roi, writes from Menan that he is going on to Ostende, to pay his duty to his Majesty, & to endeavour to recover some portion of his lost health – for which purpose he has the permission of Monsg^r le comte d'Artois.

I shall surely join him there, unless his duty paid, he thinks it better to come hither. He was already, in fact, made unfit for the campaign by his previous fatigues, for since the disembarkation of the barbarous Destroyer, he has never known rest, & by doing the double service of Garde du corps au chateau,[10] & the artillery officer at la Cazerne, l'ecole militaire, he was very hardly employed almost night & day; &, by a zeal beyond his force, but which he could not controll, he was so altered & exhausted before he began his late march, that with a grain less of spirit & of loyalty, he must have declined to undertake it:[11] – & alas his strength had never been restored since his cruel accident at Calais.[12]

Le nouveau Roi,[13] in his public entry, passed yesterday before my window. There was no species of enthusiasm, but great respect & decorum, & moderate cries of *Vive le roi*. The unhappy dethroned monarch so near saddened all hearts, & I do not, therefore, augur ill from the want of apparent warmth, which, I hope, was only the effect of a contrast repressing to all demonstration of festivity. He may be better, perhaps, served than the injured King who was received with such triumphant exultation. Worse, he cannot be! I am inexpressibly anxious for M^e la D^{ss} d'Angouleme; of whom no News is known here. We wait for intelligence through England! An English lady, who found means to leave Paris for this place Sunday the 26. relates, to a lady who has repeated to me, that the 1st 3 days of B[onaparte]'s return were passed in utter consternation, but that the nomination of so Jacobinical an administration – Savary – Real – Dâvoust – carnot – caulaincourt – &c had struck with a panic that renewed all the horrour in the minds of the Inhabitants, of the reign of terrour. The soldiers were quartered in the houses, as if B. had entered as a foreign Conqueror.[14] He was seldom seen, & working always with his Ministers, & wearing an air the most *sombre*. If the Allies are but quick; if the D. of Wellington heads them,[15] the universal belief here is that he will – *par les siens même*, be culbuté. But that if he gains *time*, his activity & resources are such, that he will again, for a period, reinstate himself upon the Throne.

I shall make this pass, under cover to Mr. Rolleston,[16] by the English minister. *My* Letters – should I be so happy as to receive a line, will be sacred & safe, directed to *me* Chez la comtesse de Maur[ville], a most honourable Friend, at Brussels.

I dare attempt no apology, – no conclusion – but I am ever

[End of draft.]

113

[320, rue de la Montagne,
Brussels, *post* 31 March]

To M. d'Arblay

Mon ami – mon amico – mon *ALL*! have just had your delightful
Letter – delightful in defiance of all its painful mixture of misery &
suffering. – My Ist joy & gratitude at sight of your hand writing to M^e
de Maurville can NEVER be equalled; but my present less tumultuous
happiness fills me with a thankfulness for your preservation that ought
to tincture with determined philosophy all the rest of my existence, in
opposition to all the evils of *any other description*, that may assail it. I
cannot, however, rejoice, after such fatigues & such illness & such
strength-consuming toils, that you have again proferred your services,
when I thought you fixed to retire, for the present, to the neighbourhood
of our Alex, for repose & recruiting.

But – you have not had any of my Letters? You know not, therefore,
either my exquisite felicity at your Ist handwriting, or my cruel difficulties
how to give up, or *not* give up, all hopes of recovering any part of our
property? La Morte dans le coeur – a *sort* that I rescued not one of my
letters nor a single of my many trinkets – nor our bibelots nor my shawls!
– Excess of disorder robbed me of all recollections that we had them, in
the hurried moment of unexpected departure – I have written all this AT
LENGTH to Ostende post restante directed à M.M. Le. Chev d'Arblay,
Marechal de Camp, et Lieut des Gardes du Corps, du roi de France. If
you can send for the Letter, pray do, as it contains many things that were
written in the belief you only would read them! I sent a rough duplicate
also to *Gand*. pray enquire – to M. le General de Lux[em]bourg, & one
– I sent thro the post, though not *post Restante*! & I wrote also to Ypres,
& to Lille, received 1 only. I bless & save it in requite – If you can come
hither, *do now*, I have much I should ask – should I <receive> any dire
medical advice back, I trust you will remember that to demolish yourself
is not to serve your King: & the hard service of the present moment, when
the War planned & threatened once begins, really demands the endurance
& vigour of youth to save its operators from being its victims.

How am I charmed with M. le Duc de L[uxembourg] – that much
of his quick feeling regard, in jumping from his carriage to embrace you,
winds me round him in grateful attachment for-ever.

If you can come hither you have a right to a ROOM – & when once
sure here – a BED – for our house is taken for a month between La P^{ss}
M. de Lally & myself. La P^{ss} has a Man & a Maid, M. de L. his valet

– & we have hired a helper in common, our account is to be paid, in partition, de même – I like it not – how at first to do better, I knew not, but at the end of the month [I resolve to] seek some cheaper way of life. Two – I will not go over *without you*, while I can communicate with & have news & Letters.

My journey, though in the carriage of the P^sse cost me 6 nap[oleon]s – in Gold coin for horses, Inns, dinners, &c.

I have no clothes! I only possess a small change of linen, & 2 mourning Gowns! Ceaselessly but too late I regret not having had a better foresight of migratory destiny!

And all my MSS! – My beloved Father's! my family papers! – my Letters of all my life! my Susan's Journals! – !!! – our Argenterie – Linen – BOOKS – prints – *curiosities*.

But my consternation in being forced to quit Paris so abruptly, without any means of learning where you were – or acquainting you with my own destination – & my absence indefinite from our Heart-dear Boy – all this, gave me a sort of stupor – of indifference to every other consideration – O, for what an Animation is it NOW exchanged!

[The second leaf is missing.]

[320, rue de la Montagne,]
Brussels, 27–[31] March 1815

To Alexander d'Arblay

Addressed: Angleterre/Alexander d'Arblay Esq/Caius College/Cambridge.
Re-addressed: at Mr Lock's Norbury Park/near Dorking/Surry.
Docketed: the last folding down of this – to keep –

March 27th
1815.

I know not whether my poor Alex has received my first Letter – begun at Tournay, & ended at Bruxelles? If not, This must give him the disastrous tidings of my separation from the best beloved of BOTH our hearts – who left me on Sunday the 19th March, to go to a Review of all La Maison du Roi on Le Champ de Mars. He had not yet received any order for departing – & I flattered myself to the last moment he would once again, at least, return! – but he had less hope! he prepared entirely for a Military expedition, had a noble War Horse, a servant well mounted on another Horse, splendid new accoutrements – arms, Baggage, &c – &c – Oh Alex! what a parting was ours, in defiance of my ignorance of the impending horrours, & delusive belief better days were quick approaching! Your name was nearly the last he pronounced as we separated – he forgave you, my poor Alex – & said *'Embrassez le pour moi – & dites lui que je l'aime – Je crois – plus que jamais'* –but, he then, in a low voice, added, that he would not write to you, because he felt too angry at your inconceivable negligence to write without a reproach which, at such a moment of precarious existence, he should be sorry to utter. Oh my poor Alex! how do I pray to Heaven the kindest of parents may be spared to receive – & you to offer some amends! I feel sure, sure of your desire. Then, after joining our hopes for a speedy – with our solemn prayers for a Future, an eternal re-union, he quitted me – yet, at the door, turned back, to cry, with a Face & voice reviving to his duty, *'Vive le Roi!'* – I echoed, with what energy I could assume, the call of Honour – & I have never seen him since! –

He had made me promise to quit Paris in 3 days, if he did not return – he had engaged me a place in the *voiture* of the P^{ss} d'Henin, who had decided to be gone, if Buonaparte arrived. An officer, sent upon recognizance by the Minister de la Guerre, had told Mr Victor, before me, that B[uonaparte] could not reach Fontainbleau[18] for 3 days – On this I had relied, for time to arrange my affairs, if forced to depart: but – – I was yet absorbed in grief & horrour at what I had to fear from the impending battle to which your dear Father believed himself hastening, when M^e d'Henin came to inform me B. was already at Fontainbleau – & that we must be off with all speed. She did not determine whether our route should be to Bordeaux, where was La D^{ss} d'Angouleme, or to Brussels, where she should join her niece, M^e La Tour du Pin – I made ready a small packet of linen, & 2 mourning Gowns – and This is ALL I now hold of my so numerous hoards & possessions in France! unless some happy return to Right & Justice takes place, we shall have the World to begin again – for we have neither cloaths, plate – Goods – Chattels – Linnen – nor any single circumstance necessary for house-keeping & living. But to be joined again to my two dear Alexanders will reconcile me to bearing with every privation.

My poor little packet made, I went to our excellent Gen La Tour Victor de Maubourg, to take leave of Me de Maisoneuve. I found her much disturbed for Maxime, – who always retains his friendship for you – & who was at Metz – under Marechal Oudinot, reported to be faithfully loyal, but ill surrounded. Gen Victor had been so thunderstruck by the reports that had reached him of defection & treachery, that he was quite ill: he was engaged with sundry officers, endeavouring to form some rallying point. While here, came Charles, his Brother, from la Cazerne de la Maison du Roi – whence he brought me this billet from our beloved

'Tout est perdu! – Je ne puis entrer dans aucun detail, mais, de Grace, partez! le plutôt sera le mieux! – '

It was 9 o'clock at night. I had not yet seen Gen Victor[19] – but demanded a moment – he was then equipping himself to wait upon *le Roi*, with an offer of his ultimate services. We shook hands through his door – I could only say 'Je pars! – ' & only replied 'Bien des choses de ma part à Alexander!' How kind! but he always honours you with an affection [tear]. He concluded I was going to England. But I was on[ly] destined to wander <1st> ANY whither from Paris – [and] next – to seek our dearest Friend. I then went [to] Mad^e d'Henin. & at 10 at night we set off – with no fixed purpo[se h]ow far to go, or what to do, but to change & settle our projects according to circumstances. The 21st on arriving, at Night, at Amiens, we found that *le Roi* had passed by, in going to Abbeville, but procured no news de *sa maison*. B[uonoparte] had entered Paris the 20th. But no orders had yet arrived at *Amiens*, where the Prefect came & supped with us. – All here was loyal, but apprehensive, & inactive. As every where else! We travelled nearly all night, & stopt to a long Breakfast at the Prefect's at Arras – where all the troops & Inhabitants were for *le Roi*: & the General who commanded them told me he had dined the preceding day at Beauvais with the Princes, the Prince de Poix, the ducs de Luxembourg, *Wagram, Tarente, Raguse,* &c – But the *Maison du Roi* could not travel so fast, & was not arrived!! Think of my inquietude! – As yet, however, there was no pursuit. From Arras we proceeded to *Orchies*, the last frontière town of France. Here the wheel of the carriage broke, at 11 at Night. every Inn was full – it could not be mended under 4 or 5 hours – & it rained continually. In this desperate situation, the almost unequalled humanity of a good woman who heard voices in distress, after she was in Bed, led her to arise, & come to our assistance. She made us enter her little parlour, lighted an excellent fire, got each of us a Pillow to rest our heads against a Chair & a Table, & poured us out basons of warm Tea! – With this model of true hospitality, we stayed till 6 in the morning – & at about 9, on the 23d Mars, we left hapless, disordered France, & entered Flanders by *Tournay* – w[h]ere new scares & alarms awaited me – *Le Roi* was at Lille – I saw M. de Viomenil[20] – but no news of your Father – The Prince de Conde came to Tournay – in his flight towards Brussels – but no news! I saw an *English* General, whom I addressed – & he assured me *La Maison du Roi* had never reached

Lille! – & was seeking another direction to the Frontieres!!! We came on the next day to Brussels – & stopt at Mad^e de Maurville's – whence we are now settled in a small house at our united expense, for I brought away all I could of money, though nothing of any other value. I am waiting – with feelings I would not for the world describe, intelligence of our Beloved. *Le Roi* is at *Ostende* – le duc de Berri is here – *la Maison du Roi* is dispersed! *Monsieur* has declared there is no power left for supporting it, & given to each officer his own option to follow, *by his own means,* the Roi – or return to his family, & wait for better days. But some have been lost in a dreadful *marais* where they plunged to rise no more![21] – some have been betrayed by a Traitor – others to go seek their wives & children – & others, *à toute frais & risque,* have pursued the royal tracks. That this last has been the resolution of *OUR* beloved, if not overpowered with fatigue, we cannot doubt –

March 29th I kept this back – & not in vain, I bless Heaven! to add some tidings – I have had the unspeakable consolation & joy of seeing once more your Father's handwriting, in a Letter to Mme de Maurville dated *March 27.* & enquiring news of your mother. The *Maison du Roi* has been broken up,[22] as a Body, from inability to sustain itself, in the midst of treachery & desertion! Many have returned – licensed by the Princes, to their homes – some have fallen victims to fatigue & direful accidents – others have been betrayed to the Enemy – others have betrayed themselves – your beloved Father – through difficulties that nearly overpowered him – got at last to the King at Ghent – wh[en]ce – finally – I have a Letter from himself. Joy for [*wafer*] me, my dear Alex – & write – Write – Tell me when you exhibit – &c – yrs ever

<FB ly>

direct

à Madame <F> Burney Bruxelles, Madame d'Arblay – chez Madame de Maurville, à Bruxelles.

[286 rue de la Montagne],
Brussels, 8 April 1815

To Esther Burney
Addressed: Angleterre/Mrs. Burney/Turnham Green/Middlesex/
near/London.

Brussels – Ap^l 8th 1815

Ah, my dearest Esther, when am I to write to you a chearful Letter?
A Day longer than I was first offered for writing to England being given
me, I cannot refuse myself using it to again address you, though still –
alas! alas! only in the sackcloth & ashes of grief – distress & alarm! – a
frightful paragraph of a contagious fever at Cambridge has chilled my
blood, & added so direful a weight to my already so loaded mind that
every minute seems to linger out an hour – though I do all, all I can to
smother my apprehensions, not further to oppress my *Partner in All*;
himself but just escaped from a malady, the effect of his long fatigues &
nearly outrageous exertions, which threatened him with the most serious
consequences. I had hardly had time to bless Heaven in grateful fervour
for his safety – after our critical & dread separation on the 19th of March,
when this so unexpected blow came to quash again all remittance from
evil! – for the best is but remittance, since the congée of M. d'A. has only
been granted, or asked, for the recruit of his shattered health, & that he
may procure himself a fresh equipment for his military service! all his
original most expensive equipment – his papers, Baggage, military Books
& stores – his Horses, & his Domestic – All, in short, but his weapons
& uniform, have been left en route, at Bethune, near the frontières,
whence the whole *Maison du Roi*, i.e. gardes du Corps, issued with the
belief of a Battle – which, however, did not take place. The pursuers,
Buonaparte's guards, being but 200, against as many thousand, then
making a parade of approach & defiance, suddenly called out *vive
l'Empereur* while the Duc de Berri cried *'vive le Roi'* – & precipitately fled.
It was concluded, however, that this was a feint, & that they had sufficient
force near at hand; the Duc, therefore, ordered the *Maison du Roi* to march
on, without stopping to retake either Baggage or Domestic. To us this
has been peculiarly unfortunate, for *I* had already left Paris, with only a
handful of linen, & 2 mourning Gowns – and now M. d'A. also is robbed
of every thing! Yet oh – if of Him & my other Alexander I am *not* robbed
– if once we have a safe re-union in any peaceful spot, away from
Revolutionary events & sufferings & terrours, – methinks I shall be happy
under every privation.

Adieu! my dearest Esther – my best Love to Mr. B[urney] who I hope continues mending, & to Amelia – & when you write to Maria in particular, & to dear Sophy, Cecilia & Fanny²³ –

How our affairs go on in England I know not – & never yet were money matters so important to me – Not a line has come to me relative to our now unfortunate Cottage – nor to the so long impending 2ᵈ *Edition* that was sold *before publication*! nor from Charles for our residu at White's, Leigh's, & the Museum! – nor from Mr. White for the goods we left to be sold from West-Humble – nor of the Irish business – nor whether the Mortgage of Mr. Lewes²⁴ had been deemed worth struggling for. Certainly we are greatly injured, & in a very considerable Sum (I speak of you & me,) if Mr. Lewes keeps a debt so undoubtedly due to our dear Father: Oh, my dear Esther, what succession of mortal & bodily sufferings have been mine, from the time of his loss, to its anniversary next Tuesday! I had always kept in mourning, as we had agreed – & 2 mourning Gowns, with a small change of Linnen, is ALL I have saved from All my possessions in Paris! And, since, M. d'A. in his short & *triste* Campaigne, with *La Maison du Roi,* a tout perdu! – military Equipments – Baggage, Books, Maps, papers, Horses & Domestic. &c – all left at Bethune [where] he thought himself preparing for a Combat!

[1358, Marché au bois, Brussels]
15–19 June 1815

To M. d'Arblay
Addressed: *Treves*/À/Monsieur le Général d'Arblay/officier Superieur du Garde du Corps/de sa Majesty Le Roi de France/Chevʳ de Sᵗ Louis, &c &c/À Treves.

June 17ᵗʰ 1815.

Oh my beloved Ami – what dreadful times are these! May you but still be at Treves! – & quickly, quickly be able to let me see that date which is now my fondest desire – for I have just received your Letter of the 12ᵗʰ where you answer to M. le D[uke] de L[uxembourg] – & I entirely enter into your reasonings & feelings, – they are now, indeed, *my own*, so completely they have operated upon my mind: & others, which I cannot now write, that the change of affairs has given rise to, combine to make me earnestly desire your continuance with Gen Kleist at Treves. So be it! Amen! – –

To the present state of Brussells.

*Thursday, the 15th* – early in the night, a Bugle Horn called me to the window:[25] I saw a few soldiers, & thought them collecting for some change of sentinels: but about 3 in the morning I was awakened by a *Hub bub* in the street, that made me rise, & run hastily again to the window: it was not light, & a sound of a few voices, in passing stragglers, made me once more conclude there was nothing material & go quietly to Bed again. But at six o'clock *Friday the 16th* the same sounds called me forth to examine the neighbourhood, & enquire of the maid, who was arranging the sallon, what was the matter? Can you conceive this flemish phlegm? From *FLEMISH, PHLEGM* must certainly be derived! She answered that she knew of nothing; & the Masters of the house gave me no species of intelligence though well aware of my deep private interest in public matters! & I forwarded to you my Letter without any communication upon a subject which was then known all over Bruxelles, except to my lonely self!

You will certainly have learnt, long ere this can reach you, that the Enemy has broken into La Belgique. No clear account of the particulars has yet been published. M. de Beaufort came to me immediately with an offer of services; Mme d'Henin came, also, to say she would remove herself to Malines, or anvers,[26] & lend me Therese to attend me, if I wished it: & Mme de Maurville offered me a Bed in her house, if I preferred staying, yet not resting alone. Every body revived into friendly attention. To the Boyds I went myself.

What a day of confusion & alarm did we all spend! In *my* heart the whole time was Treves! Treves! Treves! That day, & *This*, which is now finishing, June 17th I passed in hearing the cannon – ! – seeing the wounded & disabled return, & the ready-armed & vigorous victims march forth to the same destruction! – I was with the p^ss^ at least 10 times – spent 2 Hours chez M^e^ La Tour du Pin, – who was returned to Brussells, – calling upon & receiving the Boyds & Me de Maurville – as well as M. de Beaufort – joining in & changing plans 20 times in an Hour – &, while occupied thus variously in words & actions, filled, entirely filled within one sole only all concentrating thought – of Treves! Treves! Treves! –

Finally, it is arranged This Day

Sunday,[27] June 19th – Exactly 3 months since I flew from Paris.

That I shall set out to-morrow, at 5 o'clock,

If Danger here approaches

with the family of the Boyds, for Antwerp. (Anvers.)

If better prospects arise, I remain at Brussells.

As also if – unhappily, our conveyance fails us!

Direct always in future à Mad^e *de* Burney,[28] post Restante, Anvers.[29]

For Heaven's sake, one line each way! *no* signature!

I have just – at last – had a Letter, delicious for us both – from our Alexander. – still, alas at James's –

At Anvers, Mr. Boyd says I can draw upon the Danoots, here, or from Hoare's in England, without difficulty. How soon I must do it, if we do not meet! – for I have only 10 napoleans left in all.[30] And travelling – & incidental expences in removals will soon swallow them up.

You, also, Mon Ami! mon cher ami! will always be able to draw upon the *tight*,[31] *without* me, if M. de Feltre fails you – & if this place should be taken. Since I have *heard* – since I *HEAR* the canon![32] – Oh mon ami! – one line! *one word!* –

Daily!

Daily! –

For the present awful moment! –

all the people at Brussels LIVE in the streets or at the windows – the whole population is in constant view.

They assure us the Chiefs on each side are in constant view, too, of one another!

The poor Duke de Brusnwic[33] was killed close to the side of the D. of Wellington. – & le Comte de Vincent, the austrian minister extraordinary, has been wounded to day in the same position.

Sunday Night.

The various News of this horrible day has altered my projects every hour. All, at first, was ill – & I accompanied the Boyds to the water side, to embark in a Barge for Anvers: but our vessel was siezed for some wounded officers, & we could get no other.[34] The news then changed, &, in the Evening, I was assured Lord Wellington & M Blücher united had gained a complete victory. 800 prisoners were brought in[35] – made by report as many thousands – But now, the last news of all, tells us the Enemy is working at turning the right wing of Lord Wellington,[36] who is in great danger, & that Brussels is threatened with being taken to-morrow morning!

I am come therefore, to the Boyds, to be in readiness for departing for Anvers to-morrow – or rather This morning at 4 O'clock. We none of us go to Bed, but they are all gone to lie down, in their cloaths; & I have tried to do the same, but excessive inquietude prevents my sleeping. I must now make up this confused scrawl, with repeated petition for a Line to Mad^e *de Burney, poste restante,* Anvers. Heaven bless & preserve you, O mon ami! – and grant that, This frightful storm weathered, we may be re-united in dear, soft, gentle & confiding peace for the rest of our mutual days! Amen. Finished *Three o'clock* on *Monday Morning, June 19th*

We have all been employed in making Charpie! – Ah, ma chère Mad^e de Tessé! – ! –[37]

Mr. Boyd & his family have been upon La place Royale to see the prisoners who were almost all severely wounded, & were in immense numbers. & to see 2 tri-coloured Drapeaux, & two large & beautiful Eagles.[38] The English have continued arriving, on foot, in carts, & on Horse back, grievously wounded also. NEVER yet, all agree, has there been so bloody a battle fought! We have had as yet no consistent details – but the continued sight of the maimed, wounded, mutilated & tortured victims to this exterminating warfare is shocking & afflicting beyond description.

P.S. I open my Letter to say, that, just as we were setting off for Anvers, an English officer brought us word the Enemy had so been pushed & routed at *Wavre* that he had fought his way en retraite back to Genappe[39] – and that Brussells is saved! – though the *War* is only beginning. I must run to Copy you a bulletin that I am told is just published. I have this moment read it. Added to what I have told you of the *position,* is 100 pieces de cannons *present* from the Enemy! – I stay here, therefore, decidedly – so direct as usual, only *Bruxelles, sans rue.*

P.S. 2^d No official news is given since 3 in the morn^g of the 19th – ! Lord Wellington & M Blücher were then both following the Enemy.[40] We are terrified lest they have gone too far! I will write again to-morrow if I can learn any tidings. We think Bruxelles as safe now as before the War. Oh for equal satisfaction from Treves! Treves! – Treves! –

[1358, Marché au bois, Brussels]
22–23 June 1815

To M. d'Arblay
Addressed: Treves/A/Monsieur le Genéral d'Arblay/Offi^r superieur des gardes/de sa Majestie le Roi de France/Chev^r de St Louis, &c &c &c/ à Treves.

Jeudi, Juin 22^d 1815.

How more than ever precious is now the sight of your hand! – I received it to day with a joy inexpressible.

Can I grieve you have not accompanied your favourite General?[41] No, alas, no – for good as *He* is, his party, I am told, is all inflamed against ALL France so as to be bent upon granting no quarter! We have had scenes even here, with stragglers, that frightfully avow their schemes of exterminating vengeance!

I will write directly, according to your desire, to Gand; & to our friend; for I am ignorant whether M. le Duc[42] is there. He was here lately; but nobody now can be found.

The Duke of Wellington is gone entirely from Brussells. He merely arranged for the Hospitals, & ordered off all that could bear, & find, arms, belonging to him.[43] His Quartier général, when I heard last was at Wavre, or Waterloo: but I have been able to get no news of it to-day with certainty.

The dreadfulness of the late Battle exceeds all precedent! *Piles* of Dead – heaps, Masses, *hills* of Dead! French, English, Belge & Prussian, are horrible. The wounded still are coming in – & the *Charettes* are now sent back for the sick & maimed Prisoners. The English who *began,* passed 2 days & a Night without food! There was no cessation of slaughter!

The accounts of individuals vary so, that all I have told you is contradicted, & new tales are current. But there are no leading persons here who affirm or make positively known anything.

Sir Charles Stuart also is gone to Gand. There is no longer any English Ambassadour here. But I had the great satisfaction, by the most happy chance, to send a packet to the tight by the last Courrier who went hence.[44] I called myself, with a long Letter for the Bonne et Belle, at Sir Charles's, to make enquiry how I might act – & heard he was gone entirely from Brussells, as were all the Secretaries, & even domestics. Much disappointed, I was coming away, when they mentioned a courrier going for London – I begged to see him – Times of disturbance give me courage. He was getting his Horse, & had not a moment. I followed to the stable yard. He came to me, & proved to be a most Gentleman-like man, who had served, under Lord Burghersh, all the last campaign. I had a long discourse with him, & he took my packet, & promised it should be delivered by himself immediately on his arrival. How fortunate! for I may now have no other opportunity.

'Tis to Gand Sir Charles is gone. I suppose he will accompany le Roi to the Frontiers. It is supposed He will make his entry by Lille,[45] as that is thought the place that will first declare for him.

I see no more of the Gardes du Corps here now. They are gone to their destination.

Oh how are you to appear in safety in a French Uniform! – pray, for Heaven's sake, consider to what dreadful mistakes it may make you liable!

In the last Battle, near Night, the Belgians, from the likeness of their uniforms,[46] were taken for French by the English, & fired upon! A wounded soldier here told me the English were quite in despair when they found their mistake.

All the Prisoners I have seen here look a complete set of dirty, ragged, coarse Jacobins! in soiled old carter's Frocks.

I am since told that these Frocks were cast over them after they were taken, & had been despoiled of their uniforms by their captors! –

The garde imperiale were all cut up & killed,[47] that did not escape by B[uonaparte]'s side! One whole regiment went, every man!

The poor brave Highlanders have fared little better!

Yet B. has got back to Paris & has published a bulletin that he has conquered Lord Wellington! – !!![48]

He mentions, you will believe, only the surprise upon Charleroy, where he took 1500 men & 6 pieces of cannon: but not a word of LOSING every one of them, with *ALL* the material of his army! Baggage, &c &c.

I have just seen an English wounded soldier who had been made Prisoner on the 18th Sunday; I asked how he became free? he answered he had been carried into a Wood, with many others, where he was very ill & roughly used, stript of all his baggage, & of his shoes, & whatever did not leave him naked; but that in the Night, they were in too much trouble to watch, & he crawled upon all fours out of the wood, & crept on till he joined a party of his comrades.

I have written to de Boinville to plead that I be taken to you with M. Durand now in defiance of all ambition even though at first I joined in your objections;[49] but since I have had each fresh proof of the almost universal deviation from right in All quarters, thus I shall be comforted. For all things else if I know you by the name of one who truly feels his real duty, to whom each will find no hesitation, prepare your utmost firmness of purpose – for that which sickens us must unavoidably be resolved as what to any and each *French* man would at this moment be deemed a disgrace, a *personal* quarrel! You must act & think for yourself, mon ami, in this uncertain time, & rather shew by your example than by your precepts what ought to be done.

M. & Mme de la T[our] du P[in] returned yesterday, I have heard, from Anvers; & Mme d. H[enin] comes back to night. The Boyds have not yet re-appeared. I can give you no account of Mme de Beaufort's Will: Public affairs are so absorbing, I have had no opportunity to enquire. M. de Beaufort I hardly ever see; but he is always polite & obliging, & interested for you: but instead of less, he grows *MORE triste,* – *much* more. – Mr. Kirkpatrick is too busy & troubled now to think of sending me the N[ews] papers, which I miss cruelly. At this moment I am going to subscribe for *reading quick,* if possible, to the Oracle⁵⁰ – for I cannot live without any intelligence.

How kind, how very kind (and reviving) is your attention in writing! I should certainly *succomber* without it! I shall write myself by every post, i.e. 3 times a week, during this critical situation – for I well know – & have *always* & at *ALL* times known that my dearest ami can never suppose me in any great distress or embarrassment & not be wretched if without intelligence.

A new Regiment, the 43^d of English, has just passed before my Eyes! *pour remplacer* their poor slaughtered Countrymen! – *Every* major was killed! 2 colonels, one after the other! the brave Gen Picton, who was in all the victories in Spain!

Heaven bless you, mon ami! – Heaven preserve & bless you! – not once a day, once an hour, once a minute such is my prayer – but *all* day long – but *every* moment! –

Finished Friday morning 23^d June – all here quiet, scarcely a military unmaimed to be seen!– except the just arrived from England, or elsewhere, to march on! –

Your colleague de Namur, *M. de Castries,* was at Brussels a few days ago: & perhaps may be here now.

[1358, Marché au bois]
Brussels, 26–28 June 1815

To M. d'Arblay
Addressed: TREVES. À Monsieur/Monsieur le Général d'Arblay/
Off^r Supérieur des Gardes du Corps/de sa Majesty le Roi de France/
Chev^r de St. Louis, &c – &c/à TREVES.

BRUXELLES.
Ce Lundi,
ce Blessed Lundi, June 26. 1815.

Why have I not a Balloon to be the first to tell you this enchanting news! – or rather, Wings to fly to you with it myself! Buonaparte has yielded to Lord Wellington! – – –[51]

The particulars – how, which way, &c, are told too variously for building upon their correctness – but the Fact SEEMS undoubted – SEEMS, I am compelled to say, for nothing official has been here printed. The sleepiness of this quiet & good, but most drowsy & hum drum people exceeds belief: Especially when I consider que les Francs et les Belges came from one parent stock i.e., the *Germains*.

O Mon Ami! will not PEACE re-visit us! My hand shakes – & my spirits are agitated past all description, with an inward fear that all this will not be confirmed. O for an English Gazette! –

The whole City, in spite of its apathy, looked smiling, & even, some few, grinning with contented joy, as I walked out early. I except some others, evidently & gloomily overset. But these last are few. The people of this house, & every shop-keeper had heard the news, though without positive authority.

But, about noon, I had a visit from M. de Beaufort – who came, kindly smiling himself, to bring me the first of the news. He had *JUST* learnt it, at the Commandants' – M. le Colonel Jones. His account was that Buonaparte had sent to the Duke propositions, by an officer General. *1st* To Abdicate, in favour of his Son & a Regency: or *2dly*, in favour of Prince Eugene,[52] the great favourite of the Empr of Russia; *3dly,* In favour of the Duke of Orleans!

The Duke sent him word he must yield at Discretion, or Fight. He had nothing to do with *Abdicating*, for he was NOTHING! He *had* already Abdicated, when he was Emperor.

The Army then sent a deputation, demanding a TRUCE to prepare a Peace, for sparing the further effusion of human blood.

The Duke answered, Their King might spare it, when reseated on his Throne; but that *FOR THEM,* & *FROM* Them, the application was now too late.

After this, I spoke all the kind things you have written of M. de Beaufort, who heard them with tears in his Eyes, & who is still & evidently more melancholy. Does he feel her loss more than he felt her presence? I have heard no relation of the Will; but it is impossible for me to doubt that so very attached a wife should have failed in the tender duty of shewing a regard beyond the Grave.

In the course of the Morning, came the P^ss escorted by M. de Lally. They gave me, & kindly came on purpose to give me, the same particulars: with many added, of deep interest – but of a sort I shall not write till I am sure my Letters come straight into your hands: & you talk so often of their *following* you, that I durst run no rash risks at such a moment.

After all this, in the Park, whither I went to breathe an instant, at it's epoch of real emptiness, 5 o'clock – I met a Gentleman whose face I thought I knew. He looked a reciprocal look of a similar idea, but walked on. Presently, however, we both looked back, & caught each other making the same second investigation – He then returned, & seizing my hand, with an air of cordial affection, exclaimed 'Mon Dieu! Mad^e d'A:! –' & I then recalled our old friend le voisin [M. de Boursac].

He was extremely affectionate & kind. He had escaped the same day that we did: but *ses dames sont toujours à Paris.* I believe he is with M. le P[rince] de Condé. He has promised to come & see me speedily; he enquired most heartily after you & said he had done so already, & had learnt you were at Treves. He told me further news –[53]

That in *Les Chambres,* various voices had demanded army intelligence, & where was the Emperor. At first, the Ministers present said Les Nouvelles were not mauvaises; the *Emperour* was with his army; but being hard & hardily pressed, Carnet acknowledged *all to be bad,* & the Emperor in Paris! – After much dissention, & contention, & [violence,] a Majority took imperious lead, & declared Buonapart *déchu.*

A Committee was then formed to make a proposal to the Allies – THREE took the lead – And said They would make any sacrifice to recover peace – resign the Emperor; – become a republic; take another & new form of Government – or revert to a free Monarchy – *ANY THING*, for Peace – except – reinstating the late Power! – – – oh mon ami – I hope this is exaggerated – & surtout that it is FALSE, entirely false that one of these Three is one of our most valued Friends! – – Not Victor, you are very sure – nor yet his Brother – – but – – M. de La Fayette!

Difficulties – contrarieties – Factions – Mischiefs we must expect – & meet with fortitude – but ONE voice, clear & UNIVERSAL, in a chorus angelical, cries, affirms, & confirms, That the Armies fight no more! –

If you were to see me in this happy, happy Moment – you would not know me – I have not felt so blyth since – – – since when? – Since the

Evening you came home from the first short & frightful Campaign – when happiness – after long – long Journeying elsewhere, suddenly & sweetly made me a visit –

Tuesday, June 27th I have again seen M. de Boursac, & I have been to the Boyds, once but no *new* News is afloat to day. The King is at Cateau Cambresis, under the immediate protection of Lord Wellington – whose proclamation[54] if I can possibly procure I will copy for you to-morrow early. How amazing that on the *21st* you should not have heard, at Treves, of the Invasion of les pays bas! – I am truly sorry for Gen: Kleist: but oh how happy to think & hope *you* still at Treves! – I am happy, also, I decided against going to Anvers: already, I am forced to tell you I must have recourse myself to Messrs Danoots in a short time. With my most scrupulous œconomy, I can only hope to wait till I hear from you next, as an answer is always 12 days in arriving. I have been compelled to purchase some few matters of wearing apparel, – nothing coming from Paris – though merely matters of necessity, for I live more retired than ever, & have NO pleasure in ANY expence of which neither you nor Alex partake. The Aegide, ou plutôt, *les siens,* would much have disappointed you; had you seen them *de plus prés.* When you come to *close quarters,* they are ordinary & uninteresting; I mean in *discourse.* I except, however, the Eldest, who is far the best fashioned of the tribe. But I am truly glad not to have been forced upon beginning an intimacy it would have been a burthen to me to sustain.

Wednesday, June 28! – O how *il me tarde* d'avoir de vos nouvelles! & to know your destination! I shall love Treves all my life! To-morrow is post day, Dieu merci! – – & my kind Ami has not once failed his impatient suffering athanase since this alarming period, that would make failure almost mortal. I cannot get the Proclamation till next post! I hope it will reach you otherwise. I have no room to relate the pourquois; for I have another thing to tell you. I enquired of our voisin how it happened that *you* had received no order to move, when one of your Collegues, M. de Castres, certainly had, since he had been at Bruxelles. He answered me – That M. de C. had received no order, for he had seen him, & believed he was even here still: but when the Fr[ench] arrived, or were undoubtedly arriving before Namur, he came away of his own accord, *AS A THING OF COURSE,* & of *common sense,* since, had he been taken, he must instantly have been shot by the Buonapartists, on account of his mission: & that without serving any purpose, as he had no troops, & no command.

The Maison du Roi IS, or is to be, *dissoute:*[55] I asked what was become of its members? He replied Those who had *leave,* or *orders,* accompanied the King: the others addressed M. de Feltre, & waited where was most *convenable* for directions. But ALL, of ALL descriptions, have left Gand. At Alost there is still a Depôt.

With respect to the person *fusilé* for M. de L[ally]'s *Manifest,*[56] it was M. de L. HIMSELF who told me. But happily, it has proved a misinformation. NOTHING, at this moment, must be QUITE CREDITED, but upon *proof:* – is it not *THEREFORE* that you QUITE credit the tender faith of your inalterable

F B d'A. – y? –

De Boinville is with the D[uke] of Feltre in France – by mistake, he missed my letter, for he must else have answered it. I have much uneasiness at the moment relative to the *parties divers* –![57]

Le Voisin tells me le Duc de Bourbon has been all this time in Spain – but is now certainly in La Vendee. M. d'Angouleme still in Spain at the last News.

[1358, Marché au bois]
Brussels, 1 July

To M. d'Arblay

Saturday, Ce 1ʳ Juillet

Ah mon ami – q'êtes vous donc devenu et que n'ai-je de vos nouvelles? Have you quitted Treves? – could not François – if you were too hurried, write one line? – I am a prey to the most terrible uneasiness & so must remain till Monday! for to-morrow there is no Post. I will send this – since you bid me continue writing to Treves – but know not how to add any thing more –

Yet – should you be there, & have no quicker intelligence I ought to tell you that I read last night the King's Proclamation,[58] drawn up by M. Talyrand, which is perfect!

He will pardon *ALL* but Individuals peculiarly culpable – of those he will select very *few,* & only the *worst,* to banish or bring to Justice.

He declares he has *himself* forbidden *All the Princes of his house* to accompany the Allies into France.

And has himself restrained the ardour of all his faithful adherents, who would have fought for him *avec l'Etranger.*

B[uonaparte] – is said to be trying to escape to Havre, or some sea port,[59] with all his surviving officers.

If he be suffered, – in 2 years he will again lead us the same dance of death he has so frightfully taught us at this moment. The numbers of dead, whether of Conquerors or Conquered, have not yet been counted! – nor even all the wounded – many are still on the field of Battle, where they are dressed, – their wounds, I mean! – while waiting for carriages, which are constantly on the road!!

Brussels is a Walking Hospital! Maimed & Wounded unhappy men of War are met at every step, either entering, carried in Casts, from the Fields of Battle, or the adjoining Villages, to be placed in Infirmaries, Work houses, Churches, & also at private houses. Every body is ordered to receive all their Dwelling can hold. It is even written on the doors of most houses how many are already refuged in them. The Belgians behave with the utmost humanity to the miserable objects of fallen Ambition, – or contentious strugglers on either side. Almost all the Natives prepare to run from the City, in apprehension of some Contagious fever, from the multitude of Sick! –

O Write! My best beloved! my noble husband! Write – or make François write –

At so fearful a time not to have certainty of your health & your position is Agony! nothing less, – mon trop cher ami!

[1358, Marché au bois]
Brussels, 3–[10] July

To Mrs. Waddington
Addressed: ANGLETERRE/À Madame/at Madame Waddingtons,/
Lanover,/Near Abergavenny,/Monmouthshire

July 3ᵈ
Bruxelles.

How is it that my ever dear Mary can thus on one side be fascinated by the very thing that, on the other, revolts her? how be a professed & ardent detester of Tyranny; yet an open & intrepid admirer of a Tyrant? O had you spent, like me, 10 years within the control of his unlimited power, & under the iron rod of its dread, how would you change your language! by a total reverse of sentiment! yet was I, because always inoffensive, never molested: as safe There, *another* would say, as in London; but *you* will not say so; the safety of deliberate prudence, or of retiring timidity, is not such as would satisfy a mind glowing for freedom like your's: it satisfies, indeed, NO *mind*, it merely suffices for *bodily* security. It was the choice of my Companion, not of my Taste that drew ME to such a residence. PERSONALLY, for the reason I have assigned, I was always well treated, & personally I was happy: but you know me, I am sure, better than to suppose me such an Egotist as to be really happy, or contented, where Corporal Liberty could only be preserved by Mental forbearance − − i.e. subjection.

The panic impressed upon all the Inhabitants, whether native or visitors, by the late Invasion, & its consequences, would have cured any one not absolutely incurable of a revolutionary taste; & my dear Mary has too fair & too liberal propensities ever wilfully to blind herself against visible facts, or to deafen herself against powerful, yet candid conviction. The Belgians have for so many Centuries been accustomed to sanguinary conflicts, & violent, or mercenary, change of masters, that I really thought, from the placid state in which, when seeking here an asylum, I found them, that they were utterly indifferent to the result of the neighbouring struggle, & would just as willingly have fallen again into the hands of Buonaparte as not. They never, of their own accord, opened upon the subject, nor considered nor treated us poor fugitives but as common Visitors. I imagined they had gone through too many political changes, to deem one, or two, more or less, an addition worth ruffling their serenity. And Buonaparte, whether from hearing of this passive philosophy, or whether from motives yet unknown, certainly expected not alone that they would not oppose, but that, on the contrary, they would join him. This idea, with respect to the Belgian troops, was, indeed, spread, & most alarmingly, here. The Duke of Wellington was warned by several persons not to trust them: & it is generally understood That he determined They should neither be trusted in front, lest they should join the Enemy, nor in the Rear, lest they should run away from their friends. Nevertheless, when the day of the most bloody battle that ever Rival Warriors fought, arrived, I found I had taken the calm of their Natures for mere indifference to their fate; [for when] a cry was shouted through the streets That The French were come! That *Buonaparte et les Français étoient à la porte de la Ville!* − the consternation that ensued, the horrour that was depicted on every Countenance, shewed they were alive at least to the evils that menaced themselves − and how few, how very few are really awake to any other![60] We do not appear to be asleep, because our Eyes are wide open; but dormant lies every feeling that belongs to whatever is not animated, in some or other shape, by SELF, except in the very, VERY few whom Nature has gifted − or condemned − 'to feel for OTHER's woes'.[61]

132

[10 July] It is now within 3 days of 2 months since I last saw M. d'A: he has been sent upon a mission, of the King's, first to Liege, next to Luxembourg, & then to Treves, where he has passed 6 weeks: he has now left it, but I know not, yet, for what other destination. You will not believe me very tranquil in the ignorance; but I am tranquil in nothing during this wandering, houseless, homeless, Emigrant life. This is no siecle for those who love their home, or who have a home to love. 'Tis a siecle for the Adventurous, to whom Ambition always opens resources; or for the New, who guess not at the Catastrophes that hang on the rear, while the phantom Expectation allures them to the front. –

The 2^d restoration seems now fast advancing. I have just had a Letter from the quarter General of the King from *Roye*, written by a friend in the King's *suite*, who says His M[ajesty] has been received there with enthusiasm. – I, you well know, must hear that with pleasure, for my only consolation during the[se] tremendous conflicts, & prospects eternally va[ryin]g, in which of late I have lived, has been that the principles & feelings of M. d'A: have coincided with his duty. You were quite right not to have had a doubt as to the line he would pursue; belonging to the *Maison du Roi*, & having ALWAYS refused to serve Buonaparte, he must not only have been perfidious, but indefinable to have hesitated. I am extremely glad, therefore, you would take no measure for MY affairs but with MY concurrence, for whoever, at that period, remained in Paris, & in power, must both think & act so very differently from M. d'A: that he would have been offended to have owed to them even a solid benefit. He is *très* what those on the other side of the question call *exalté*[62] – & oh what painful scenes must we go through if we get back to our deserted home! You will wonder to hear me say *IF*; prosperous as all now seems; but the changes which this Country has now for so long a time gone through, have been so astonishing, so sudden, so unexpected, that they take at least away all presumption, if not all confidence in public transactions. The various parts, from various circumstances as well as propensities, taken upon the late Eruption of Mount Corsica, will have severed asunder half the families amongst my best friends! In particular she who is most dear to me[63] – a very sister in tender affection, useful friendship, & endearing sympathy, will stand between two Brothers, each equally loved by her, who have decidedly & actively taken two opposite sides! – With regard to a very very delicate subject, my dearest Mary, upon it now I have nothing to fear of rashness: I flatter myself, therefore, she will weigh – & then, I am persuaded, make a decision which seems circumspect – all with her fond devotion to those who so entirely love you. You make me wish to see Waverley[64] – Alex, also, writes to me of it with rapture. Sismondi's 'Literature' also I should like to see. But I am out of the way of Books, & Book people. I subscribe, nevertheless, to a Library,[65] but it has almost no foreign works. How vexing that Alexander should have so endless a vacation just when he cannot pass it with us. Your angelic Emily I still must hope will *weather the storm.*[66] Embrace her for me with tenderness; but I am alarmed for my bright Augusta! What has she to do with headaches? does she apply too much? My wise, prudent, yet so kind hearted & feeling Name sake alone seems fashioned to sustain the siege of application in her elaborate studies. M. d'A is quite chagrined to miss the Drawing & Letter so obligingly designed for him. You may imagine how impatiently I desire – yet tremble to know the actual state of my affairs in Paris, & the state of my MSS. I have had no sort of information. Whenever the King gets to Paris, the post will, of course, be again open. Should you go to town, you will see, I hope, my excellent sister Broome, & my very dear Fanny Raper, and, probably, my excentric Alex, for he goes not to Cambridge till the end of October. I dare not ask if you have had any more recent account of him – Yet nothing would more usefully serve & oblige me than to know.

Adieu, dearest Mary – for
Life yours truly,
FB d'A.

[1358, Marché au bois]
Brussels, 4–5 July

To M. d'Arblay
Addressed: Nº2/Au/Chevalier d'Arblay –/&c/Nº 2.

Tuesday, *July 4th*
Midnight –

Mon ami! mon Cher ami! what joy! what extacy! – Just as my Letter was filled, & folded – & our house all retiring to rest – a ring at the door gave an alarm – & in rushed – into my room, & my arms – the princess d'Henin to tell me all was arranged, by That Angel Lord Wellington! – that the King should enter Paris next Thursday, July 6th without ANY of the allies – without even HIMSELF! (Lord W.)

M. de Lally, who has followed the King, & been admitted to an Audience, & to all the Counsels, has stolen from them to write this – & 3 pages of detail – with ink flowing through tears of Joy! – –

M. Mounier, he says is crying like a Child – M. de Jaucourt *subdued* with excess of happiness – All round do nothing but embrace – & laugh – & weep! – The Letter is the most affectingly delightful I ever read. But, what astonishment! – B[uonaparte] is NOT ONCE mentioned in the Letter! –

Neither is he in one M. de Jaucourt, with the same exquisite News, has written here to his wife!

Nor yet in one received from the King's party by the D^ss d'ursel. –

It is supposed he is with the *debris* of his army, behind La Loire.[67] The King is now proclaiming That Army *dissoute*. Valenciennes still holds out – so do various places – because not knowing, or not believing this divine event.

Lord Wellington has done the Whole! as Masterly in the Cabinet as in the Field! And he has done it, by going on at all risks foremost, – for had the Prussians, &c arrived, it is probable his negociations would have been overpowered by the earnest desire of plunder. –

The Messenger sent by the Governor of Paris – that horrible d'avoust, with acceptance of the terms of Lord Wellington, his Grace desired might be well treated; that no *acharnement* of *l'amour propre* might mar the treaty. He dined, therefore, with some of the King's Gentlemen.

I shall gather all possible particulars for the next part, – pray give very attentive orders about the safety of your Letters, should you leave Treves while any are on the road: I shall continue writing till you tell me not: – It is such a consolation to *me* to hear you say my Letters procure any to you! my dearest dearest amico! what a blessed termination at length of so much misery! – Pray write for I can only wait for the next post, before I take up money, as I have at this moment but 30 Nap[oleons] left in the world. I cannot take up less than 20 – for many reasons – unless your next letter gives me some direction how to do otherwise – Heaven bless you, caro mio ben! – caro carissimo! –

Wednesday July 5th

I kept this for a Bon Jour – <and> – viz. demain – Thur^s our Bon Roi ENTRERA – every body now will say, notre bon Roi! – <am I last to hear I wonder?> I want to share in your pleasure! My enjoyment is only half till I know yours –

FLORENCE NIGHTINGALE

The Crimean War (1853–56) began with a dispute over the Holy Places of Turkish-controlled Jerusalem. Tsar Nicholas I claimed the sole right to protect Orthodox Christians within the territories of the Ottoman Empire. When the Ottomans rejected this the Tsar occupied Moldavia and Wallachia, resulting in a war with the Turks. Britain and France, fearing Russian expansionism in the Middle East, moved into the Black Sea after a Turkish flotilla had been destroyed and declared war on Russia when Russia refused to withdraw from the area.

With the beginning of the Crimean War the British public were for the first time given almost instantaneous news from the front by telegraph. William Howard Russell, special correspondent of *The Times*, had sent outraged reports on the high incidence of cholera and other enteric diseases and the scandalous conditions in military hospitals. The newspaper launched an appeal for funds to supply the sick and wounded with necessities, and the public response was immense. Florence Nightingale (1820–1910), who had trained briefly in nursing at Pastor Fliedner's school for nursing in Kaiserswerth, Germany, and had, in 1853, been appointed Superintendent of the Harley Street Hospital for Gentlewomen, was asked to go out with a group of nurses, first by the philanthropist Lady Maria Forester, then in an official capacity by her friend Sidney Herbert, Secretary-at-War. Women had never been allowed to serve officially in the army, and the sick and wounded in military hospitals were traditionally served by pensioners and recovering soldiers. The fact that nursing was considered an immoral and undisciplined profession, not fit for respectable women, was an added complication in the difficulties faced by Nightingale.

Florence Nightingale left for the Crimea on October 21 1854 with 38 nurses, accompanied also by her friends Selina (nicknamed Sigma by Florence) and Charles Bracebridge, who stayed in the Crimea until the summer of 1855. Readers of *The Times* donated £7,000 for her personal use, and Nightingale herself donated her annual allowance of £500, paid by her family, to the work. This money became central in improving hospital conditions, but was also a source of friction with the army personnel who opposed Nightingale.

Nightingale's party arrived on 3 November, to find utter chaos at the Scutari hospitals. Her genius for organization came to the fore, but she made enemies in the process. Her initial tactic was to play a waiting game. After her first offer of help was refused by the medical officers, she waited for them to come to her. After the Battle of Inkerman, when masses of sick and wounded poured into Scutari on 9 November, the doctors turned to Florence Nightingale and her nurses for help.

To Elizabeth Herbert   1854
                                        1 Upper Harley St 14 Oct 1854

My dearest

I went to Belgrave Sq. this morn'g, for the chance of catching you, or Mr. Herbert even, had he been in town.

A small private expedition of nurses has been organized for Scutari & I have been asked to command it. I take myself out & one Nurse. Lady Maria Forester[1] has given £200 to take out three others. We feed and lodge ourselves there, & are to be no expence whatever to the country. Lord Clarendon[2] has been asked by Ld Palmerston[3] to write to Ld Stratford[4] for us, & has consented. Dr. Andrew Smith[5] of the Army Medical Board, whom I have seen, authorizes us, & gives us letters to the Chief Medical Officer at Scutari. I do not mean to say that I believe the Times accounts, but I do believe that we may be of use to the wounded wretches.

Now to business –

(1) Unless my Ladies' Committee feel that this is a thing which appeals to the sympathies of all, & urge me, rather than barely consent, I cannot honorably break my engagement here. And I write to you as one of my mistresses.

(2) What does Mr. Herbert[6] say to the scheme itself? Does he think it will be objected to by the authorities? Would he give us any advice or letters of recommendation? And are there any stores for the Hospital he would advise us to take out? Dr. Smith says that nothing is needed.

I enclose a letter from Sigma. Do you think it any use to apply to Miss Burdett Coutts?[7]

We start on Tuesday *if* we go, to catch the Marseilles boat of the 21st for Constantinople, where I leave my nurses, thinking the Medical Staff at Scutari will be more frightened than amused at being bombarded by a parcel of women, & I cross over to Scutari with some one from the Embassy to present my credentials from Dr. Smith, & put ourselves at the disposal of the Drs.

(3) Would you or some one of my Committee write to Lady Stratford to say, 'this is not a lady but a real Hospital Nurse', of me. 'And she has had experience'.

My uncle went down this morning to ask my father & mother's consent.

Would there be any use in my applying to the Duke of Newcastle[8] for his authority?

Believe me, dearest in haste
ever yours

F Nightingale

Perhaps it is better to keep it quite a private thing & not apply to Gov't qua Gov't.

To William Bowman, Surgeon[9]

Barrack Hospital.
Scutari 14 Nov 1854

'I came out, Ma'am prepared to submit to Everything. to be put upon in Everyway. But there are *some* things, Ma'am one can't submit to. There is the caps, ma'am that suits one face. and some that suits another. And if I'd known, Ma'am about the Caps, great as was my desire to come out as nurse at Scutari, I wouldn't have come, ma'am'. – Speech of Mrs Lawfield

Dear Sir time must be at a discount with the man who can adjust the balance of such an important question as the above – & I, for one have none: as you will readily suppose when I tell you that on Thursday last we had 1715 sick and wounded in this Hospital (among whom 120 Cholera patients and 650 severely wounded in the other Building, called the Gen'l Hospital, of w'ch we also have charge, when a message came to me to prepare for 510 wounded on our side the Hosp'l who were arriving from the dreadful affair of the 5th Nov'r at Balaclava, where 1763 wounded & 442 killed, besides 96 Officers wounded & 38 killed. I always expected to end my days as Hospital Matron but I never expected to be Barrack Mistress. We had but 1/2 an hour's notice, before they began landing the wounded. Between one and nine o'clock, we had the mattrasses stuffed, sewn up, and laid down, alas! only upon matting on the floor, the men washed and put to bed, & all their wounds dressed – I wish I had time or

I would write you a letter dear to a surgeon's heart, I am as good as 'Medical Times'. But oh! you gentlemen of England who sit at home in all the well earned satisfaction of your successful cases, can have little idea, from reading the newspapers, of the horror & misery in a military Hosp'l of operating upon these dying exhausted men. A London Hosp'l is a garden of flowers to it. We have had such a sea in the Bosphorus, and the Turks, the very men for whom we are fighting are carrying our wounded so cruelly, that they arrive in a state of agony – one amputated stump died two hours after we received him, one compound fracture just as we were getting him into bed, in all 24 cases on the day of landing. We have now 4 miles of beds – & not 18 inches apart. We have our quarters in one Tower of the Barrack & all this fresh influx has been laid down between us and the main guard in two corridors with a line of beds down each side just room for one man to pass between, and four wards. Yet in the midst of the appalling horror, there is good. And I can truly say like St. Peter 'it is good for us to be here' – tho' I doubt whether if St. Peter had been here, he would have said so. As I went my night-round among the newly wounded that first night, there was not one murmur, not one groan the strictest discipline, the most absolute silence & quiet prevailed.

Only the step of the Sentry & I heard one man say 'I was dreaming of my friends at home', & another said 'and I was thinking of them'. These poor fellows bear pain & mutilation with unshrinking heroism & die without complaint. Not so the officers, but we have nothing to do with the Officers. The wounded are now lying up to our very door & we are landing 540 more from the 'Andes'. I take rank in the army as Brigadier General, because 40 British females, whom I have with me, are more difficult to manage than 4000 men. Let no lady come out here who is not used to fatigue & privation – for the Devonport Sisters, who ought to know what self-denial is, do nothing but complain. Occasionally the roof is torn off our quarters, or the windows blown in & we are flooded & under water for the night. We have all the sick Cookery now to do – & have got in 4 men for the purpose, for the prophet Mahomet does not allow us a female. And we are now able to supply these poor fellows with something besides Gov't rations. I wish you w'd recall me to Dr. Bence Jones[10] remembrance, when you see him, and tell him I have had but too much occasion to remember him in the constant use of his dreadful present. In all our corridor I think we have not an average of three units per man, and there are two ships more 'landing' at the Crimea with wounded, this is our phraseology. All who can walk come in to us for Tobacco – but I tell them we have not a bit to put into our own mouths – not a sponge, not a rag

139

of linen, not anything have I left. Every thing is gone torn to make slings & stump pillows & shirts. These poor fellows had not had a clean shirt nor been washed for two months before they came here & the state in w'ch they arrived from the Transports is literally *crawling*. I hope in a few days we shall establish a little cleanliness. But we have not a basin, nor a towel, nor a bit of soap, nor a broom. I have ordered 300 scrubbing brushes. We are getting on nicely in many ways. They were so glad to see us. The Senior Chaplain is a sensible man, w'ch is a remarkable providence. I have not been out of the Hospital wall yet. But the most beautiful view in the world I believe lies outside. If you ever see Mr. Whitfield the House Apothecary of St. Thomas's will you tell him that the nurse he sent me, Mrs. Roberts, is worth her weight in gold. There was another engagement on the 8th, & more wounded, who are coming down to us. The text w'ch heads my letter was expounded thus Mrs Lawfield was recommended to return home and set her cap, vulgarly speaking, at some one elsewhere than here, but on begging for mercy, was allowed to make another trial. Mrs. Drake is a treasure. The four others are not fit to take care of themselves nor of others in a military Hosp'l. This is my first impression but it may modify, if I can convince them of the necessity of discipline and propriety in a drunken garrison. Believe me dear Sir your very truly & gratefully

Florence Nightingale

This is only the beginning of things. We are still expecting the assault.

To Sidney Herbert

Barrack Hospital, Scutari
25 Nov 1854
British Sisters Quarters

Private

Dear Mr. Herbert

(1) It appears that in these Hospitals, the Purveyor considers washing both of linen & of the men a minor 'detail' – & during the three weeks we have been here, though our remonstrances have been treated with perfect civility, yet no washing whatever has been performed for the men either of body linen or of bed-linen except by ourselves, & a few wives of the Wounded, & a story of a Contractor, with which we have been amused, turns out to be a myth. The dirty shirts were collected yesterday for the first time, & on Monday *it is said* that they are to be washed, – & we are organizing a little Washing Establishment of our own – for the bandages

&c. When we came here, there was neither basin, towel nor soap in the Wards, nor any means of personal cleanliness for the Wounded except the following.

Thirty were bathed every night by Dr. MacGrigor's orders in slipper-baths, but this does not do more than include a washing once in eighty days for 2300 men.

The consequences of all this are Fever, Cholera, Gangrene, Lice, Bugs, Fleas – & may be Erysipelas – from the using of one sponge among many wounds.

And even this slipper-bathing does not apply to the General Hospital.

(2) The fault here is, *not* with the Medical Officers, but in the separation of the department which affords every necessary supply, except medecines, to them – & in the insufficient supply of minor officers in the Purveying Department under Mr. Wreford, the Purv'r Gen'l, as well as in the inevitable delay in obtaining supplies, occasioned by the existence of one single Interpreter only, who is generally seen booted.

(3) Your name is also continually used as a bug-bear, they make a deity of cheapness, & the Secretary at War stands synonymous here with Jupiter Tonans[11] whose shafts end only in 'brutum fulmen'.[12] The cheese-paring system which sounds unmusical in British ears is here identified with you by the Officers who carry it out. It is in vain to tell the Purveyors that they will get no 'kudos' by this at home. See Note A

(4) The requirements are, unity of action & personal responsibility.

It is a sad joke here that a large reward has been offered for any one who is personally responsible, barring the Commandant.

(5) Another cause is, the imperfection of distinct order in England as to *packing*. The unfortunate 'Prince' who was lost at Balaklava had on board a quantity of medical comforts for us which were so packed under shot & shell as that it was found impossible to disembark them here & they went on to Balaklava & were lost at the same time as your Commissioner Dr. Spence.[13]

(6) In consequence of the Duke of Newcastle's letter to Mr. Cumming,[14] the latter has not taken the command here, & in consequence of Dr. Spence being lost on board the 'Prince', the Commission of Enquiry has not yet begun its labours. Mr. Maxwell visits us *en amateur*.

(7) Two or three hundred Stump Pillows, ditto Arm Slings, ditto *Paddings* for Splints – besides other Medical Appliances are being weekly manufactured & given out by us – & no provision appeared to have been made for these things before.

All the above is written in obedience to your *private* instructions. Do not let me appear as a Gov't spy here which would destroy all my usefulness & believe me, in great haste,

Yours ever truly

F. Nightingale

P.S. Lord Napier[15] & the Visitors generally remark that the Hospital is improved since we came.

Note A –

The habits & the honor of the Purveying Department, as inferior officers, fix their attention upon the correctness of their book-keeping as the primary object of life.

Note B –

Mr. Osborne & Mr. Macdonald have been profuse of offers. We have accepted wine, shirts, flannel, calico, sago, &c – delay being as fatal to us as denial in our requisitions.

Entre nous, will you let me state that Lady Stratford, with the utmost kindness & benevolent intentions, is, in consequence of want of practical habits of business, nothing but good & bustling, & a time waster & impediment. As the Commission is not yet doing anything, the Ambassador should send us a *man* who, with prompt efficiency, can also defend us from the difficulties & delays of mediating between conflicting orders in the various departments – to which I ascribe most of the signal failures, such as those in washing &c, which have occurred.

F.N.

P.S. Mrs. Herbert gave me a fright by telling Mrs. Bracebridge that your private letter to me has been published. That letter was shewn to no one but my own people & it appears to me impossible that it can have found its way into any other hands.

P.P.S. We are greatly in want of Hair Mattrasses or even Flock, as cheaper. There are but 44 Hair Mattrasses in store. Our very bad cases suffer terribly from bed-sores on the Paillasse, which is all we have – while the French Hospital is furnished throughout with mattrasses having an elastic couche of Hair between two Flock & a Paillasse underneath.

To Sidney Herbert

Barrack Hospital, Scutari

Private   10 Dec 1854

Dear Mr. Herbert

With regard to receiving & employing a greater number of Sisters &

Nurses in these Hospitals, I went immediately (on reading Mrs. Herbert's letter of the 23rd, addressed to Mr. Bracebridge,) to consult Mr. Menzies, the Principal Medical Officer, under whose orders I am.

He considers that as large a number are now employed in these Hospitals as can be usefully appropriated, & as can be made consistent with morality & discipline. And the discipline of forty women, collected together for the first time, is no trifling matter – under these new & strange circumstances.

He considers that if we were swamped with a number increased to sixty or seventy, good order would become impossible. And in all these views I so fully concur that I should resign my situation as impossible, were such circumstances forced upon me.

For our quarters are already inadequate to preserving in health our number. More quarters cannot be assigned to us. The sick are laid up to our door. We had even to give up a portion of those quarters which had been assigned us (at the General Hospital) to the Wounded.

With regard to taking a house at Scutari, the Medical Officers considered it as simply impossible. Regularity could not be preserved, where the Sisters & Nurses were living from under our own eye – the difficulties of transport are what no one in England would believe – & the going to & fro between the two Hospitals is becoming daily less easy. That I should not accept a responsibility, which I could not fulfil, is equally the opinion of the Medical Officers & mine.

If, in the course of the winter, we have out ten or twenty more, & send back some of those we have, the Medical Officers are of opinion that that number will be sufficient, i.e. forty efficient ones being picked out eventually for the two Hospitals averaging 3000 sick.

Lastly, I have found from this last month's experience that, had we come out with twenty instead of forty, we should not only have been less hampered with difficulties, but the work itself would have been actually better & more efficiently done. About ten of us have done *the whole work*. The others have only run between our feet & hindered us – & the difficulty of assigning to them something to do without superintendence has been enormous. It is the difference between the old plough with the greatest amount of power & the greatest loss in its application – & the Gee-ho plough with reins – accomplishing twice the work with half the power & much more efficiently.

We were so alarmed at the general terms in which Mrs. Herbert described the nurses as instantly to be sent off – that we held council & decided on writing the enclosed to the Ambassador as the only means of protecting them & ourselves. In other words we could neither house nor keep them.

English people look upon Scutari as a place with inns & hackney-coaches & houses to let furnished. It required yesterday (to land 25 casks of sugar) four oxen & three men for six hours – plus two passes, two requisitions, Mr. Bracebridge's two interferences, & one apology from a Quarter Master for seizing the Araba, received with a smile & a kind word, because he did his duty. For every Araba is required on Military-store or Commissariat duty. There are no pack-horses & no asses, except those used by the peasantry to attend the market 1¼ miles off. An Araba consists of loose poles & planks extended between two axle-trees, placed on four small wheels, & drawn by a yoke of weak oxen.

There is not a Turkish house which is not in a fragmentary state – roof & windows pervious in all directions – there is not a room in our Quarters which does not let in the rain in showers, whenever the weather is bad. We can only buy food through the Commissary & are sometimes without wood or charcoal.

For want of a carpenter & a man to put up a stove, in the absence of all hands (the workmen available being all employed in repairing the sick Wards, the matter of first importance) we have been unable during the last week to effect the move of some of our nurses into the Gen'l Hosp'l, or even to get in a few poor soldier's wives into our little Lying-in Hospital, which the pressure of the misery of these poor women had compelled us to begin.

All this will tend to explain the impossibility of having more women, & especially ladies, out here at present.

Mr. Bracebridge has put down some Memo'a as they occurred to him. What we may be considered to have effected is
1) the kitchen for extra-diets, now in full action, for this Hospital – with regular extra-diet tables sent in by the Ward-Surgeons –
2) A great deal more cleaning of Wards – mops, scrubbing-brushes, brooms, & combs, given out by ourselves, where not forced from the Purveyor –
3) 2000 shirts, cotton & flannel, given out & washing organized – & already carried on for a week.
4) Lying-in Hospital begun
5) widows & soldiers' wives relieved & attended to.
6) a great amount of daily dressing & attention to compound fractures by the most competent of us –
7) the supervision & stirring-up of the whole machinery generally, with the

full concurrence of the chief medical authorities – & the practical proof which our presence has given that Gov't were determined to know all they could & do all they could –

8) the repairing of wards for 800 wounded which would otherwise have been left uninhabitable. And this I regard as the most important.

The Government could not do otherwise than send a number of Female Assistants worthy of it – viz 30 or 40. Of these, at most 16 are efficient. The personal qualities of five or six have effected (under God's blessing) the results already obtained.

I am willing to bear the evil of governing (& preventing from doing mischief) the non-efficient *or scheming* majority, which is my great difficulty & most wearing-out labor – because I acknowledge the moral effect produced, which could not have been produced by smaller numbers. But I am not willing to encounter the crowding greater numbers to exhaust our powers & make us useless & incapable – by wasting our time & nervous energy in governing that which cannot be governed.

Lastly at the moment we came out, the 'Times' commissioner & his fund were prepared immediately to go into opposition – as they have actually done at Balaclava, where the 'Times' supplies have been refused – as well as admission to Mr. Stafford – whereas here, instead of opposition, we have had support. Nothing has been given here except through us & we have had abundant supplies, more than we asked, from Mr. Macdonald & Mr. Osborne – who have held daily consultations with us. Mr. Stafford, who was on the point of going into extreme opposition, has shewn nothing but kindness & zeal.

The great fault here lies in our geography – in our being on this side of the water. Four days in the week, we cannot communicate with Constant'e, except by the other harbour, 1¼ mile off, of Scutari proper, to which the road is almost impassable.

I add the Pièces Justicatives –

The grand administrative evil emanates from home – in the existence of a number of departments here, each with its centrifugal & independent action, un-counteracted by any centripetal attraction – viz. a central authority capable of supervising & compelling combined effort for each object at each particular time.

Excuse confusion In great haste

    ever yours

F. Nightingale

P.S. The remedy which was proposed in making Mr. Cumming Inspector

General was distinctly neutralized – 1st by his own caution in not assuming a power not legally his & waiting for Ld. Raglan's orders 2nd by the D. of Newcastle's letter assigning him the post of Head Commissioner, which arrived at the same time as Ld. Raglan's reply. The result has been that Mr. Cumming has not acted as Insp'r Gen'l & that the Commissioners were three weeks before they began to sit – having replaced poor Dr. Spence by the selection of an efficient Medical Officer here.

Mr. Cumming's habit of mind & delicacy towards Mr. Menzies led him to be very chary in giving advice till the arrival of your letter, since which he has given it *as* advice.

1855   To the Nightingale family

Scutari 5 Mar 1855

Dearest people

I saw Athena[16] last night. She came to see me. I was walking home late from the Gen'l Hosp'l round the cliff, my favorite way, & looking, I really believe for the first time, at the view – the sea glassy calm & of the purest sapphire blue – the sky one dark deep blue – one solitary bright star rising above Constantinople – our whole fleet standing with sails idly spread to catch the breeze which was none – including a large fleet of Sardinians carrying up Sardinian troops – the domes & minarets of Constantinople sharply standing out against the bright gold of the sunset – the transparent opal of the distant hills, (a color one never sees but in the East) which stretch below Olympus always snowy & on the other side the Sea of Marmora when Athena came along the cliff quite to my feet, rose upon her tiptoes, bowed several times, made her long melancholy cry, & fled away – like the shade of Ajax. I assure you my tears followed her.

On Wednesday 28th Feb, we had the sharp shock of an earth quake. It is indescribable. One does not feel the least frightened, but I felt quite convinced our old towers must come down. Two hundred patients jumped out of bed & ran into the Main Guard – two jumped out of window – some got out of bed who c'd not get in again. When next we looked across to the other side, two minarets of Constantinople had disappeared. Half Bursa is in ruins, & the accts. of killed & wounded there, where statistics are none, vary from 3000 to 800. One man here with comp'd fracture seriously injured himself by scuttling out of bed. We have had several slight shocks since.

Please pay £5 (which torment me) due to Harley St. for board of self & Mrs. Clarke from Michaelmas till the day of our going, *and* my £5.5 Sub'n. for 1855.

ever yours   FN

To Parthenope Nightingale

Scutari 8 Mar 1855

My dearest   I hope you are doing something about the Monument.[17] The people here want to have a Cross – they do not see that immediately will arise the question, Greek or Latin Cross – that we cannot have our own Cross in a country where all Xtians are Greeks – still less can we have the Greek Cross – besides the ill grace of our setting up a Cross at all who are fighting for the Crescent. But these people cannot be made to see this. I should like Trajan's column – or Themistocles' *broken* column, only that nobody would see the sentiment of it.

The whole of this gigantic misfortune has been like a Greek tragedy – it has been like the fates pursuing us. Every thing that has been done has been a failure & nobody knows the reason why – the Gods have punished with blindness some past sin & visited the innocent with the consequences – for 'our God is a jealous God' &c how like the Greek & the Jewish Mythology!

But this great tragedy must now, one would think, be near its close.

Please put yourself *at once* in communication, dear Pop, with the Chaplain-General Gleig, to get us working drawings for our Public Monument & Private Chapel in the British burial ground now to be enclosed on cliff looking over Sea of Marmora – first ascertaining from Herberts whether Queen wishes to interfere. If she has no commands, set to work at once. I should like 'Wingless Victory' for Chapel – one single solitary column for monument to greet first our ships coming up the Sea of Marmora. It is such a position – high o'er the cliffs we shall save in vain. I should have liked the Temple of Sunium – but a miniature never does – & they want a Cross.

I have told Herberts & Chaplain General you will put yourself in communication with him. *Let us live* at least in our dead. Five thousand & odd brave hearts sleep here – three thousand, alas! dead in Jan. & Feb. alone – here.

But what of that? *They* are not here. But, for once, even I wish to keep their remembrance on earth – for *we* have been the Thermopylae of this desperate struggle, when Raglan & cold & famine have been the Persians, our own destroyers. *We* have endured in brave Grecian silence. *Let* the 'Times' avenge us. I do not care. We have folded our mantles about our faces & died in silence without complaining. No one can say *we* have complained.

And as for myself, I have done my duty. I have identified my fate with that of the heroic dead, & whatever lies these sordid exploiteurs of human misery spread about us these officials, there is a right & a God to fight for & our fight has been worth fighting. I do not despair – nor complain. It has been a great cause.

We cannot yet believe in the death of the Emperor,[18] telegraphed from Bucharest yesterday – though it is believed at the Embassy – it is so like the dénouement of a Novel – too good to be true – how rarely do the fates of Nations hang upon the life of an individual & how rarely does that individual die in time to be of any use.

ever thine

F.N.

Please date your letters

To Elizabeth Herbert

Barrack Hospital Scutari
16 April 1855

Private[19]

Dearest – I am sorry to be obliged to tell you that Thompson & Anderson, two of the Presbyterian nurses from Edinburgh, went out drinking with an Orderly on Saturday night. Anderson was brought back dead drunk. But Thompson I believe to be the most hardened offender. This was such a catastrophe that there was nothing to be done but to pack them off to England *directly* – & accordingly they *sail* this morning by the Gottenburg. It is a great disappointment, as they were hard working good-natured women. I sent them to the Gen'l Hosp'l, & alas! I find that under any guardianship less watchful than mine, I can hardly depend on any Nurse. Yet no one else is of any use.

Only one week's wages was due to them, which I have not given them, of course, as by rights they ought not to have a free passage home. There were *no* extenuating circumstances. Should they come to you to have their fares paid down to Edinbro', you will perhaps extend that as a matter of mercy, but pray do no more. They were engaged on March 9. You paid them the first month. I discharge them on April 16.

I think the other five promise well. I like Sinclair particularly. Miss Wear is gone to Balaclava, Miss Stanley rejected her at Koulali. I fear she is too eccentric to be of real use.

Will you tell Mr. Herbert Milton has with-drawn his paper, requiring me to sell the free Gifts, with an apology, compelled, I believe, by Ld. W.

Paulet – & that since Mr. Herbert's letter to him, he has been much less red-tapy.

Ever your FN

To the Nightingale family

Black Sea 5 May 1855

Poor old Flo steaming up the Bosphorus & across the Black Sea with four Nurses, two Cooks & a boy to Crim Tartary (to overhaul the Regimental Hospitals) in the 'Robert Lowe' or Robert Slow (for an uncommon slow coach she is) taking back 420 of her Patients, a draught of convalescents returning to their Regiments to be shot at again. A 'mother in Israel', old Fliedner[20] called me – a mother in the Coldstreams is the more appropriate appellation.

What suggestions do the above ideas make to you in Embley drawing-room? Stranger ones perhaps than to me – who, on the 5th May, year of disgrace 1855, year of my age 35, having been at Scutari this day six months, am, in sympathy with God, fulfilling the purpose I came into the world for.

What the disappointments of the conclusion of these six months are, no one can tell. But I am not dead, but alive. What the horrors of war are, no one can imagine, they are not wounds & blood & fever, spotted & low, & dysentery chronic & acute, cold & heat & famine. They are intoxication, *drunken* brutality, demoralization & disorder on the part of the inferior – jealousies, meanness, indifference, *selfish* brutality on the part of the superior. I believe indeed & am told by admirable officers in the service, that our Depot & Barrack at Scutari – in which to live for six months has been death, is a disgrace to the service & our Commandant the worst officer in the service, (had & solicited for by Ld. Stratford because he would have a man of rank). But our Scutari staff, military & medical, content themselves with saying that the English soldier *must* be drunk & not one thing is done to prevent him. Nothing has been done but by us. We have established a reading room for the Convalescents, which is well attended. And the conduct of the soldiers to us is uniformly good. I believe that we have been *the most efficient* – perhaps the only – means there of restoring discipline – instead of destroying it, as I have been accused of. They are much more respectful to me than they are to their own officers. But it makes me cry to think that all these 6 months, we might have had a trained schoolmaster & that I was told it was quite impossible. That, in the Indian

149

army, effectual & successful measures are taken to prevent intoxication & disorganization, & that here, under Lord W. Paulet's very windows, the Convalescents are brought in emphatically *dead* drunk, for they die of it, & he looks on with composure & says to me, 'You are spoiling those brutes'. The men are so glad to read, so glad to give me their money to keep or to send home to their mothers or wives. But I am obliged to do this in secret.

On the 1st May, by the most extreme exertions, our Washing house opened, which might just as well have been done on the 1st November six months ago.

I am in hopes of organizing some washing & cooking for the Regimental Hospitals – & am going up with Soyer,[21] dollies & steaming apparatus for this purpose for more than for any other.

Mr. Bracebridge goes with us. Mrs. B. keeps the bear-garden at Scutari. Four vessels of Sardinian troops go up with us – one vessel, the Argo, with Artillery & horses, ditto – but went aground in the Bosphorus & could not get her off.

I have more & more reason to believe that this is the kingdom of hell – but I as much believe that it is to be made the kingdom of heaven.

Beware of Lady Stratford

yours ever

FN

To Parthenope Nightingale

(Balaclava) 10 May 1855

My dearest/   My days at Balaklava have been so busy as you may suppose. I have made a tour of inspection of Regimental Hosp'ls in camp – besides re-organizing the two Hospitals under our care, which were terribly 'seedy' – Nurses all in confusion.

The camp is very striking – more so than any one can imagine or describe. Between 150,000–200,000 men in a space of 20 square miles all obeying one impulse, engaged in one work – it is very affecting. But to me the most affecting sight was to see them mustering & forming at sun-down for the trenches – where they will be for 24 hours without returning. From those trenches 30 will never return. Yet they volunteer – press forward for the trenches. When I consider what the work has been this winter, what the hardships, I am surprised – not that the army has suffered so much but – that there is any army left at all, not that we have had so many through our hands at Scutari, but that we have not had all as Sir John McNeill[22] says. Fancy working 5 nights out of 7 in the trenches. Fancy being 36 hours in them at a stretch – as they were, all December – lying down or half lying down often 48 hours without food but *raw* salt pork because the *exhausted* soldier *could not* collect his own fuel, as he was expected, to cook his own ration. And fancy, thro' all this, the army preserving their courage & patience – as they have done – & being now eager, the old ones more than the young ones, to be led even into the trenches. There was something sublime in the spectacle. The brave 39th, whose Regimental Hospitals are the best I have ever seen, turned out & gave Florence Nightingale three times three, as I rode away. There was nothing empty in that cheer nor in the heart which received it. I took it as a true expression of true sympathy – the sweetest I have ever had. I took it as a full reward of all I have gone through. I promised my God that I would not die of disgust or disappointment if he would let me go through this. In all that has been said against & for me, no one soul has appreciated what I was really doing – none but the honest cheer of the brave 39th.

Nothing which the 'Times' has said has been exaggerated of hardship.

Sir John Macneill is the man I like the best of all who have come out. He has dragged Commissary General out of the mud. He has done wonders. Every body now has their fresh meat 3 times a week, their fresh bread from Constantinople about as often.

It was a wonderful sight looking down upon Sevastopol – the shell whizzing right & left. I send you a Minié bullet I picked up on the ground which was ploughed with shot & shell – & some little flowers. For this is the most flowery place you can imagine – a beautiful little red which I don't know, yellow Jessamine & every kind of low flowering shrub. A Serj't of the 97th picked me a nosegay. I once saved Serj't —'s[23] life by finding him at 12 o'clock at night lying – wounds undressed – in our Hosp'l with a bullet in his eye & a fractured skull. And I pulled a stray Surgeon out of bed to take the bullet out. But you must not tell this story. For I gave evidence against the missing Surgeon – & have never been forgiven.

Sir John McNeill, whom you must not quote, it was who told me that it was . . .[24]

P.S. There is some Cholera in Camp, but not much. I want very much to hear how Blanch is. I was very much disappointed that Aunt Mai did not write. I heard it through a common newspaper, till I had a note from Mama.

151

To Mrs. Maria Hunt[25]

Barrack Hospital, Scutari
6 Sept 1855

Dear Mrs. Hunt,

I grieve to be obliged to inform you that your son died in this Hospital on Sunday last, Sept'er 2nd. His complaint was Chronic Dysentary – he sunk gradually from weakness, without much suffering. Everything was done that was possible to keep up his strength. He was fed every half hour with the most nourishing things he could take, & when there was any thing he had a fancy for, it was taken to him immediately. He sometimes asked for oranges & grapes, which quenched his thirst, & which he had, whenever he wished for them – he spoke much of his Mother, & gave us the direction to you in his last moments. He was very desirous that you should be written to about him. His great anxiety was that his Mother should receive the pay due to him, & should know that he had not received any pay since he had been out, which he wished his friends to be told that they might apply to the War Office for the whole of the pay due to him. He was very grateful for whatever was done for him, & very patient. You may have the satisfaction of knowing that he had the most constant & careful attendance from the Doctors & the Nurses of the Hospital. The chaplain and myself saw him every day. He died very peacefully & sorrowful as this news is for his bereaved Mother. May she find comfort in thinking that his earthly sufferings were over, & in the hope that our Almighty Father will receive him into a better world through the blessed promises of our Lord. With sincere sympathy I am

Yours truly

Florence Nightingale

Barrack Hospital
Scutari
December 1/55

Madam

That Your Majesty's sympathy is given to every man of your troops none know better than myself, who have seen the tears which the expression of that gracious sympathy has called forth in these brave fellows, who have never had one tear to shed for their own sufferings.

That the feeling is unanimous & constant in these men, – not an enthusiastic madness but a deep, unfailing purpose & determination to see

Your Majesty's wrong righted & the offence against the liberties of Europe put down, – I can assure Your Majesty who have but just returned from the Crimea where all hearts are steady & all wills stanch. We would stand ten years of war, should Your Majesty require it of us.

That Your Majesty's sympathy should have extended to me, I could hardly have expected. I have done what I could. But it is indeed impossible to me to express how much the believing in that sympathy, which, I know, arises from a real interest & enquiry into the cause of the soldiers will be an abiding support amidst difficulties which appal & perplexities which dishearten me.

Your Majesty's beautiful present will be to me an object of tender affection recalling the assurance that our Sovereign's heart is in this cause.

The expression of my gratitude was delayed, on account of my absence from Scutari at the time that Your Majesty's letter arrived. I was then at the Hospitals at Balaclava under my charge. I was there, living in the midst of, seeing day by day, hearing from those in the very heart of it, the evils & difficulties which beset & almost threaten to disorganize Your Majesty's brave army.

For the re-action of bravery & over-strained endurance is depression & love of drink in uneducated minds. And this is the real pestilence with which *this* winter we have to struggle in an Army, idle & rich.

Such is our experience & conviction of Your Majesty's deep interest in the welfare of your Army that I will venture, even without apology, to speak to Your Majesty of some impressions left on me by what I saw passing in the Crimea.

The reasons for the increase of this vice of intoxication are two

   (1) plenty of money to drink

   (2) time undisposed of – trench-work & road making being, I thank God, at an end.

The remedies are

   (1) to give the men every facility for remitting money home. They complain that there are delays in the remittances – that they cannot trust *themselves* to keep their own money till the day for remitting it comes – that they do not wish their comrades to know of these remittances, otherwise the money would be borrowed.

That these are not mere excuses is proved by the fact that I rarely remit home a smaller sum than £200 per week for the men in petty sums of 20/- or 30/- shewing that they will avail themselves of an easy opportunity.

   (2) employment & amusement to dispose of their unoccupied time.

Useful & amusing books

A warmed & lighted Hut for each Regiment to read them in, which might be used also as a Church, a school-room, with reading & copy-books, – & even as a Theatre.

Practical lectures with plain illustrations,

Diagrams &c two or three evenings in the week

I understand that Your Majesty's Government is already about to act in this direction – lending out lecturers, diagrams &c

Every thing which tends to soften & cheer the soldier's imagination tends to diminish the vice of intoxication. The games & books & newspapers which Your Majesty has sent, the prints of Your Majesty & their Royal Highnesses the Prince Albert & the young Princes which I have hung on the walls of the Reading Huts which already exist, (so deep & true is always the feeling of duty towards Your Majesty in these hearts) the Illustrated Shakespeares & Miltons, combined with the more comfortable pleasure of a good plate of bread & English cheese & cup of coffee – all these things have tended visibly & materially to lessen the curse of our Army.

But still, in the Crimea, even our Patients in the Hospitals are nightly taken to the Guard Hut drunk.

Yet the soldier is not degraded. He is only idle & uncultivated.

Employment, facility for sending his money home, difficulty in obtaining spirits – *certain* & *immediate* punishment for drunkenness, the cordial co-operation of the Officers may do much to discourage the besetting sin.

These latter matters do not, indeed, strictly belong to my business. Yet that business, when carried on at Balaclava, in presence, as it were, of Your Majesty's army, forces them on my observation – which I hope may be my excuse when I trust to obtaining Your Majesty's gracious permission to allow me to mention what I believe will have interest for our Sovereign.

(1) the necessity of strict military surveillance over the Canteens & Canteen keepers, depriving them of their license, if the police regulations be infringed – a Committee of Officers over them, if possible

(2) a correspondence between the Chief of the Staff in the British Army, on the means of preventing *international* drinking, with the same Officer in the French & Sardinian camps. It is chiefly in these camps that *our* men obtain spirits, & often sell their clothing for drink

(3) the men are rich, they boast that they will spend their *field* & *working* allowances "on their bodies". Had *these* allowances been laid up for them at home there would not have been so much money to spend in spirits. It might appear, perhaps, almost a pity that the soldier should have been paid

for what is as much part of his trade as going on Guard.

I do not know whether these remedies be practicable. Tho' I have ventured to speak as one who has seen & lived among these things, & has seen, too, the interest of our Mistress in our welfare. *We* obey *our* Sovereign, with love & devotion, the Russians theirs with superstition & fear.

I can assure Your Majesty that your brave troops are sound at heart. They want only care.

I do not know the etiquette with which subjects write to their Sovereign, & must crave pardon for blunders. But I know the feeling with which I am

Madam,

Your Majesty's dutiful, most grateful & devoted subject

Florence Nightingale

To Her Majesty

the Queen

[RA F4/15]

To Sidney Herbert   1856

Crimea 3 April 1856

Dear Mr. Herbert

I received your letter of March 6 yesterday.

It is written from Belgrave Square. I write from a Crimean Hut. The point of sight is different.

I arrived here March 24 with Nurses for two Land Transport Hospitals 'required' by Dr. Hall in writing on March 10, but owing to the severe gales of wind, the Transport could not get up the Bosphorus, & our arrival was therefore delayed – tho' announced by return of mail.

We have now been ten days without rations.

Lord Cardigan was surprised to find his horses die at the end of a fortnight because they were without rations & said that 'they chose' to do it, obstinate brutes!

The Inspector General & Purveyor wish to see whether women can live as long as horses without rations.

I thank God – my charge has felt neither cold nor hunger, & is in efficient working order – having cooked & administered both Hospitals the whole of the Extras for 260 bad cases ever since the first day of their arrival.

I have, however, felt both. I do not wish to make a martyr of myself; within sight of the graves of the Crimean Army of last winter (too soon forgotten in England) it would be difficult to do so. I am glad to have had the experience. For cold & hunger wonderfully sharpen the wits. But I believe that it is difficult to those who never, by any possibility, can have imagined either, (except by the side of a good fire & a good dinner which they will have every day of their lives) to imagine what is the anxiety of being responsible for the lives & healths *and the efficiency* (for the sake of the lives & healths of those we are come to nurse) of those placed under men's charge when the means to feed & warm them have all to be obtained by irregular & private channels. During these ten days, I have fed & warmed these women at my own private expence by my own private exertions. I have never been off my horse till 9 or 10 at night, except when it was too dark to walk him over these crags even with a lantern, when I have gone on foot. During the greater part of the day, I have been without food necessarily, except a little brandy & water (you see I am taking to drinking like my comrades of the Army) the snow is deep on the ground. But the object of my coming has been attained, & my women have neither starved nor suffered.

I might have written to the Commander of the Forces, who came to see me the day after my arrival. But this would only have marred our work by making a quarrel.

I might have accepted presents which were poured in upon us, for all, Military, Medical, Clerical in the Land Transport are our sworn friends. But this would be against a rule which I have been obliged to make so strict that nothing but sheer necessity would induce me to break it.

I might have drawn upon the Extras for the Patients. But then the whole would have gone into the Account of *Nurses'* Expenditure as their extravagance.

I believe it, on the whole, best for our work to do as I have done, notwithstanding the urgent pressure upon me from others to adopt one of these courses. But I do not think that that work can be said, pursued thus, to have been pursued in a 'vehement or irritable spirit'.

I received your letter at 10 o'clock P.M. on my return to our hut upon a pitch-dark snowy night after having been 15 hours on foot or on horseback & almost without food.

I confess it cost me a sleepless night thinking over within myself, Have I injured the work by shewing 'vehemence or irritation', by not bearing persecution, moral & physical rather than not complain, except when the very existence of the work itself was perilled?

I thought & considered – and I determined that I had not. I think I can prove my assertion.

About this matter of the rations, foreseen to a certain extent by me, so that I had brought up with me from Scutari, every article for cooking, furnishing, warming the huts, even stoves, & every article of food that would keep.

Every formality not only of routine but of politeness had been observed by me – within 24 hours of my arrival, the rations had been settled by me in person (after having been 'required' in writing from Scutari) with the P.M.O. of the Land Transport in the office of the Deputy Purveyor in Chief Fitzgerald – had received the approval of Inspector General of Hospitals – & by a curious coincidence of the Commander of the Forces from his calling upon me while in the Purveyor's Office. Every form was observed there & then. Both the Purveyor's Clerks, both the Medical Officers in charge at the two Land Transport Hospitals were visited by me, distant some miles from Balaclava & not together, in company with Dr. Taylor, the P.M.O. Every form was there strictly observed. The rations were to begin from the day before. Every day since, I have ridden some miles, or walked, in the severest weather, with driving storms of sleet & snow, to see the Purveyor in his office on these businesses. I have never brought him a yard out of his office on my business. I have never 'prévaloir'd[26] myself, even on my quality of woman, to avoid hardships or fatigue, or allow him to say that I had entailed either on him. Never, by word or look, can he have detected that I knew how he had slandered us.

Why do I give you this detail, you will ask, which can be of no use.

It is not because I ask you to do anything. It is merely because I wish to leave on record some instance of that which nobody in England will believe or can even imagine. But we in the Crimea know it. And we know, & knew at the time, *what* filled the Crimean graves last winter – K.C.B, I believe, now means Knight of the Crimean Burying-Grounds –

As I stood yesterday on the Heights of Balaclava, & saw our ships in the Harbour, so gaily dressed with flags, while we fired the Salute in honor of peace, (it was a beautiful sight), I said to myself, More Aireys,[27] more Filders,[28] more Cardigans,[29] more Halls[30] – we are in for them all now – & no hope of reform.

Believe me when I say that everything in the Army (in point of routine versus system) is just where it was eighteen months ago. The only difference is that we are now rolling in stores. But indeed we were so then only most of them were at Varna.

'Nous n'avons rien oublié ni rien appris.'[31]

2. Those who say that there is a 'Popish plot' are quite mistaken. It is not a Popish plot, but a split of the R. Catholics against themselves.

Of all the Oriental mysteries which I have been made acquainted with since I have been in the East, this has been not the least curious.

The seculars are divided against the regulars. This we have often seen before but never so much as now.

But, as the old Whig families are said always to have a Tory heir apparent, in order to be 'in' both ways, so the R. Catholics have one set of priests & nuns *with* the Gov't & one *against* it.

Mrs. Bridgeman & the Jesuits are against, the secular priests & Bermondsey nuns for.

Mrs. Bridgeman & her 11 Irish Nuns have been instructed to resign & go home & make themselves martyrs, which they will do, I am afraid, on Saturday – tho' I have piped to her & done the Circe in vain.

The Rev'd Mr. Duffy, Jesuit, has been instructed to refuse confession & therefore Holy Communion to, or even visit those Bermondsey Nuns, whom I brought up with me from Scutari to one of the Land Transport Hospitals, & he calls them, among other epithets in a note to themselves, a 'disgrace to their Church'. For none can be so coarse as a R.C. priest. This note we have forwarded to Dr. Grant, Bp. of Southwark, [32] for approval.

Cardinal Wiseman has recalled the Rev'd Mr. Unsworth, Senior R.C. Chaplain here, who always took part against the Jesuits & Irish Nuns 'under these circumstances'.

On the other hand, the secular priests repudiate the Irish Nuns, & do the civil by the Gov't & me & the Bermondsey Nuns – with principal & interest – & even Father Cuffe, who used to call me 'Herod', now licks my hand, as the Provost Marshal says, 'like a good 'un'.

Irish 'Regulars' are little else than 'Rebels' as has truly been said here.

Such are a few of the premises. You say that the English like to draw their own inferences. Here they have done it already – and here Deputy Purveyor in Chief Fitzgerald is supposed to be the tool of the Jesuits & the Irish Nuns.

The 'Confidential Report' is not a secret to any one here.

3. You say this is but one bud of the bed of roses upon which Secretaries of State are wont to lie. I have just seen enough of Gov't to know what that bed must be. But, till Secretaries of State have known what it is to have the reputations of their wives & daughters slandered, for party purposes, till you have known what it is to be uncertain for many days where you should get food or warmth for those *beautiful children (*My poor Nurses are not 'beautiful' – *Bien s'en faut*. [33] But they are not less my charge.) who are

158

standing round your table, & to feel that grinding anxiety for the responsibility of the lives & healths of those under your charge, & to doubt whether you are not sacrificing them, in your turn, to considerations for the good of the work, I deny that you can cull one bud from my bed of roses or even imagine its fragrance afar off. Had I told but half the truth in my answer to Mr. Fitzgerald, you would have said, What a fool she was not to make her complaint before!

But no one in England has yet *realized* the graves of Scutari or the Crimea – or their causes.

4. I deprecate most earnestly your judgement that 'the highest proof of success is when a mission is carried thro' without producing attack' as being against all experience & all history from the Sacred history down to the fable of the 'wolf & the lamb', which was the incarnation of a pretty wise experience too. I beseech you to reconsider your opinion. I am not a lamb – far from it. But I have been a lambkin in many instances, & principally in one, & yet have not 'avoided attack'.

I know that yours is the principle of most governments now, & that to steer clear of 'attack' & to promote & praise both sides, if possible is its theory. But I do not see that it succeeds even in averting attack. A 'quarrel' always, it is true, vulgarizes both sides (witness Sir J. Graham & Napier[34]). But I don't see that the lamb could help the *attack* if Joan of Arc had been said to have had a *'quarrel'* with the D. of Bedford or the lamb with the wolf, it would have been a misapplication of the word.

I will give one 'instance'. In all the Hospitals of our Army which I have seen where women have not been, the Doctors go round so late* (*notwithstanding the Queen's Regulation) that the Diet Rolls cannot be made out in time for the men to have their dinners before 3 or 4, & their Extras before 5 or 6 o'cl. It was (*partly*) on this account that I have insisted so strenuously on our Extra Diet Kitchens. The Drs do not like sending their Diet Rolls in to us late – & the men always get consequently their Extras at 12 & their dinners at 1 from our Kitchens – making the difference for a weakly man between waiting for his Beef Tea from 8 A.M. till 4 or 5 P.M. & waiting till 12 or 1 P.M. I have never, in one single instance, got in my Diet Rolls except as a 'lamb', never reported a Medical officer for being late, but I know the Medical Officers have opposed our Extra Diet Kitchens in many instances like 'wolves', on this account, tho' no single case can be found against us of having given any thing but upon Diet Roll to Patients. Yet this is the ground alledged against us.

5. You may well say that Sir John McNeil's Report is the model of a Report. It is indeed – accurate, lucid, cool & conscientious. But had Sir

J. McNeil made nothing but a Report, he would have done little. But he put his hand to the plough & did much out here. So did Col. Tulloch.

It still remains to be seen whether his *Report* will do *anything*. Hitherto nothing has been done but to promote those reported on – to make Ld Panmure say 'I am very sorry, but I did not know that these men had been promoted', to make Ld Hardinge[35] say, 'I am very sorry. I did hear that the Army had suffered. But I did not know that their sufferings had been at all attributed to these men.'

In 6 months, all these sufferings will be forgotten. And I *indeed* agree with you that, in the presence of that colossal calamity & of the national disgrace of promoting the authors of it, the promotion of that petty offender, Mr. Fitzgerald, tho' in some respects, his offences are not petty, (for none dare offend him, because he can starve any Hospital in the Crimea, & leave, as he recently did, 130 typhus fever cases for 24 hours without wine,) but compared with our other disgraces, *his* promotion sinks into the shade – and I feel more shame than will ever crimson his face at having but mentioned it.

Oh! Lord Stratford – oh! Kars[36] –

And now, what do I want?

Not that you should do any thing, not, ten thousand times *not*, that you should alter your opinion of me – (though I own I am anxious that you should not pre judge a work because it has been 'attacked' – anxious too to believe that I have not injured the work.)

But all I wish is to leave some record of what will not be believed in the homes of London, a twelvemonth hence – of what, tho' a trifling instance, is a true example of what ruined our Army.

Believe me, dear Mr. Herbert, (and if I have used some strong expressions, let me say that there is no more comparison between Sr J. McNeil's case & mine than between the calm review of a historian of the causes of a war, & the officer in the heat of battle providing for his men's safety,) believe me very truly yours,

Florence Nightingale

ELIZABETH MACKENZIE

Elizabeth Mackenzie (1816–92) was the daughter of the Reverend Dr. Thomas Chalmers, an eminent Scottish divine. She married John Mackenzie, minister of Dunkeld, in 1839. She served as a nurse during the Crimean War.

Therapia Hospital 6th May   1855

My dear Aunt,

    Your box has at length arrived safely & its contents are most useful & acceptable. They are sure to be of use & much appreciated. I was rather alarmed at not getting it sooner after hearing it was on its way but all has come right at last. If you see Anne or any of the girls tell them I am much pleased with the things that are for myself, such as my gowns & the ribbons etc. The shoes are rather large but that is a good fault & it is cool for the feet. I am amused with the list, for it brings so many people before me & many of the things they have done are like them. We have still only a few patients but our Nurses are diminished in number & there is always one or other of them ill. I hope I have not done wrong in writing to Lady Foulis to beg her to get two more for us. It is so great a thing for me being allowed to ask my friend to do so, instead of getting them through the Service – some dreadful set from London without any character in particular. We have got on well on the whole as to this, but I have been much grieved about Mrs. Vine. She has been sent away with dreadfully varicose veins – but I fear her character has been injured by being out here & so much liked. & she was such a nice creature when she came first & the dearest nurse we had. I do hope Lady Foulis will know something about Nurses. I know she visits the Infirmary & Dr. Foulis may know such people. Dr. Davidson likes Scotch women best if of good character. I never now get a moment of quiet to write. This room begins about 6 in the morning & people are in it all day & only leave about 11 at night – so I am always half asleep when I am writing letters & they have got very

stupid. This has now lain for two days. & I have got time to go through
& arrange the contents of this box & am much interested in the names
upon the things. I am much obliged to you for the coffee & Curry powder
which are both most acceptable. We have lived upon small half starved
creatures for about 5 months & only vary the entertainment by varieties
in the cooking – but we have had no curry yet. Poor Frank has had to
go home on sick leave, but so suddenly that I have not seen him & feel
anxious to know his precise state. He has had fever & ague so often. We
now hope the siege is to go on in earnest. We got in 9 patients today all
sick. I am sure you would be a most capital Nurse among them though
you would never be strong enough for the ward duties & all have to
conform to the service arrangements. I am less homesick now than I have
ever been when on a visit or in lodgings, from having so much to do, but
I often think of all who are at home & feel as if one day there would be
such a refreshment. Patrick Watson was here one evening last week, quite
strong & well. I have been very glad to have seen so much of him. I am
sorry to hear Mary has been so poorly but I trust she is now better. We
are all getting on quietly & well at present, & I am much stronger in mind
than when you saw me – that is, I sit calm in storm & keep up much
more heart than you can ever believe of me. I go out in caïques alone &
don't mind either Turks or Greeks. As to sailors & marines, they are the
easiest of all beings to deal with. Not I believe by their officers so much,
but certainly by ladies. Anne will be gratified to hear that our various
servants highly approving of her taste in my gowns.

I am sorry about poor Fanny who appears to have fallen back again
& they do not write often enough to me for I get quite starving for letters.
It is such a disappointment when the bag is opened & none for us. I hope
Uncle Charlie is in better health. Give him my best love & tell him I would
have been much the better of him here at first, as a support. Now it is
better as far as that goes. & the country is so beautiful & as yet the Climate
is good – but no patient gets on well who has disease of the lungs & they
send them off whenever they can to Malta. I am surprised it is so for the
weather here is dry & not too hot. The fireflies are most brilliant in the
garden and the nightingales sing most beautifully, but at the same time
the croaking of the frogs almost overpowers every other sound. The scene
is very gay – such crowds of ships going up loaded with stores & troops.
I do not know what will come out of it all, but the spirits of the troops
have risen greatly since the fall of Kertch and the success in the Sea of Azoz
– we hear less here than you do at home. I am growing very stupid about
letter writing & am always sleepy from about 1. o'clock in the day. We

get up so early & there is such a blaze of light from our nine windows about 5 in the morning. I hope you will thank Lady Elphinstone & all other kind friends from me. I will see that every thing is put to its proper use & profitably given. I am much obliged to David & was interested in seeing his name upon some shirts today & Uncle Charles' upon the Bunches. Nothing delights the nurses so much as the Bunches & I distributed some of them immediately.

With kindest love to all
Believe me ever
my dear Aunt
yours most affectely
Eliza Mackenzie
Make John write!

ANNIE CECILIA ELD

Annie Cecilia Eld belonged to a family of long-time squires in the village of Seighford near Stafford. Her husband was serving in the Crimea.

1854

Seighford Hall
near Stafford Dec. 25th:

My very dear Frederick

This is "Christmas Day" – and I sit down (not to wish you a *Merry One*, fearing it would appear to you a mere mockery of words) but to express a *sincere hope* that long 'ere the next arrives we shall have the extreme delight of meeting and that we both may be spared to spend many many many happy ones together in peace and quietness and our dear child to add to our bliss by her loving and dutiful conduct – The morning unfortunately was wet but Rose & I with your brothers succeeded in getting to Church all right – it is scarcely necessary for me to say that I had you in my prayers frequently & could not forbear allowing the *many happy* events of the past to cross my memory – & though they did so in *quick succession* still my heart was saddened to a degree, and I could not bear to compare the *sad present* with the joyous past, – but this giving way to *useless* grief will never do, and we must hope & trust that all things will turn out for the best: – After Church Frank Chambers & I called upon Caroline. She is suffering from her *old attack* I am sorry to say and in consequence of which we shall not have the pleasure of their company at dinner today. – This afternoon has become quite fine and mild, darling Silla is out walking with her cousin *John* and so are all the rest of your family – Your dear father is well and intends driving over to Sidway Hall on Wednesday with Edward – he was delighted to hear of your safe arrival and desired me to give you his best love & good wishes; – I think dearest if you can find time to do so, you should write him a few lines for I know he likes hearing from you *himself*. – My last letter to you was sent off the day before I received yours; and I assure you the sight of your dear hand writing once more filled me with gladness – but I have to give you a *severe scolding* for not telling me *more of yourself* – and you do not mention one word about your poor Horse, – pray how is he now? better I hope; and how truly delighted I shall be to hear that you are both safely put up: do dearest write to me *constantly* for you cannot conceive what a comfort your letters are to me, and please to inform me when you next favour me with one whether *I trouble you too often* with mine? This is my *third* remember. Mary wrote to you a few days since – I see by the Newspapers that *our relation* Major Norcott has been promoted for his services out in the ''Crimea'' – perhaps you may make his acquaintance soon. – Richard Chambers' ship has arrived at ''Portsmouth'' and he hopes to get leave shortly, but does not expect to do so just at present as he is the *first* lieutenant on board and they say it *does not look well* for them to take the first leave – *a very hard case* is it not, when people are anxious to see those they love – poor fellow! I hope he will not be sent out again – Do tell me darling what you think of the War and whether ''Sebastopol'' is likely to be taken soon? There are so many different rumours afloat that one does not know what to think. – I fear dear Frederick you will think my letters so *excessively stupid,* but really I hear & see so little at Seighford, that it is quite impossible to write anything that would at all interest you; however perhaps to hear that those most dear to you are well will in some slight measure console and comfort you; and perhaps repay you for the trouble you are put to by reading a dull uninteresting epistle. – I wish you dear when you write to inform me *when your next allowance* is due and let me know whether you took the ''Memorandum'' Book with you? – We *constantly* send you Paper which I hope you receive. – Once more let me beg of you dearest to *write often,* and with many apologies for this stupid *effusion*.

   Pray believe me ever to remain your
         fond and most truly affectionate wife
         Annie Cecilia Eld
P.S. Silla and *all* your friends join in very kind love to you and many happy returns of the season –
                     Adieu dearest Pet
2nd P.S. Mr. Thompson has just told me that the 90th Regiment is to be joined to the 2nd. Division which is commanded by our old friend General Pennefather. I am so glad of this, and I hope dearest you may have a prosperous career and return to us with laurels –
   Once more Adieu.

My darling Frederick – Your dear letter of the 21st December has just reached me, the first I have received since you wrote to inform me of your safe arrival at "Constantinople". I have *already* sent you *four letters,* all of which I hope you have 'ere this received. When you acknowledge the receipt of my letters, pray always mention the *date of each* as I *keep* them & I would know directly whether any *were lost* – how truly I regret to hear the account you give of our poor men, the dear old 90th I fear will be entirely disorganized if so many deaths continue to take place in it – God forbid that it should be so – My dearest I cannot think *what to advise,* with respect to your retiring upon full Pay – pray do as *you consider best* & I shall be satisfied. I fear it would not be allowed at present. The accounts this morning are rather more cheering (*if true.*) The "Papers" say the Emperor of Russia *has* accepted the terms of peace proposed to him which is *confirmed* in all the morning papers – This being the case I presume, and sincerely trust the War will be brought to a close without delay – I have not ventured to speak to poor Francis about it for he is so distracted just now with different affairs – May the Lord in his goodness preserve you dearest from all harm and grant that you may return to us in safety – Poor old Hockerly *how sorry* I was to hear of his death: do enquire dear whether any one has written to inform his poor wife of the *sad event* – he was *so kind* to her & his poor little child. – I think dear Fredk you had better write to your brother Francis don't you think so? – I will write to you again shortly, all your brothers & sisters are well and desired to be *most kindly* remembered to you, dear Silla is well & sends her best love to you & many kisses. – Do love allow me to get *you some warm Clothing* & send out to you – could easily do so: & pray take the greatest care of yourself for *our* sake. *Write often, if only a line* to say how you are. And believe me dearest to remain ever your fondly attached & loving wife

Annie Cecilia Eld

QUEEN VICTORIA

These letters were written to Leopold, King of the Belgians, during the Crimean War.

Buckingham Palace
May 22. 1855

My dearest kindest Uncle,

Many many thanks for your dear letter of the 18th duly received on Saturday. – The prospect of seeing you, dearest Uncle, shortly, is an *immense* pleasure, & I need not tell you with what joy we should receive you with Philippe & Charlotte. – We are going today for 8 or 9 days to Osborne to spend my *very* old *birthday* there, returning here on the 30th or 31st. – Good Feo[1] means to stay till the 12th when she had intended paying you her respects at Brussels. When would you choose to come? *After* that – about the 14th or 15th or sooner?

The state of affairs is uncomfortable and complicated just now, but our course is *straight* – we cannot come to any peace unless we have such guarantees by *decided* limitation of the Fleet which would secure us against Russian preponderance for the future.

Ernest will have told you what a *beautiful* & *touching* sight & ceremony – (the 1st of the kind *ever witnessed* in England) the Distribution of the Medals was. – From the highest Prince of the Blood to the lowest Private, received the same distinction for the bravest conduct in the severest Actions, & the rough hand of the brave & honest private Soldier, came for the 1st time in contact with that of their Sovereign & their Queen! Noble fellows – I own I feel as if they were *my own Children*, my heart beats for *them* as for *my nearest* & *dearest*!

They were so touched, so pleased, many, I hear – cried – & they won't hear of giving up their Medals – to have their names engraved upon them for fear that they should *not* receive the *identical one* put into *their hands by me*, which is quite touching. Several came by in a sadly mutilated state. None created more interest or is more gallant than young Sir Thomas

Troubridge, who had – at Inkermann, – *one leg* – & the *other foot* carried away by a round shot – & continued commanding his Battery till the Battle was won – refusing to be carried away, – only desiring his shattered limbs to be raised in order to prevent too great a hemorrage!! – He was dragged by, in a Bath Chair & when I gave him his Medal, I told him I should make him one of my Aides de Camp for his very gallant conduct, to which he replied: "I am amply repaid for every thing."! –

One must revere & love such Soldiers as those! The account in the Times of Saturday is very correct & good. –

I must however conclude now, – hoping soon to hear from you again. Could you kindly tell me if you could in a few days forward some letters & papers with *safety* to good Stockmar?

Ever your devoted niece

VR

Balmoral Castle.
Sept: 11. 1855.

My dearest Uncle,

The great event has at length taken place. *Sevastopol has fallen!* We received the news here last night when we were sitting quietly round our Table after dinner. We did what we could to celebrate it, – but that was but little, for to my grief we have not *one* Soldier, no Band nothing here to make any sort of demonstration. What we did do was in Highland fashion to light a *bonfire* on the top of a Hill opposite the House, which had been built last year, when the premature news of the fall of Sevastopol deceived every one, and which we had to leave *unlit*, and found here on our return!

On Saturday evening we heard of one Russian Vessel having been destroyed, on Sunday morning of the destruction of another, yesterday morning of the fall of the Malakoff Tower, – & *then* of *Sevastopol*. We were not successful against the Redan on the 8th – & I fear our loss was considerable. Still the *daily* loss in the Trenches was becoming so serious that no loss in achieving such a Result is to be compared to that. – This Event will delight my Brother & faithful Ally – & *friend*, Napoleon III. I may add – for we *really* are *great friends;* this attempt,[2] though that of a madman is very distressing & makes one *tremble*. –

Many thanks for your dear, kind letter of the 7th. We arrived here safely that day & find our new House really *very* pretty & very comfortable

168

& with a beautiful view which the *old one* had *not*. –

I still wish you would let Philippe go to Switzerland; it is *not fatigue* but *change* of *air* which he wants. Leopold is an instance of the want of sufficient change, & I fear much, Philippe at the present moment when he has grown so immensely may likewise get into that delicate state in which Leo is. It is, depend upon it – of the greatest importance to *change* air often & to let children & young people have *bracing* air.

We expect the young Prince Fritz Wilhelm[3] of Prussia on a little visit here, on *Friday*.

I must now conclude, with Albert's love,

    Ever your devoted niece

VR

CHARLOTTE CANNING

Charlotte Canning (1817–61, *née* Stuart) was the wife of Lord Canning and was Lady of the Bedchamber to Queen Victoria from 1842 until Charles Canning took up the Governor-Generalship of India in 1855. She chaired the committee which appointed Florence Nightingale as Superintendent of the Institution for the Care of Sick Gentlewoman in Distressed Circumstances, and also selected nurses to be sent out to Scutari during the Crimean War.

During the Indian Mutiny Charlotte Canning's letters to Queen Victoria were regular and detailed, and were described by the Queen as 'universally considered as the *best* which are received from India' in a letter from Victoria to Charlotte. In a sense Charlotte deputized for her husband during this crisis by keeping the Queen fully informed of events.

In 1858, when the government of India was tranferred to the Crown from the East India Company, Lord Canning became the first Viceroy. Charlotte Canning died of fever in 1861, and the news reached Queen Victoria as Prince Albert was dying.

1857   Calcutta August 24

Madam

Your Majesty's very kind letter of the 5th of July has arrived & given me great pleasure, and I thank Your Majesty most sincerely for writing to me. I look forward with delight to the promised Photographs but they have not yet reached me.

By that steamer Sir Colin Campbell arrived, to our great surprise! He accomplished his long journey in a month and a day! We had no expectations of the news of Gen. Anson's death being known in England so soon. Sir Colin is very well and in his usual high spirits, and is most agreeable, he must long to be in the field, and to have a sufficient force to enable him to move & strike a decisive blow but it must yet be some time before troops from England can arrive. We have a hope of seeing 3 more of the China regiments early in next month. Sir Patrick Grant remained with us a week after Sir Colin's arrival. They seemed to be working very zealously & happily together until he sailed for Madras, his intimate knowledge of the officers of the Bengal army & all other Indian army concerns, must have made his store of information most valuable & he was *a*lways anxious to impart it. We liked him very much indeed & I am sure the Madras people must be glad to see him back after his 2 months of absence. There is always much suspicion & alarm at the Mussulman population in that presidency tho' they are tolerably confident with regard to the Sepoys. The Moharrum has now begun, the latter days of the feast when the processions in commemoration of Hussein & Hussein's funeral take place, are the alarming time, for the fanatics work themselves up to furious excitement helped by doses of bang which make them almost mad. This year they are so much warned to keep within bounds that we may hope it will pass off safely.

Lord Elgin is still with us, the steamer prepared for him has kept him waiting, and he is anxious for the next English news before he proceeds to meet the French Ambassador or Commissioner at Singapore towards the middle of September. He has left us the Shannon for a time & Captn Peel is now on his way up the river with his naval brigade, 10 great guns, & 400 men. We went on board his ship before his departure & he paraded his fine crew, he, & they, in the highest spirits. It will be a most efficient reinforcement even if it proceeds no further than Allahabad, if they land, Elephants will come into play & 3 or 4 will move one of the great guns with ease!

Some things are rather better than a fortnight ago. Bengal is now perfectly quiet, & the mischief done in that rich tract of country proved less than was feared – the mutineers after being defeated by Major Eyre on two occasions hid themselves & skulked in a chain of hills behind Mirzapore, & have either dispersed altogether or gone towards Delhi.

From Delhi there are very late & cheering accounts, up to August 14, the rebels are believed to be despirited & quarrelling, & without a leader. Their ammunition falling short, & it is supposed they can throw no more shells for want of fuses – the Mussulmen are outraging the Hindoos & they have a story that bullocks will be slaughtered in Delhi at the feast. Our camp is secure & the troops in spirits, reinforcements in a very fair scale were at hand from the north, & all was well, excepting a good deal of sickness.

The great anxiety now is for Lucknow & the thought of it haunts me day & night, we know it is strictly hemmed in, & it is quite uncertain for how long they have been able to provision themselves. A native has a cheering report on that point, but no recent letters have got thro' & the truth of this good report cannot be proved.

General Havelock's attempts to relieve it were most gallant! his little band repeatedly defeated fresh and large numbers of the enemy, but his force was too small to bear this constant & harassing duty, with unceasing exposure & much cholera in his camp. At last he recrossed the Ganges to Cawnpore, (on the 13th, I think) having beaten the enemy the day before & no attempt was made to molest him. The sickness at Cawnpore has been very great I regret to say. –

Sir James Outram has been heard of from Dinapore, he commands that & the Cawnpore division & will strain every nerve to collect enough force to make an attempt to save those poor people in Lucknow – so there is still a ray of hope, the residency buildings are strongly fortified & they alone are now held. The only force I believe to be the 32^d regiment & some artillery. There are many wives of officers and civilians & numbers of children who crowded there from all parts to take refuge. They must already have had a time of great suffering & anxiety & one must indeed earnestly pray for their rescue.

I am sure Your Majesty has felt deeply for all these sad events – and I trust I do not err in writing so often & at so much length. I am even inclined to send Your Majesty some very touching narratives of the escape of some of the poor refugees & sufferers. I hope there will be much sympathy felt for them in England and that there will be subscriptions opened both for them and for the widows & orphans of soldiers, in fact a renewal of the Patriotic fund.

I think the small society here has shewn much generosity: full 15000£ having been collected. Sir Colin Campbell has given me a most delightful account of the distribution of the medals "for Valour" by Your Majesty. I hope Your Majesty will find some of your soldiers in this country deserving of the same great distinction.

Your Majesty's gracious expression of confidence in Lord Canning is most cheering to him & most gratefully appreciated & I trust that his hearty & zealous endeavour to do his duty in Your Majesty's service will be wholly successful. He & Sir Colin are quite sure to work well together, and as there has been no lack of energy with small means, I trust in a month or two hence a brighter & very different account of the state of things here will be laid before Your Majesty.

With every good wish to Your Majesty, the Prince the Princess Royal & the rest of the Royal Family,

I am Madam
   Your Majesty
      dutiful humble servant
         C. Canning

I venture to add that I made a most foolish mistake of the name of the straits where the Transit was wrecked in my last letter. I had never seen it written & caught up the sound quite wrongly.

[RA Z502/15]

Calcutta Oct 9. 1857

Madam,

There is nothing doubtful in the good news of which I trust Your Majesty heard the beginning by the last mail and the completion by this.

It is with heartfelt joy that I congratulate Your Majesty on being once more in possession of Delhi, and on the relief of Lucknow.

With grateful hearts we thank God for permitting such enormous difficulties to be overcome, & the happiness of these events after such intense longing for them for months past, is far beyond words.

Lord Canning has now a grateful duty in cordially thanking Your Majesty's brave soldiers who have so gloriously conquered in this unexampled struggle, and have triumphed over obstacles such as never were attempted in this climate & in this country before –

I well know how much Your Majesty & the Prince will rejoice! & so will all England.

The little army relieving Lucknow has been too small to attempt to keep open the road to Cawnpore and to take possession of the city, but now almost all the China troops have arrived & a force is hastening up with all speed to reinforce Gen. Outram & to complete what he & General Havelock have begun so well. They did not arrive a moment too soon for besides scarcity of provisions, one shudders to hear that mines were found, stretching far within the works, ready to be loaded, and another day might have been too late to save that devoted garrison.

It was very distressing not to have a list of the persons rescued to send home, & we must believe that the messenger taking it to Cawnpore was cut off – a private letter reached Benares with a few names of the friends of the writer. So I was glad to know of the safety of *"the Coupers"* I suppose the son of Sir George. The death of Gen. Neill is a sad drawback in this success, & I am sure Your Majesty will lament the loss of such a brave good soldier. His regiment came from Madras, I think the first of all the reinforcements after the outbreak & he passed on at once & Lord Canning and I never saw him to our great regret. He was from Ayrshire & is described as a most quiet silent man, a thorough soldier, & with a will of iron. I believe when away on furlough he had a brigadier's command in the Turkish contingent in the Bashi Bazouks. He leaves 9 children, one son has arrived since his Father's death to join his regiment and another is expected immediately in the Royal Artillery.

There is more enmity in Lucknow than was expected, or else the sepoys are very successful in keeping the town & country people away from communicating with our troops, for there appears as yet no symptom of a wish to submit & the rich chief *Manu Singh* who was supposed to be friendly is now said to be wounded in fighting against us. There are extraordinary anomalies in this struggle, for Sir J Outram mentions no less than 10 chiefs in Oude who have protected Europeans – A person told me an extraordinary story of the pains taken by a chief in saving a Mr & Mrs Probyn & their children, he had a boat prepared with hollow places in which they could lie down and he covered them over with planking at the bottom & in this way he sent them down the river to a place of safety. I am not certain if he belonged to Oude or the other bank. I fear the loss in men & officers at Delhi has been very great. Gen. Nicholson's wound was supposed to be mortal but it is hoped he may now survive. Lady Lichfield's son is wounded but slightly.

The soldiers inflicted tremendous retribution in Delhi & private letters begin to tell of enormous slaughter of men, but they always spared women & children I am glad to hear, & they also say so many men are killed, or have fled that none remain to be seen in the town.

The Headquarters are in that Palace said to be so very beautiful & where there is still a Peacock throne. There was a great dinner of Officers and Your Majesty's health drunk till the walls resounded with the cheers & the soldiers took it up & even the Goorkhas joined. The old king is in close imprisonment & I suppose will be tried, the amount of his guilt is not quite certain but it looks much as if his helplessness was an appearance assumed. 3 sons were shot – Does Your Majesty remember the story that Lord Ellenborough sent to offer to pay him a visit once, & received a reply that he was willing to see him, but he could not allow him to sit down in his presence!

Of the fugitive sepoys one detachment was pursued & beaten going Eastward, & another on the way to Agra is said to be entrenched near Muttra – there will still be plenty of work for the great army from England

174

when it arrives, & harassing difficult service in pursuing & dispersing the fragments of Sepoy regiments besides quieting the country & punishing those rajahs who took part against us, but no very determined resistance seems likely, & I trust the soldiers from England will be generous enough, if they are disappointed, not to grudge the small remnant of the army here its great Triumphs. Sir Colin is so full of its praise and in such great delight at its success, and the fact of these successes taking place before the arrival of more than 2 China regiments who went up to Lucknow, is believed to be sure to have the best effect upon the native mind.

A few days ago the first ship arrived direct from England, of all the great force on its way, it is the Nile a sailing ship with recruits. A wing of the 13th, & some artillery has come from the Cape & the Governor shews his zeal in affording help by completing the number of horses the steamer could bring by adding a team of his own! & hearing of a scarcity of artillery officers he spared his own military secretary who volunteered to come & serve with his battery from Ceylon. I sent Your Majesty a narrative of the escape of a poor Mrs Mawe. I cannot resist mentioning that this poor woman has gone to England by this packet carrying with her a very fine boy born about 6 weeks after all these extraordinary adventures – It is quite wonderful how many stories of the kind I hear every day. Many of the poor babes have died but still I know of 6 or 7 in good case! The last steamer has largely added to the number of officers Generals Wyndham & Dupuis are arrived & numbers of others, many of the R. Artillery. We have made acquaintance with such numbers of Officers that I feel as if the whole Army list passed before me. It is so pleasant to see how joyfully they almost all come to this service & in what spirits they are. Captn Peel has had many annoying adventures in steaming up the river in a sort of "flat" a large covered barge. Many days were passed on sand banks. At last he is garrisoning and commanding the Fortress of Allahabad and all the soldiers are gone on the road beyond it. I am sure he is disappointed in not having a shot at the walls of Delhi with his great guns, but still he is doing us useful service.

I have put off my letter to the latest moment and trust Your Majesty will excuse its haste and its length.

With very respectful remembrance to his Royal Highness & the Princesses

I am, Madam
     Your Majesty's
          dutiful humble servant
               C Canning

[RA Z502/20]

Calcutta Oct 23. 1857

Madam,

Your Majesty's very feeling and kind letter has given me great delight, and I thank Your Majesty most heartily for it. I believe Lord Canning will himself express the gratitude he feels for Your Majesty's gracious words expressive of confidence in him. I well know how cheering and encouraging it is to him in all his difficult and heavy duties & cares to be assured of such support.

To tell the poor sufferers of Your Majesty's warm sympathy with their sorrows & misery will be a pleasing task for me & I shall take care that all I can reach may know of Your Majesty's kind words. I have told several of them and they seemed quite pleased and soothed by them. All the generous subscriptions from England shew the same warm kind feeling & it will be very much appreciated. It was very good of the Emperor to give so generously & promptly.

A good many women and children are already gone to England. Their passages being paid wholly or in part and a small sum left in hand to take them to their friends. Here a good deal has been done in the way of giving clothing & loans & supporting persons in houses of refuge, 11 in number. A great many are supported by the Fund in other places. I still think we do not know the full amount of distress. We know that in those districts where the mutinies broke out all the Officers & Civilians had to fly with merely the clothes on their backs & lost all; but merchants & planters & contractors also must have lost all their works & buildings & no subscriptions or compensations can reach them. There will also be many refugees from Oude & other parts when the road to the North West is open. I see many stories in the English papers quite new to me & grieve to think how much additional pain must be given by the strange delight of some persons in exaggerating horrors already so terrible. A quite untrue story of some poor girls being kept alive in Delhi, and that one had written to me, has reached England, & made a family quite miserable who had begun to be resigned at the thought, of the quick tho' violent death of their poor girl. There was not a shadow of foundation for the story.

There have been few events in the last fortnight except the successes of Col. Greathed's column in pursuit of the fugitives from Delhi. These have been most brillant & at Agra they routed a fresh force from Indore, and followed them until they dispersed them completely, taking all their guns ammunition & plunder. And that after long & weary forced marches! They are now about to come down to Cawnpore & reopen the Great Trunk road & these same regiments may perhaps still do some good service at Lucknow. The 9th Lancers & 6th Carbiniers have, with some infantry, most of the credit of these great feats. There is still much to be done before Lucknow can be left by all these poor women & children who are there still. They must feel far safer, but their position will be somewhat anxious as provisions are not plentiful and it will take a large force to bring them safely away. The town surrounds the residency on all sides but one & the river which is not yet fordable is on the other side. The list of survivors will go home by this mail & comfort many sad hearts, but, tho' they say it is incomplete, how I feel for a poor man who comes here repeatedly to ask for a wife & children not named in it!

For the last week the great steamers have begun to arrive from England, it is quite an exciting race. The Thebes came first. Then the Golden Fleece in 68 days & without any sick list! & then the Caledonia & the Sydney to-day. It is most cheering to see such magnificent reinforcements. The cold weather is nominally beginning for the North wind blows & the rains have long ceased, but the days are too hot for the troops to be put into tents here & all lodging is not yet quite exhausted. I must tell Your Majesty of a humble military Spectacle in which I bore a part. I am afraid the photographic representations are not successful enough to send.

It was to present colours to the Calcutta Volunteers Infantry and Cavalry. I gave them on horseback reciting my speech, not very correctly I am afraid, but few heard! Sir Colin was much pleased with the little Corps & the pains every man took to do his very best. There are about 600 Infantry 180 Cavalry & 4 guns, and the privates are gentlemen & clerks & shop keepers, English or East Indian (which is the polite term for halfcaste). My cortège would have been brillant enough for Your Majesty for I had 5 Generals & staffs in attendance. Sir Colin, Gen Mansfield Gen Wyndham Gen Garrell & Gen Low, the member of Council. Gen Dupuis could not come being laid up with a slight accident. I am told 20000 people were present! & the moral effect of this sort [of] little force being seen is supposed to be very good. I think all the sorrows & horrors in India must have weighed sadly in Your Majesty's mind, but I trust Your Majesty is now cheered by the repetition of better news by every succeeding mail. Lucknow is certainly a cause for some anxiety still but I trust for much hope too and by the middle of next month we may trust to hear that Oude is quite subdued again.

I hope Your Majesty has been much the better for passing a little time again at Balmoral. How thoroughly enjoyable it must be. With many sincere & grateful thanks for the kind messages from the Prince & the Princess Royal,

I am
  Madam
    Your Majesty's
      dutiful humble servant
        C. Canning

[RA Z502/21]

Calcutta Nov. 25. 1857

Madam

   I am sure Your Majesty will have rejoiced most heartily at the good news of the relief of Lucknow, which is announced by this mail. This time we may really trust that the Garrison is safe, for we hear not only of Sir Colin's meeting with Sir James Outram & General Havelock, but that he has safely deposited all those much tried women & children with the wounded in the rear of his force. It will be a great comfort to know of them safe across the Ganges, & still better to see them arrive here! They have had nearly 6 months of terror and anxiety to say nothing of the constant misery of being in the midst of fighting & living crowded together with bad scanty food & probably sickness. The last list of survivors was a far better one than we dared to hope for, but this last month must have been sadly trying.

   The fighting in Lucknow was tremendous, & gives one hope that the example will tell in the struggle for the rest of the town, it is not fortified and it is likely enough that the sepoys & other rebels will forsake it. It is said that 1500 bodies of sepoys were picked up in one spot.

   Sir Colin's wound we are thankful to hear is very slight & does not disable him, but it makes me dread to think that he cannot resist exposing himself to risk in a manner very wrong in a Commander in Chief. As he & I are always great friends I venture to write him my sentiments on this subject, & I should think Your Majesty's must be the same! I am sure he must have been in some most forward & dangerous spot (very likely with his favorite 93rd Highlanders). The two Alisons who are on his staff and sure to be close to him were both wounded, one severely. We have no details and as there is no mention of the loss of rank & file, & from the wording of the telegraph, in which Sir Colin's wound is first named, it seems likely that a message is missing. To carry the telegraph wire along with the troops thro' a country in which nearly every soul is hostile, was in itself a new experiment, and one need not wonder at occasional interruptions of the line. –

178

Lord Canning has been always looking forward to the time when his presence here should not be absolutely essential, & that he could go up towards the North West Provinces, where he has much to do. – He has settled to go to Benares & Allahabad almost immediately. I am afraid it will be 2 or 3 months before I get leave to follow him, for as he is very severe in prohibiting other persons from taking their wives & putting them "in the way" I am bound to give a good, rather than a bad example, & must be left behind. I expect my cousin Colonel Charles Stuart & his wife in a very short time which will be a great comfort to me, he is to succeed Dunkellin as military secretary when he has to go home to attend Parliament.

I am very glad for Lord Canning's sake that he will have this wholesome change, it will be so cheering & good for him after his ceaseless work and anxiety. During the last fortnight the great bulk of the troops from England have arrived. We were anxious that they should be *seen*, but it often was difficult to manage, for they arrived usually in small detachments & had to be sent on at once. Still the natives began to say "the Sea was spawning soldiers". We wished very much that the Highlanders should be seen, but only half the 42^d was here, even that was paraded the evening before moving up. But last week ships crowded in. The Champion of the seas, & the James Bains, those enormous Clippers Your Majesty saw, they were full 30 days beyond the promised 70 days! but they brought each full 1000 men in perfect health & comfort. Many others came, & General Garrett arranged a most beautiful little review of infantry. Not a man however was delayed for it, indeed the 20th landed & marched that very morning. The 19th, 54th & 97th were on the ground & the last half of the 42^d & most of the 97th Highlanders half the 3rd Battalion of the 60th rifles & 2 companies of the Rifle Brigade & the Calcutta volunteers to their intense pride & delight. I know Your Majesty's love for Your troops so well that I am not afraid of giving too many particulars. The whole of Calcutta came out to see the sight, & I believe so many English soldiers were never assembled here before, they went thro' many evolutions & formed squares & a Highlanders charge was a sight & sound I should think not likely to be soon forgotten by the natives. They look upon them with terror and amazement still.

There is very great activity going on in all departments and this precious cold weather has to be made the most of. One great want is of horses. The Himalaya is bringing as many as she can carry from the Cape. Some are on their way from Australia (I think private speculations), & Burmah is made to contribute ponies & Elephants. I shall be curious to

179

see the ship loads of the latter & their landing. The public works of course are at an end for the present but I hear of barracks beginning to be built in all directions & roads making and there is every exertion for the future comfort & safety, in point of health, of all the soldiers who have been sent. I do not hear of any more arrivals of wounded men, & of those we saw in Hospital only one has died – a bad case of dysentery. Miss Nightingale writes that she is ready to serve here & if there is work "in her line of business" she would start at 24 hours notice. I am sure her offer is hearty & true, but it would be wrong to encourage her to come. The Hospitals must be scattered & 3 months hence there will probably be little fighting exept perhaps with the different columns marching over the country.

Very few wounded officers have come & I am told we need only expect those who intend to go home. I wish some very good nurses were available for them, preparation are making for them when they are sent down. Your Majesty will regret I am sure to hear that the young midshipman of the Naval Brigade killed at Lucknow is not as reported "Damien" but Daniell, & I fear he is the same who had the Victoria Cross for his conduct at Sevastopol & for saving the life of Captn Peel. Arthur Clinton (the D of Newcastle's son) is slightly wounded & Lady Lichfield's son Captn Anson has again a slight wound. He is Aide de Camp to Brig^r Gen. Hope Grant.

The communications with the North West are still rather uncertain, but many persons who have come down with the column from Delhi & Agra speak of the country looking really prosperous in many parts and covered with crops – and revenue begins to be collected about Agra. Central India is much disturbed & petty rajahs fight amongst themselves. The troops will be welcome in the district between the Nerbudda & Jumna about Saugor.

We could hardly have expected that even now a fresh mutiny should occur, but only yesterday there came news of the rising & departure of the remaining 4 (I think) companies of the 34th which was at Chittagong when the rest was disbanded the beginning of May. These men had vehemently protested against the conduct of their comrades, & now at the eleventh hour, they do even worse. I believe they secured some treasure but no lives (but one police man) were lost. The Gwalior troops were uncertain where to go & remain on the Jumna, some with 18 guns are believed to have crossed it. I wish they would attack Gen Windham who is left to take care of Cawnpore, he would deal satisfactorily with them & finish them off.

I think it possible that Your Majesty has lately seen some photographs of Dr Murray of Agra, he left 800 negatives with Hogarth to Print & has just returned here. I hope he will be immediately employed to photograph everything to be demolished at Delhi, he is an enthusiast in his art & a first rate surgeon – My recollections of Balmoral have been vividly refreshed by a collection of stereoscopic pictures he has brought from Aberdeen by Mr Wilson some of the falls of the Gairvelt & the Balloch bue & the Cluny burn &c &c are like the reality. I have received with delight the collection of Portraits Your Majesty has so very kindly given to me. They are excellent & give me such an idea of the change & growth of the Princes & Princesses in the 2 last years, especially in the Prince of Wales & Prince Arthur, & also in the Princess Royal. I am so glad to have Prince Frederick's[1] portrait, everyone here wished so much to see it.

May I beg to offer my respectful remembrances to the Prince & the Princess Royal & with many thanks for Your Majesty's kind thought of me, I am

Your Majesty's
dutiful humble servant
C. Canning

[RA Z502/24]

MARIA ('MINNIE') WOOD

Maria Lydia Blane (1835–89) was the daughter of a civil servant and grew up in Slough. After her father's death in 1852 her mother moved to Bath, where Minnie married Captain Archibald Wood of the 14th Bengal Native Infantry in 1856. Shortly after their honeymoon in Torquay the couple sailed for India. Whatever Minnie may have expected of her new life, and her letters suggest a conventional and rather limited person, she certainly could not have expected to confront the terrors of the Indian Mutiny, which erupted shortly after her arrival. Her attitudes are not ours, and will often give offence to a modern reader, but nevertheless it is impossible not to feel some sympathy for a young woman facing not only a foreign climate, frequent childbirth and a less than idyllic marriage, but also the fear of brutal massacre. She had to fear not only for herself and her husband, but the children she gave birth to in quick succession.

The Woods survived the Mutiny, but the marriage did not, undermined by growing debts and Archibald's inability to manage their family finances. Minnie gave birth to three sons and a daughter, the last being born on the journey home from India. The children were brought up in Bath with their grandmother and, after a divorce in 1874, Minnie married again. Astonishingly, she married a Colonel Vyvyan of the 7th Bengal Native Infantry and returned to the India she had hated so much. After his retirement the couple settled in Naples with Minnie's daughter.

1857   *Jhelum, 17 May*

My own darling Mama,

By the same mail as this letter will be received in England the dreadful intelligence of the horrible massacre at Delhi, Meerut, etc., and the fearful state the country is in from these brutes of Sepoys. Our lives are not now worth much, for although our regiment, thank God, are faithful as far as we can tell, still no one is certain from one hour to another whether we shall not be murdered by the natives.

You can have no idea, dearest Mama, of the state of mind one is in from one day to another. My dear husband looks ten years older from the anxiety he suffers on my and darling Sonny's account. Poor fellow, he hardly sleeps at night. At the least sound he is up, revolver in hand, for we have that loaded by our bedside, and his sword hung at the foot.

Our kind friend, Mr Frazer, was killed at his desk, and Mr Jennings, the Chaplain, with his daughter, a very sweet girl of twenty, were speared as they were returning from church in their buggy, poor things. Although we only met en route here, still we took a mutual fancy to each other. I have felt dreadfully shocked at her untimely end.

Two of our fellow passengers on the ship have been murdered at Meerut, Mr and Mrs Dawson, I believe, slowly burnt to death in one of the houses the mutineers fired, and would not allow them to escape from.

Is this not enough to appal officers who have been toiling here for years, treating the natives kindly, and then this is the return they get. It is abominable.

Nothing is thought of or spoken of now but these mutineers. Our little station is becoming desolate, the 39th Native Infantry having left last week, as it was not considered advisable to have three native regiments on the same station, and no Europeans.

My darling child is quite well and looking so pretty, dear wee thing. Oh, I wish you could see him. His lungs are the thing which I consider too powerful!

[The letter continues in Archie Wood's handwriting.]

30 May

The mutiny, I regret to say, is spreading from Barrackpore, which is but fifteen miles from Calcutta, up to our Frontier station, Peshawar. About twenty five Sepoy regiments have been false to our Government. The 9th Native Infantry have joined the mutineers at Delhi, and they have *murdered their European officers*!!! They, the mutineers, have butchered every white man, woman and child in the city. The last accounts are most heart-rending. More than fifty women and children, Christians, who took refuge for safety in the King's Palace there, have all been murdered. Such revolting atrocities, etc., have never been heard of before.

[Minnie here continues her letter, crossing the fresh lines over her earlier ones, a habit of the period.]

Our hot season, dearest Mama, has commenced with a vengeance, which makes everything worse. We can open no door or window between nine in the morning and seven at night, in an effort to keep the house bearably cool. The Thermantidote is going all the time, a most ingenious contraption of fans, etc., which blows a little air about, but it is stifling.

The mail is leaving. I hope it reaches you.

My love and many kisses,

Your fondly attached child,

Minnie Wood

2 June, from Jhelum

My dearest Mama,

We are, thank God, still alive and quiet in our little station, but the fearful accounts which reach us daily of the atrocities committed by these barbarians

keep us in a state of the greatest anxiety.

My beloved husband is away on Treasure escort, that is travelling with the money that is used for paying the troops, a hazardous duty in these days. Poor fellow, he feels much at leaving me and my babe at such a time of trouble. Our Colonel and his wife, the Gerrards, are most kind and wished me to stay with them during his absence, but I do not like leaving our house to servants at this time, so I just spend each day with them and come back for the night.

The Colonel has allowed me a guard of Sepoys to be constantly on our premises so now I have no fear of anything being stolen, as I do not think the men of the 14th would allow any ill to befall any of us. At present all is going on well, and we hope to hear of the reduction of Delhi in the next day or two.

I have just been told that our corps marched off from Jullundur with all their arms, and last evening at Peshawar 150 mutineers were blown away by artillery. This is the kind of punishment due to such brutes for they are nothing else.

We have not yet had your letters by the steamer of April 29th. Those wretches have stopped all traffic so the letters are detained in Agra until the road is cleared. This is yet another trial, as one longs to hear from one's relatives.

I am suffering from terrible boils and can wear neither shoes nor stockings, and little Sonny has caught them from me. Nevertheless he is thriving nicely, and becomes more precious to us each day. I wish sincerely he was safe with you instead of out here. How you would love his sweet little face, and he has such pretty attitudes that I sit for hours looking at him.

It is now next day, June 3rd, and I have just arrived at the Colonel's and heard the startling intelligence that Goolab Singh in Kashmir has collected 10,000 men and is coming down on Jhelum. Consequently all the ladies and children are to be packed off to Rawalpindi, and we are to have everything in readiness to start at a moment's notice. Dearest Mama, I am almost beside myself. My husband away, and I have to superintend everything, and that while I cannot speak fluently, and while I am not at all well, and with my little one to take care of.

Pray for us all, dearest Mama. God knows if we shall be spared by these wretches. If we had the money we, baby and I, would be in England in a very short time, for Archie says he will take us home as soon as he can. Several of our officers' wives are going home sharp, as they do not like being exposed to monsters, and yet we hear the roads are not safe to travel on. Oh, what is the best to do?

How are you all? I have just received a parcel containing papers and a London Journal. They started from Bath on the 30th March, that is over two months ago, which is not too bad.

I cannot write more as the mail is going out. I trust my news will be better next time.

With my most fond love and many kisses,

Ever your most affectionate child,
Minnie Wood

P.S. I am off tomorrow night at ten o'clock as the Chief Commissioner has telegraphed to say all ladies must leave immediately, or they will run great risks. Consequently I am very busy. I shall travel in my little carriage drawn by bearers, three camels with luggage, and two Banghy budars, that is a pole carried on the shoulders of the bearers with goods attached to it. What servants will agree to go with me I shall take, but no furniture, not even a chair. Shall we lose all our belongings?

Jhelum again! 18 June

My last letter to you, my darling Mama, was written when on the point of leaving for Rawalpindi. Well, thanks be, I am back again after only a few days to please some old croaker here, who advised the ladies should be sent away he said, just to hasten us, that he was sure the 14th would mutiny. I shall advise him to pay the expenses of our trip, for it has amounted to 200 rupees. I could cry to think of our having thrown away so much just to please him. Heaven knows we have enough to do with our money without scampering about this wretched country in the hottest month of the year, under a broiling sun, for a pack of rumours. It really is abominable.

Well, now for our travels. I and my baby and ayah, and the Sirdar bearer, started at 8 o'clock in our little carriage drawn by twelve bearers, and five men to carry my traps on the evening of the 10th June. We travelled all night, as the heat is too intense in the daytime. The road was frightful, up and down hills all the way, in some places almost perpendicular, and in other places on the brink of the most horrible precipices with only a foot or two between ourselves and destruction. But these bearers are as sure footed as mules, and I really was not much alarmed.

By six next morning I was within ten miles of my darling husband who was encamped at a place called Googir Bhan, where I was also to halt at the bungalow for travellers until the evening.

Imagine my horror on arriving at this place where my relay of bearers ought to have been waiting, to find not a single man to take me on to Googir. I was in a pretty fix, for the men who were with me refused to take me a step further. This nearly set my brain on fire, and I had the prospect of spending many hours waiting if no one came to my assistance, which was not likely, seeing I was miles in the jungle from any human being.

However, after remaining one hour and a half, persuading these black brutes to take me on, and after promising to give them baksheesh (a present), they dragged me on, but had it not been that dear Archie sent out fresh men to meet me, I think I should never have arrived.

Oh, the delight of a cup of tea when I reached his tent! I was feeling dreadfully knocked up with the heat, which I can assure you was something frightful, the thermometer being at 120 in the tent, and my dear baby suffering from a bowel complaint as well as the heat. You people in England have no conception what an Indian summer is, and fancy our having to leave our comfortable house with Punkahs, tatties[1] and a Thermantidote, all able to battle with hot winds and dust storms. I did not remain with Archie but went on to 'Pindi where a Mr and Mrs Brown kindly took me and mine in until our movements were decided.

Later I took half a house with our Doctor Cole's wife, and of course in *three days time* I was ordered back to Jhelum again! And here we are, safe and sound, thank God, and our regiment is behaving admirably. I sincerely hope nothing may go wrong here, but we cannot now say what a day may bring forth.

It has been discovered that letters were sent to every regiment from Calcutta to Peshawar desiring that on the 1st of June they should rise en masse and murder every European in this country. How we have been preserved I know not. Matters are getting worse and worse. Three more massacres have just taken place, one at Bareilly, Saharanpore, and Morabad in Rohilkand, and we have just received intelligence that Lucknow, the capital of Oude is burned to the ground. Mr and Mrs Martin are there, also the Reverend Polehampton, who officiated at our wedding. I really dread looking at the papers. The atrocities are awful at Delhi and Meerut, poor little infants and children were thrown into the air and received back on spears, and ladies first had their clothes set on fire, their breasts cut off and then hewed in pieces. Can anything be more dreadful, more revolting?

I feel very sad when I see my pretty little baby to think of what his fate might be.

[The rest of this letter is written by her husband, giving more news of the mutiny. Minnie, he said, 'is behaving like a soldier's wife'.]

Jhelum, 22 July

My dearest Mama,

We are the only people left in this station now besides Doctor Cole and his wife, and I know not from one day to another what will become of us. Arthur Roberts, kind as usual, is anxious that I and my dear baby shall reside with him at Lahore, but my husband could not accompany me, so it is out of the question, as I have not the nerve to travel alone at night in these dreadful days. Yet, dear Mama, we have much, very much, to be thankful for in having escaped in the last outbreak here. It was miraculous.

I was nursing my sweet son in bed when the firing commenced, and had only time to slip on the skirt of a muslin dress, the body of another, and rush barefooted into the carriage. Oh, Mama, you can little know how fearful it is to feel at any moment you may be murdered in the most cruel and bloody manner. I thought of you all at home, and prayed we might meet in Heaven, for I never expected to live, and indeed it was only through the mercy of God we were permitted to survive.

Even as our little carriage *flew* through cantonments, the guns of the

Artillery under Lieutenant Cooke opened out, and *boom* they went, carrying death at every sound. It was awful. I shall never recover from the terror, aye, worse than terror I endured that dreadful morning. It was worse than any battle, everyone says. We ladies were all sent to the Deputy Commissioner's house in the Civil lines, and then to a village a mile further on, where we had to remain until twelve in the boiling sun. I was almost naked, for I was obliged to take off my chemise to put on baby, who was dreadfully wet, and I had no napkins, in fact *nothing* with me. It has been dreadful work. Even now matters look anything but cheerful, and until Delhi falls things will be no better.

Every day we hear of some fresh mutiny or massacre. It certainly is a most fearful time for us all. The Punjabis and Sikhs are staunch, if there is such a thing among blacks. Strange that the very people against whom we fought only a few years back are those to whom we now look for protection. We have a guard of Sikhs always, fine strong young men, more like us in their habits, drinking spirits, etc., and eating meat. Indeed, they found a bottle of *Eau de Cologne* and drank it! I like them and their appearance is frank and open.

You can't think how miserable and deserted this station is. I can hardly believe that in the space of a few hours it could become so changed. The day I returned it resembled a charnel house, and the stench was awful, as many bodies were still lying about the lines, and in this great heat decay is rapid.

I do not think there can be many of our mutinous men left. Numbers are being shot, and blown away from the guns whenever they are brought in. A terrible death, if instantaneous, but one that the Sepoy on religious grounds dreads more than any other. It is an awful thing to hear the volleys of musketry, and to know that human life is being taken.

The other day twenty men were blown from guns here in the lines. They are tied by threes with their backs to the mouth of the cannon, and then the word is given. Unfortunately we were taking our drive that evening and came upon them all on their way to the lines. It certainly sent a shiver of horror through me when I thought of them being so fearfully deprived of life, but they deserve it richly, for they have taken others' lives, and had I not escaped that morning from my house, they would have killed me.

I have a cannon ball which fell at Archie's feet the day of the battle.

I know you will be sorry to hear that since my confinement I have been very unwell, indeed at one time it was proposed to send me to the Hills for a change, but I am thankful to say I have managed to do without that, as it would have put us to great expense. It has been 'piles', but now I hope I have got over the worst, but the agony I have endured during the last three months has been intense.

Thank you for all the papers you send, and I have just today received Cissy's letter of June 1st. I should so much like to bring my dear baby to England. You, dearest Mama, can easily imagine what a dreadful fear I have, for after all the atrocities committed on women and infants, my mind is never quiet. Just at the least sound I am on the alert, and this state of anxiety is very trying, besides which my dear husband knows not from one moment to another where he will be ordered, for orders and counter-orders are continually coming in. He is supposed to be here now until after the trial of a hundred of our men who have been caught in Goolab Singh territory, that is Cashmere. They are expected daily, of course only to meet the same dreadful fate as their companions.

I send by this mail some more scraps of newspapers, which you will find interesting, one written by Mr. Roberts. You would be so charmed with him. I should like very much to be with him in Lahore as I would be taken good care of, but it is utterly impossible that baby and I should travel.

One has to put up with so much now from one's servants. They are most insolent, and think nothing of telling you that soon we shall all be in the service of the King of Delhi. One of our kitmaghars left us saying he was going to enter the service of his King where he would get much better pay. I doubt it, and he may well be caught and treated as a Sepoy.

Please will you send me in your next letter five yards of two or three kinds of lace to trim my little boy's caps with, as in the winter he will wear them. Also could you give me some idea of what warm dresses are made of for children of his age, and some paper patterns as my Dirzee is a very good workman and can make anything. Should you have any braid patterns for little dresses I should be much obliged if you would let me have some, and a pattern of children's leggings. I cannot procure a thing here as all shops are closed.

It is most awfully warm here, though we are rejoicing that the weather is cooler, the thermometer at only 98!

Now I must mention the other subject which is worrying me, in fact on top of the mutiny and its horrors, it is almost the last straw that could break me.

The matter of Archie's debts. I was quite innocent that such a debt existed until a letter arrived from one of the securities begging that he would pay. The facts have caused much unpleasantness between us. That

189

my husband has acted wrongly I freely admit, and when he first proposed asking your assistance I would not hear of it, knowing how hard pressed you are for money since the death of poor dear Papa. I have been really angry with him, and he had no business to bring things out from England knowing how badly off he was, and then expect others to pay his debts for him.

By a letter we have just received from William Wood, his brother, we have heard that you have taken the matter of this Bombay debt in hand, and that everything is to be settled by the 10th of this month. I need hardly tell you how immeasurably grateful I am to you for doing this and overlooking Archie's conduct. It has been a sore subject between us for weeks. I know his character well now, and for all our sakes you must *insist* that the measures he proposes by which to repay you will be carried out. This I beg you to do, otherwise he will spend all his pay.

I have been most careful of all money I have had given to me, and managed to save about 120 rupees (£12), but alas these mutineers have carried it all off, as they have so much else from our house, and I feel quite disheartened at this, my first effort, to be economical. We have lost upward of 300 rupees in these troubles, and this is a very large sum to lose in these days when we are not stationary two days together, and in our present financial circumstances, and with no pay coming to us at all.

God bless you, my dearest Mama. I wonder whether I shall ever see England and you all again. I must close this as it is time for my evening drive. Archie intends writing to you by this mail. Ever with my fondest and best love, and a kiss from my little baby who is a very great crower.

Your fondly attached daughter,

Minnie Wood.

P.S. Baby has dark eyes like you and the boys. He has a dear little face and is just beginning to take great notice, and laughs and crows with us, bless him!

Jhelum, 24 August

Dearest Mama,

Yesterday we received the joint letters of yourself and Cissy written on July 7th. Our mutiny took place on that date. Little did you think as you were writing that at that time we did not know from one moment to the next, what would happen to us.

I am not surprised to hear of the non-arrival of our letters, but we have never missed writing by every mail. Perhaps they will turn up one day.

Letters are taking twenty days from Bombay to here, which is almost as long as coming from England to Bombay overland. And now the rains being at their height, the roads are sometimes impassable, which makes more delay.

I have had a terrible abscess in my right ear. I had hardly recovered from that when I was attacked by the regular Indian complaint, fever and ague. After the three alternate days it left me, but so weak that I fainted from the exertion of moving from one room to another. I am obliged to take heaps of quinine to prevent another attack, which of course flies to my ear and sends me nearly crazy with pain. Doctor Cole is a perfect fool and knows nothing of his profession, and he is the only so called medical man here.

This is very distressing as dear Sonny is far from well. His two upper front teeth are beginning to teaze him, and I have had no one to whom I can go for advice. I wish I could get letters from you sooner, as it would be such a comfort to hear what you suggest, and I feel so very nervous about my darling.

Oh, Mama, he has such beautiful eyes, jet black, and makes the most charming little noises as he struggles to speak in his own way. Our night's rest is far from peaceful. The little man makes a dreadful noise, and cries and cries, and nothing will do but walking up and down the room with him until we are utterly tired. He generally sleeps on his stomach, and kicks and amuses himself by the hour in that position.

He has this very moment been brought to me by Ruggio, the ayah, and is lying on the sofa by me, crowing and amusing himself, and looking so sweet, whilst the ayah takes him for a little ride round the room on the sofa, which for a wonder out here has castors. He has an immense liking for his toes, which he is now trying to put into his mouth. Oh, how I wish you could see him!

Now, dear Mama, let me assure you that we have had a lesson about debts which will never be forgotten, indeed I have suffered more than I can express on this subject. Now I have a child I have much to think about. Now he is no expense, but, oh, how we are ever to educate him and bring him up, I do not know. Had it not been for this mutiny we should have done very well indeed, but, alas, not only have we lost a large sum of money, looted on that dreadful day, but our pay is *all stopped* for three months! How do they expect us to live and not to be forced to borrow money?

I have been fortunate enough to dispose of an outfit at a good price (things that are now too small for me), but in *one* hour every rupee we

191

had went, carried off by those brutes. I cannot remember if I told you that our drawers and boxes were forced open by the villains' bayonets, and then ransacked for money. All was carried off.

It is hard on one now, but I trust there is a brighter future for us. We will not fail to send you the money. I think it will be better to send you 200 rupees at a time. I promise faithfully to attend to all you have said, indeed I know the necessity of it.

You and Cissy both appear to look upon these mutinies in a very cool manner. You people in dear, quiet England, have no conception of what it is like to be out here, in hourly dread of meeting some cruel death. The accounts we hear get worse daily. At Jhansi the gentlemen were tied in a row, and their heads taken off. The ladies and children were then obliged to see them taken up by the legs and torn asunder, and after, the ladies and children were all barbarously murdered. It makes my blood boil to hear of such atrocities. Surely you and Cissy must now realize what a precarious position we are in. It is all very fine sitting quietly in one's drawing room reading about these Indian mutinies in the *Times*, and quite another thing living out here in the midst of it. Every sound one hears drains the blood out of one, and holds one for two or three minutes enduring terror indescribable. I assure you I cannot endure to hear the guns go off, it makes me so awfully nervous. I have no power over myself, and tremble as if I had ague.

Dear Mama, I cannot write more now. Our most affectionate love to you all, and a very wet kiss from darling little Cecil to dear Grandmother and Aunt Cissy.

Ever your fondly attached child,

Minnie Wood

Lahore, 11 Oct.

My dearest Mama,

I have received the missing letters of the last three mails! Most truly grateful was I to get them as I had not heard from you for so long.

Dearest Mama, I indeed feel for you as I know the anxiety under which you are suffering must be painful, though we may now look on the worst as being past, but there is no doubt that our position will remain precarious until fresh troops are dispersed all over India. We who are left without regiments are most anxious to know what will become of us. Everything is in the greatest state of confusion, and even the wisest heads think that many months must elapse before we shall be in quietude. Our officers are sent hither and thither. Our Colonel is now posted to a new regiment at Peshawar, where two of our Subalterns were sent to join the Foot Artillery. We shall never again be together as a regiment. And still the disturbances which delayed your letter are not quelled, for as one tribe is defeated another rises.

The last few days has brought the news of the relief of Lucknow. General Havelock arrived there on 25 September, but the siege continues and it may be many weeks before the whole place is free of these wicked mutineers. Food may be short and many more brave men fall before the Residency is entirely relieved. I fear that many horrors must have happened in that place, but none to equal the frightful atrocities of Cawnpore. An officer writing from that place says:

'We found arranged in rows in a barrack fifty pairs of men's feet in their shoes, 30 women's cut off just above the ankle, and numberless children's feet and hands lying about.'

Oh, Mama! can you imagine human beings being guilty of such things? I am unspeakably grateful to the Almighty for having spared us from such barbarities.

Alas, I am still a sufferer from my old pain, and though last Monday I underwent an operation under chloroform, I still am a martyr to this dreadful pain. Doctor Smith assures me, however, that I am getting better, but it will be a long time before all is healed. I have Blue Stone applied every morning. To think that neglect and ignorance by Doctor Cole and that nurse have been the cause of my distress! It is very hard that an officer's wife is obliged to employ the medical man of her regiment, whether he is competent or not.

Archie intends handing up that man Cole for his neglect of duty, and preciously glad I shall be if he is turned out of the Service. My dear husband is here, having obtained a few days' leave in order to be present when the operation was performed. Poor fellow, he is quite wretched about me, and only our Cecil, who is such a sweet pet and so interesting now, seems to divert him.

He is so strong that sometimes I can hardly hold him. He throws himself back with such violence, and, oh, has he not a naughty little temper! It is astonishing how he manages to make such a noise, and at night Papa rushes off in disgust at his son's screams, and takes refuge in a room where he can finish his night's rest undisturbed. Ayah and I struggle ineffectually to quiet him, and in the middle of the scolding the little darling looks up and gives such a sweet smile one cannot admonish him further!

193

He is to be christened directly Arthur Roberts comes in from camp. We shall call him Archibald Cecil. I am hoping to find someone who will take photographs so that I can send you a likeness of my boy.

The cold weather is setting in and I am busy getting baby his warm clothing. I have today begun wearing my flannels. Though the mornings and evenings are very cold, we have not yet given up the punkah during the day, for when it is still it is very hot.

I have been braiding a blue flannel dress for baby, and a nice little Cashmere jacket to wear over his low dresses when out of doors. I cannot procure a felt hat for the Mannie, and they are so soft and warm. I have, however, trimmed a straw hat with red ribbon and put a feather in it. You can't think how jolly he looks when he goes for drives.

I really am glad that my dear brother, Willie, is not of a proper age to come out here. I should have been dreadfully anxious were he out in this vile country.

You ask me if the Colonel's wife accompanied me to Rawalpindi. She offered to but did not in the end. I have nothing to thank her for. She has a vile temper and Archie could have had her up for defamation of character had not things been so disturbed, which would have been very awkward for her husband. Once offended she never forgives, and her tongue cannot say bad things enough of one. My only excuse for her is that she has not been in England for twenty-five years, and does not know how better to conduct herself.

Do you remember all the nice muslin dresses you gave me, unmade? They were all stolen on that terrible 7 July. Next year, dear Mama, I shall ask you to send me more muslin. The washerwomen destroy everything by beating it violently, so that those nice, cheap dresses from England are just the thing. As long as they are pretty and clean I do not mind if they are inexpensive.

This is my baby's day. At six in the morning he is taken out for a walk, and on his return arrowroot is given. He is bathed at halfpast eight and then I nurse him. He then sleeps for about three hours and then sago is given, and at two o'clock he now has a little chicken broth and jelly. Does he not enjoy that, and how he smacks his lips! I nurse him again when I go to bed, and again in the night, for his gums are now so hot that he gets very thirsty.

I have often been obliged to use soap, as you mention, as his bowels are often very troublesome, but I prefer a little cotton wool dipped in oil, it is softer and more soothing.

Dearest Mama, I have written a very long letter, I hope you can read it. Pray do not cross your letter to me. Your last were almost unreadable as they had had all sorts of misfortunes before reaching us. They were still wet, and had had a soaking on the way.

My dear husband joins me in most affectionate love and kisses, and my darling Sonny sends a kiss to you all.

My own dear Mother,
Your fondly attached and loving child,

Minnie Wood

Lahore, 2 November

My dearest Mama,

I really was distressed to think you should be so deceived about the different stations in the Punjab. People who never have been in India seem to make statements without foundation. I can assure you that neither Rawalpindi nor Lahore have strong forts. 'Pindi is nothing but a military station, and I should be sorry to place myself in the Lahore Fort, as it is most insecure.

I am living in Annakalli, a civil station of Lahore, which is distant from Mean Mur, the cantonments, about five miles. The disarmed Sepoys are between us, and should they ever attempt to rush over this way, we are ordered to make for the Fort. A somewhat faint hope.

Dearest Archie came down here to be present at my operation and the very day he was to return to Jhelum ague and fever came on so violently that we were obliged to send for our Doctor. On his appearance he immediately ordered thirty-six leeches over the sides and twelve on the temples. It appears that he was suffering from congestion of the liver, poor fellow. He had a severe attack and is now on Medical Certificates to remain here for two months, as the Doctor will not allow him to return to Jhelum at present. This illness took place in Mean Mur where we had gone to spend a day with the Cookes, and of course we could not return. We remained for a week in barracks next door to them, where we ladies in Cantonments are permitted to live, and wherein I certainly should not like it as a permanency, as it is much like a *piggery!* Sleeping, eating and the bathroom also in this small room, not so large as our morning room at home.

Christmas is drawing near and I wish I could feel as charitable as you do. It sickens me to hear people talk of Merry Christmas and showing mercy towards wretches who have been guilty of every foul deed. The

195

Sepoys in Mean Mur are actually paraded morning and evening in uniform by some person's orders (nobody seems to know whose), for fear they should forget their drill. I should say the sooner they forget it the better.

As to that old sinner, the King of Delhi, he is actually allowed the same show of royalty he had when in Delhi. It is disgraceful. You people in England are not inclined to have justice done on these brutes, and disregard the opinions of those out here in high positions who know the situation. I have heard newly arrived officers say that they are soldiers, not hangmen. Had they known my feelings and the happenings of July 7th they would not speak of 'insulting the men's dignity'. No punishment is too great for those inhuman monsters. When I think of the pretty, elegant girls and their charming mothers, and the brave men I met in Cawnpore coming up here and their terrible fates, it makes me wish to shoot every Indian I see.

It is sad on Sunday mornings in church to see the number of people in mourning and so many young widows amongst them.

Arthur Roberts came in a few days ago from his tour of the Frontier. He was at Groggra where he went to set things to rights. The tribes who have risen are the most wild, uncivilized beings you can imagine, subsisting on lizards, frogs and filthiness of every description. They are immensely wealthy in cattle, and until their pride and arrogance is subdued, they will never be quiet. However, herds of the animals are being constantly taken from them, so I hope the mail route between here and Multan will soon be safer. Our letters go down the Indus for the overland mail.

I am so grateful to you for thinking of my darling Cecil. It is impossible to procure anything for him here. A common little straw hat costs 8 rupees, that is 16 shillings, and that untrimmed. Nearly all my dresses, made and unmade, were taken by the mutineers, and also all my skirts, leaving me only the bodies. That nice warm dress with flounces, checked, has gone, and the only bonnet I have left is the one I had on when my picture was taken, the horse hair with the feathers. I am in great need of a straw bonnet, as they are the most useful things out here. My little straw hat has become quite rotten. I suppose the heat has done that. I cannot wear tight bodices, as when nursing it is worrying. I have a loose jacket of black cloth which does with any skirt.

Mrs Routh of our regiment is on her way to England with her little boy. She has taken a bag from me with things for you, dear Mama. It contains my books, which will get eaten by insects out here, my malachite ornaments we bought at Torquay, a pot of Mangoe Chutney of my own making, a pot of green chilli in vinegar, also curry powder, a chinelle [chenille] cushion, a pen case, envelope case and other things all made at Wizierabad, and a paper cutter of steel with a Persian inscription, and last but not least a cannon ball which I found in my dressing room. These, dear Mama, will soon be ornamenting your drawing room.

Please, dear Mama, do not write so closely, and do not cross your lines. It takes away half the pleasure of receiving letters when you have such difficulty in reading them, and they frequently arrive soaking wet.

I had a letter from a friend now in Delhi, and she says her husband with his men is now engaged in digging for loot. He has been most successful, having in two days dug up clothes, jewellery, articles of every description, and two lacs, that is £1,600 in gold mohurs.

I fear several of your letters and most of the *Illustrated London*'s have been lost for ever.

Dearest Mama, I must close to catch the post. God bless you.

With most affectionate love and kisses from all,

Your fond child,

Minnie Wood

Lahore, 20 November

My dearest Mama,

Plague take the mails! No letter from you to answer and the mail from here closes at five today.

Baby's *first tooth* came through *last night*! Poor little fellow, he was very unwell, sick constantly and fever hanging about him. I gave him some castor oil in the morning but as he still continued ill I sent for Doctor Smith, who gave him fever powders, and he will be here again in the morning. The tooth is in front in the lower jaw. He seems very stout and healthy, and this cold weather is setting him up beautifully.

I am in a regular fix what to do. Archie wishes to return to Jhelum, as he does not wish to lose the appointment he has there, as it may be an opening for something better. I have a great objection to going back as we have no medical man there, and I should be very nervous of having my poor baby teething and no one to consult.

Oh, this dreadful India! I hate it and an officer's life is a miserable one. I cannot let poor Archie live by himself, and if I did go and anything happened to little Cecil I should never forgive myself.

197

The little man was vaccinated the other day, but it did not take effect. Children are not brought, as in England, from whom vaccine can be obtained, but in the cold season it is sent down from the hills, and I am sure loses its power.

I am still in Arthur Roberts's room, by a roasting fire and am in a flannel dress, for the cold here when it does come beats an English winter hollow. It is very jolly though, for I can get a good walk now, and come in with my hands and feet quite dead. Such a change from the heat of a few weeks ago.

Our late Commanding Officer, Colonel Gerrard, was, I am grieved to say, killed in an engagement with the Judpore Legion on Tuesday last. Poor Mrs Gerrard is left a widow with six children. He was a good, kind old gentleman, and did not deserve to meet his end by the hands of these ruffians.

How grateful I am that my husband is with me, whilst so many poor creatures are grieving for theirs. When shall we have an end to these wars? Even travellers are not safe, for a few days ago a young officer of the 81st was brutally murdered by some blacks whilst proceeding down the Sutleg River en route to England. So many bad characters are roaming at large, and it will be years before there is quietness and order throughout this vast Empire.

I have been most fortunate in procuring an excellent English nurse from the 8th. Her husband was killed at Delhi, and her one child is going home to his relations, so she will have no encumbrances. Mrs Collins is a steady young woman, and thoroughly understands children, having had six of her own. My ayah is about to increase her family, her fifteenth child. This is the worst of Indian females, they are always having babies. You would be astounded to see the herds of little black, naked children running about the servants' quarters, their huts that is. How they all manage to live is a perfect miracle to me.

By the bye, I forgot to tell you the great bit of news. Baby was christened a few days after I dispatched my last letter. Mrs Cooke stood for Cissy, and Lieutenant Cooke is one of the Godfathers and Arthur the other. Baby was so good and struggled to get hold of Doctor Carshore's red band the whole time, and kept crowing, laughing and moving, to the utter consternation of everyone. And Mama, he ended by 'peeing' the clergyman and someone else took hold of him! He is the most awful boy for this, and nearly every moment he wets someone, laughing the whole time, and looking so cocky!

I have just invested in a small stool with a hole in it (comprenez-vous?), and he looks a regular little monkey perched on it. This is a great amusement to his Father, who takes great delight in placing him on it and carrying him round the room.

I am dying to know what our new Commander in Chief, General Wilson, will do with the Company's officers, such as Archie. I wish they would raise new regiments and officer them from the Native regiments which have mutinied.

If you see Colonel Birch in Bath pray remember me to him, and tell him that poor Richard Beecher committed suicide the other day at Barrackpore. He lost his wife and baby in August and it affected his mind so much that he took his own life.

If you can get paper like this to write on, pray use it, dear Mama, as it is stronger than yours. Whenever you have any nice embroidery patterns, or braid ditto, please send them in a letter, as light things can be sent that way, such as sewing silk, a little at a time, you know.

I am in great want of a worsted needle, none are to be had here, in fact we can get hardly anything as the Lahore merchants have not been able to procure fresh goods for some time owing to the disturbances.

Should baby continue to keep well I shall go into camp next week with Arthur Roberts. It is a delightful life, all but having to get up so early. Cissy would enjoy it as she could ride ten miles every morning. I am grateful to say I continue quite well. Doctor Smith has cured me, and my pain has gone and all my boils. In fact, 'Jack's himself again'!

Dearest Mama, I hope you get my letters regularly. I often feel quite unwilling to send them off for fear they should come to an untimely end. Dear Mama, I fear this letter is not very interesting, but it is such a mercy to live in comparative peace! My fondest love to Cissy, who I hope you will never allow to set foot in this horrid country, and to the boys, and with every prayer and wish that you may be spared to us many years,

Your fondly attached child,

Minnie Wood

199

ISABEL GORE

The First Boer War (1880–81) was the result of Boer resentment at British annexation of the Transvaal. At the end of this conflict the Transvaal was granted independence in internal affairs, but the British maintained an ambiguous 'suzerainty' over the region. The discovery of large deposits of gold in the southern Transvaal in 1886 brought a rush of foreigners (mainly British) to the area and exacerbated British-Boer tensions. When troops protecting British mining interests failed to withdraw, the South African Republic (Transvaal) and its ally, the Orange Free State, declared war on Britain. The Second or Great Boer War lasted from 1899 to 1902.

Isabel Gore came out from England during the Boer War to be near her husband, Lt. Col. St John Gore of the 5th Dragoon Guards. He was besieged at Ladysmith and published an account of the siege in 1901. Incredible as it may seem, her sister Babbs Van der Byl made a trip to South Africa during the war simply to sightsee, visit friends and relatives, and do the social season – also, perhaps, in search of a husband. All the letters are addressed to a third sister, a Mrs James Heath, in London. It is evident from the correspondence that Isabel Gore was somewhat embarrassed by the arrival of Babbs, since it revealed the Boer origins of the family – their father had been a Mr P. Van der Byl of Cape Town.

The letters cover most of the year 1900 and the early months of 1901. The two sisters took ship for England in May 1901, and the war ended a year later.

1900   Feb 27th

Dearest F.

I'm writing from here as I've been lunching here & the mail goes tomorrow and I know I shall be very busy all the time till then. I've been in town all the morning packing up kit bags for the hospital trains. We put into a little bag a suit of pyjamas flannel shirt socks hanky & a sponge bag with sponge toothbrush & soap and each wounded man gets one of these which he keeps & they say they are all so delighted with them. Just after I got into town a hooter (I don't know how to spell it!) went off which is always a sign of news & Lady Charles Bentinck & I ran like lunatics to the Newspaper Office. People from all parts of the town were running there & there was a tremendous crowd cheering & yelling God save the Queen & we certainly thought it must be that Ladysmith was relieved but it turned out to be that Cronje had surrendered.[1] The excitement all over town was wonderful, in a very few minutes the whole place was decorated with flags and guns were fired from all the ships & syrens going. What it will be like when Ladysmith is relieved I don't know. I do really think this last piece of good news must come tomorrow or the next day. I think the strain in one is almost worse now that one expects the news every day than it was before. I don't think you will know me when you see me again. I've got great lines all round my mouth & under my eyes & look about 100. Of course this vile climate has a lot to do with it. Everyone says it is an awfully liverish place & it is so frightfully relaxing and every single thing I eat gives me indigestion. Other people tell me they also have indigestion here. They say it is something in the climate. I hear also that the Transvaal is even worse so I hope to goodness we shan't have to stay out here. I wonder what will happen when Ladysmith is relieved. Some people say none of the garrison will be used again during the campaign as they won't be fit enough. Anyhow I hope St. Jack will get down here. General Walker told me yesterday they were eating 50 horses a day. I saw some people yesterday who had just come from Kimberley & it was very interesting to hear their account of things. They said they used machine oil for cooking instead of butter & it was so good that they are always going to use it. They said they couldn't possibly have held out much longer. The last 100 lb gun was so terrible. I am so glad they have got Cronje. I wonder if they have got Madame too. It will make no end of difference to us. I'm so sorry I couldn't go & meet the Staffs Yeomanry but it is almost impossible to find out when a transport is coming in. There is a Mrs. Jessop here who is Mr. Cecil Gardiner's Aunt & she is going to see them in their camp some day & I have asked her if I can go with her as I should like to see them so much. I hope I shall be able to go & see the 8th. Hussars arrive. I shall be at Mount Nelson then & it will be easier from there. I go there the day after tomorrow. Mrs. Mackeson arrives today. I am going to meet her if the boat comes in this afternoon. Mrs. Atherton is at Mount Nelson. She came out to see her husband who was ill and she doesn't know where he is & doesn't seem to care either. She is rumm. She thinks this is a splendid place. She always has several young men in attendance and is dressed up as if she were going to the Park. I don't think those sort of people ought to be allowed out here! Thanks for sending on Miss Eustaces letter. I wonder if you thought of writing to tell her to send the things she was collecting either to you or me to send out. Everybody is finding it is much better to send things to individuals instead of to the societies. The things are here but can't be got from the societies as there is such a lot of red tapeism connected with them. I hope you are telling everyone to collect for me. Money is really the best as everything can be bought here very cheap. Isn't it dreadful they have raised the prices at Mount Nelson half again as much. It is almost impossible to get a house. They are very expensive about £40 a month & servants are quite impossible to be got. Housemaids & cooks ask about £7 a month. If you come out here you will have to bring servants! It is a terrible place. I never want to see it again when once I get away. Love to you all.

Yours affectionately
Isabel

The Vineyard,
Newlands March 3rd

Dearest F.

Isn't it splendid about Ladysmith! I can't believe it is true yet and shan't be really happy until I hear from St. Jack to say he is all right. I suppose I shan't be able to get a telegram for some time as there must be such a tremendous lot of official ones to send off before any private ones and they still have to heliograph them. I rushed off into Cape Town as soon as I heard the news and the scene there was most exciting. Flags flying & crowds cheering. I was at Parliament House doing Hospital things when they mobbed us for not having a flag up & they stuck a Union Jack on the Queen's statue in her arms & then all shouted "God save the Queen". How sweet it was of you & Babbs to send me a telewag & how extravagant but I liked it awfully. I am still at this Hotel. They have behaved most disgracefully to me at Mount Nelson. My name has been down there for a room for the last two months but they would never let me know when they had a good room but kept on taking new people who just came for a night or two. The other day Lady Chermside told me she was going & she & I went together to the manager & I said I liked her room & would take it whenever she left. After a lot of fuss from which I could see that he didn't want me to come he said all right & put my name down. When Lady Chermside was going she telegraphed to me the day before saying she was going but wouldn't tell the manager till the next day. So the next day having had all my things packed & given up my rooms here I went to Mount Nelson thinking of course I was all right and when I got there the manager said he had never promised me the rooms & he was going to give them to [a] lady from England and he was so extremely rude in the way in which he said it. I never been spoken to so rude and heated like that in my life. Lady Chermside was awfully indignant & I actually burst into tears afterwards in Mrs. Solomon's room. I suppose my nerves are in a bad way & I get rather upset. Fortunately my rooms here had not been let so I just had to come back. I hear they want to get rid of all the women in the Hotel as they don't pay as well as men & they have been rude to a great many other ladies. I think someone ought to write to the papers about it and make it known. I told the manager it was all very well while the war lasted & people had to go there but afterwards nobody would go there who wasn't obliged. The strange thing is that I managed to get a room for Mrs. Mackeson so it looks as if I was boycotted for some reason or other. I can't think why though as I never even asked the price of Lady Chermside's rooms. I wonder if St. Jack will be able to come down here now for a bit or if I shall go up there. I'm longing to hear what they are going to do. I think I shall probably come to England when I have seen him. I feel so awfully pulled down. This climate is so trying. It is frightfully enervating. Today has been positively awful, frightfully close & one is always in a dripping perspiration & you know I don't get like that easily. One gets a sort of weak feeling & when [one] goes upstairs ones legs tremble as if one was recovering from a long illness. I expect Johnnie will be arriving tomorrow or the next day. There is no way of finding out when his ship arrives or I would try to go & meet him. – March 5th. I met Frank Fitzherbert at the Station here today. He had come out to call on the General & had come two stations too far out. He walked a little way with me & was very nice. Wants us to come & dine or lunch with him at Mount Nelson. He is out at Green Point in Camp right the other side of the world from here. I'm really awfully sorry I've not been at Mount Nelson all the time as one sees everyone there. I'm going to the dentist tomorrow. Three stoppings have come out of my teeth. The dentist here says this is a terribly bad place for teeth. What a wreck I shall be when I come back. I haven't heard from St. Jack yet. It will soon be a week since Ladysmith was relieved. Every day I think I must hear the next day & so it goes on. Major & Mrs. Mackeson came to luncheon with me yesterday, it was so nice seeing him again, he is such a dear and simply worships St. Jack. I like her very much too. What a lot there is to read now in the English papers. It is very funny getting news a fortnight old but the debates on the war are most interesting. Thanks for the Staffordshire paper with Jim's speech[2] & the nice photos. It must have been very exciting, that send off. Mr. Fitzherbert said he thought the yeomanry were going off from here tomorrow but if they didn't go he said he would take me there to see them one day. I don't like to go alone. Good bye. Love to all.

Isabel

Imperial Hotel
Maritzburg. June 9th

Dearest F.

I can't write a long letter this mail as St. Jack is here and I can't waste him. He has got jaundice and came down here about 4 days ago. Fortunately he hasn't got it badly but he is very yellow all the same and so terribly much worse than after Ladysmith. He wants a real long good rest and freedom from responsibility and feeding up. I do hope it is true that the Ladysmith garrison are to be sent home first. Everything feels so flat here now and one can't take any more interest in the war now. One only wants to get away from the country as soon as possible. Everybody is getting jaundice. They can't find out the cause as it has never been known here before and they say the colonists are getting it as well as the troops. I have been up to the hospital again to ask after Mr. Fraser and he was rather better, his temperature was lower. So I hope he will be all right now. St. Jack & I are going down to Durban to-morrow for a few days change. There is no other news.

Yours affectionately
Isabel

Imperial Hotel
Maritzburg. June 22nd

Dearest F.

I have just had a telegram from Babbs saying she isn't coming on here in the 'Briton'. I suspect she funks another voyage so soon. People in England don't realize what a long way off this place is from the Cape. It takes a week in a mail steamer and is just like going from England to

Cairo. I like the way in which you advise me to go back to the Cape. I might just as well go to England for all the good I'd be to St. Jack. I told you in my last letter that he had jaundice. He was with me for nearly three weeks and has now gone back to Dundee. He says he waits till he gets some loathsome disease and then comes down to me to get cured. St. Jack and I both think it has been such a mistake Babbs coming out here now and associating herself so with the Dutch and having a Dutch name which continually appears in the papers in ways like the enclosed cutting.[3] It is attracting peoples attention to the fact unnecessarily and they may think she is more nearly connected to them than she is as she has come out now and men fight shy rather of anyone Dutch. It seems rather horrid to talk like this but it is true all the same and it would be awkward for her always having to explain that she isn't nearly related to these rebels and funny people. It doesn't matter about me because I'm married and there is a reason for my being here. Don't tell her anything of this as it would only worry her now. It is very quiet here now that St. Jack has gone and I miss him dreadfully as I have nobody hardly to speak to. Mr. Fraser has not been quite so well again. He had rather a higher temperature for a few days last week but I think he is going on well except for that. I went up there a couple of days ago but they said nobody was to see him. I think he had been seeing too many people before that. I was so interested to hear about the Hunters. How they are going it. I suppose you went to the daughters wedding. Was it a very grand affair? I wonder what will happen to us when this war is over. I am so anxious to know. It would be a terrible thing if they kept us out here. Anyway I should think St. Jack would be able to get a good long leave but I don't think they would keep any of the Ladysmith garrison out here. We were lunching with the Governor a couple of days ago and he seemed to think that there would be a good deal of fighting still before it was over. I haven't heard anything from Johnnie. One hears absolutely no news here. I only heard casually from somebody the other day that Major Mackeson had been severely wounded. I never saw it in any paper. I am so anxious to hear more about it. How glad Mrs. Mac must be that she came out now. I am very glad I came. I have seen St. Jack for about 7 weeks and am ready for him here if he gets anything the matter with him. It is our wedding day today. I wish he could have been here but he had to go back although his leave wasn't up. Did I tell you that St. Jack wrote to Teesdale to take proceedings about the Villa[4] and also to Jo & Babbs telling them what he was doing and all the letters went down in the "Mexican". Now he has just written again. Isn't it a bore. Good bye. Lots of love to Jim

& I hope Vollie is getting all right again. Poor little chap. Give my love to Miss Wood if she is still with you.

Yours affectionately
Isabel C. Gore

Howick Falls Hotel
Howick. Aug 10th.

Dearest F.

Babbs and I came up here last Monday and I am awfully glad we came now as I feel miles better already. The air is so fresh and bracing. It is only 1½ hours from Maritzburg but it is right up in the hills. To-day there is a vile hot desert wind blowing but it acts just like rain and makes it beautifully cool for a few days afterwards. At night and in the early morning it is absolutely freezing and our hands get quite stiff. Just like England in winter. I never saw such changes from heat to cold. Of course it is very dull, but there are nice walks. It is a funny primitive sort of hotel. Rather like a big Public House and there are a few doctors' wives and a good many doctors in it, also some vets and farmers. Rather a motley crew altogether. They have started a large hospital here which accounts for the doctors. I have just had a letter from St. Jack saying he can come down to Maritzburg for a couple of days so we shall go down there when we hear which day he arrives and then come back here again for a week. I have kept my rooms at Maritzburg so I can go down whenever I like. I don't know how much longer Babbs means to stay here. I'm afraid she must be awfully bored but she says she doesn't mind. It is awfully nice for me having her. St. Jack won't let me go up to Newcastle as he says it is so horrid to hear the way nice men talk of the "women who follow the troops about" so I have given up the idea of going for the present. St. Jack had some men taken prisoner the other day but it had nothing to do with him as he wasn't with them and the men were not to blame either. They were taken to a farm full of Boers by an *"Intelligence"* officer who didn't know there were any Boers there. Just like an Intelligence officer. In his last letter St. Jack said he had been to look on at a fight Gen. Lyttleton's Division had and it was most interesting but I think I shall tell him he mustn't do these sort of things again as he said the bullets were flying around and there wasn't much cover. I wonder where you will go till you can get into your new house. I do so long to be back in England and see some green trees and grass. Here it is all burnt and there are nothing but blue gums and some fir trees. There are some mimosa trees in flower though which I forgot. They do remind me so of Cannes. I am so sad as I have had the Irish terrier I was taking care of back to his master. It is horrid taking care of other peoples animals as one gets so fond of them. I have never heard what has happened to our dogs. I wonder if we shall go back and do so wish something was settled. I can't help thinking we should go back to India. There seems to be no definite news yet about the Legations at Peking.[5] What an awfully anxious time poor Mrs. Mackenzie must be having. They keep saying one day in the papers that they are safe and the next day that they are [*sic*] so one doesn't know what to think. Please thank Vollie for his letter that I got by the last mail. I hope he is quite all right by now. I am nearly cured of my jaundice though my complexion isn't beautiful yet. Good bye. Love to everybody.

Yours affectionately

Isabel

Howick Falls Hotel

Howick Aug. 17th.

Dearest F.

Babbs & I came back here this afternoon from Maritzburg where I had four happy days with St. Jack. I got a telegram from him saying he was coming down to inspect the Depot! so we rushed back and he arrived on my birthday. Wasn't it splendid! and he had no loathesome disease this time! He was looking much better than when I saw him last and just a wee bit fatter. Now he has gone back to Volksrust again. I am awfully anxious to get news as there have been all sorts of reports about. One was that squadron of cavalry had been caught near Newcastle and as the 5th are scattered along the line from Newcastle to Volksrust we can't help feeling anxious. There is probably no truth in the thing! It is lovely and fresh up here & I really feel better for having been up here before. At present Babbs & I feel rather low. Our rooms are very small & cold & we've got two miserable candles and only two straight backed chairs and outside there is a most unholy row going. A lot of doctors' wives and queer men of all sorts shrieking and roaring with laughter. So vulgar! This hotel is just a sort of Public House. Rather like Rathfelders.

I've just committed a fearful act of extravagance in buying a silver jackal Kaross. There was a man who had some sent down to sell. I'm afraid I've paid too much for it. I think I shall send it back by Babbs to be mounted. We went to a Garden Party at Government House while we were down at Maritzburg. I was told it was a very funny sight as people came in such very odd garments the men especially but it was rather disappointing in that way. It wasn't very amusing so we only had some tea & came away. My first and only piece of dissipation since I have been in Maritzburg.

We were so sorry there is a hitch in the arrangement about Ashorne. I wonder what will happen. If you will get it after all. We have been writing there for several mails. It will be most annoying for you if they change their minds now after having bought such a lot of things. I wonder what you will do for the summer if you don't get it. Good bye. Lots of love to you all.

Yours affectionately
Isabel

Nottingham Rd. Hotel
Aug. 31st

Dearest F.

Many thanks for the two letters you forwarded to me. One was a most amusing one from the Indian Khansamch. You didn't write to me by this mail but I had Babbs' and St. Jacks letters to console me. He generally sends your letters on to me to read. Babbs & I like being here so much. Of course it is very quiet, nobody to speak to except a poor lady whose child has just died here of dysentry. This place is right up in the hills. There are not many trees but miles & miles of hills, as far as you can see around rising one behind the other. It is quite cold too and the air is so fresh & bracing that I feel like a different being already and don't at all like the idea of going back to stuffy Maritzburg but I don't expect I should like being here all by myself alone. Today we went for a lovely walk and saw the Drakensberg mountains all covered with snow. Babbs went into raptures over the view. Yesterday the proprietor of the hotel took us for a drive. It was just like being in Scotland on the moors with cold air blowing in ones face. So nice. I have been awfully worried by my maid giving me notice a couple of days ago. The whole time I was at Howick all the work she did was to make half a dozen tucks in a blouse (in ten days). She spent all her time flirting with different men and one evening she was seen in the smoking room sitting on the sofa with a man (officer) in the Lancashire Fusiliers. I told her it was not right and that she never did any work so she said she would go at the end of the month. I am going to see if I can get another woman here and if not I will telegraph to you to send out one as I must have one especially if I go out to India. One can't do without a maid here either as there are no servants to do anything for me in these wretched hotels. Of course as the woman has given me notice I won't pay her passage back. I really think the war will really be over in about another six weeks or two months at the latest. They seem to [be] working up for a last big fight now and I think that really ought to be the end. That would just be a nice time for us to go to India about the beginning of November. I don't think it will get very hot before then. We are going back to Maritzburg in a few days and I shall stay for a month I think and then perhaps come up here but one can't decide anything. I am so glad to hear that the doctors have given such a favourable verdict about Vollie. How delighted he will be to go back to school! I wonder what you will do now for the winter. Remain in England and have Hylda's coming out ball but if you don't get Ashorne will you have it [in] London? I am so anxious to hear if you have got the place or not.

Tommy sent us some photos of their new house and it seems very nice. I think I can remember it quite well. What good news that is about Major Mackeson! I am so glad and hope his eye really will be all right. Fancy his having a piece of shell in his cheek all this time! What a good thing it was that he went to England. I heard from St. Jack a couple of days ago. His horse had fallen with him again and twisted his ankle but it is not anything serious. He likes his new General (Talbot Coke) very much. The Boers have been giving them a lot of trouble all along the line but now they seem to have disappeared over the Buffalo or somewhere. I am so glad you liked the shell! I can't write any more as the ink is coming to an end. Lots of love to you all.

Yours affectionately
Isabel

Nottingham Rd.
Sept. 22nd.

Dearest F.

I thought Babbs had written to you & she thought I had so between the two it seems you had no letter at all and there is only a few minutes before this must be posted. I am so glad to get away from Maritzburg.

209

The heat there was getting very unpleasant and it was altogether very unhealthy. This place is up in the hills and it isn't really cold just a shade cooler than Maritzburg. Today everything is enveloped in a thick mist. St. Jack is all right again and I think the war is nearly over and we shall be on our way to India before long. We heard yesterday that Charlie Van der Byl had been wounded in both arms. I do hope it isn't very serious. I am going to telegraph & try to find out how he is today but we don't know where he is and it is quite impossible to find out. We never knew that Col. de Lisle had been wounded until we saw it in an English paper.

I expect Aunt Sara is in a terrible state about Charlie! We never knew about Guy Ward either till you wrote. Babbs is going to East London in the Kinfaun Castle on the 1st Oct. & from there to Kimberley. I'm afraid she hasn't enjoyed herself here as much as she had expected to. However she has seen Ladysmith & all that which she liked. I do hope Vollie is getting on all right. I don't think you ought to send him to school unless he is quite cured. It would be taking such a risk! I wish I was going to be in England for Xmas with you. It will [be] nice to be in a respectable house again. You can't think how I have been pigging it this last year. I feel as if I had been in Gaol. Good bye lots of love to you all.

Yours affectionately,
Isabel

Nottingham Road
Oct. 4th.

Dearest F.

I have always forgotten to wish you many happy returns of your birthday and now your birthday is nearly here and you won't get this till long afterwards. I'm so sorry. I hope you had a nice birthday. I wonder where you spent it! I was so dreadfully sorry to get your last letter and hear that Vollie wasn't any better. You will just have to find out what place suits him best and keep him quietly there till he is cured I think. I do so hope you will have a better account to give by the next mail. Babbs has gone off to Kimberley. I had a wire to say she had arrived at East London all right after a very rough night and she had found a lady going to Kimberley so I am quite happy about her. She had to leave here one night at one o'clock and it was pouring with rain and blowing a hurricane which wasn't a very cheerful departure for her. I have got my new maid. She is rather a severe looking person but is very anxious to do her best of course she has no idea whatever of doing hair but as I am only going to keep her till I get back to England that doesn't matter much. It doesn't signify in the least what one looks like here as there isn't a soul anywhere to see me. This hotel is swarming with children now. Of all ages babies that scream all day long. I shall be thankful when I say good bye to this house and the horrid kaffir servants. You can't think how dirty and disgusting they are. You can't go into your room for about an hour after they have been in it, even with the windows open. I've had half a sovereign stolen twice out of my purse as I kept it in my room by mistake when I went down to dinner. And you can't complain to the hotel people about anything as they don't care in the least and are so horribly independent. I complained that there was no hot water for my bath in the morning and the lady of the house said there was plenty of hot water at 10 o'clock. Oh I said I can't undress and take a bath at 11 o'clock. Well she said "Other people can". That's the sort of thing you have to put up with. Horrid isn't it? It will be nice to be in a respectable home again. I am actually going out to luncheon on Sunday. There are some relations of the Carr Ellisons' who are living in a farm house near here. They came out here as their children were delicate. Their name is Hughes Chamberlain and they are really very nice. I don't think they will stay out here much longer. It must be such a dreadfully dull life! I may go up to Newcastle for a little to see St. Jack but I shall keep on my rooms here in any case until I leave the country for good. I don't think I should like visiting at Newcastle altogether. There are too many smart women there and it is rather a bore when one doesn't feel inclined to be smart and hasn't got any clothes. I don't know what my new maid must think of my rags. I suppose you really will be in your new house when this arrives but anyhow I think it will be safer to send it to Cadogan Square. Good bye, love to everybody.

Yours affectionately,
Isabel C. Gore.

Nottingham Road
Oct. 12th.

Dearest F.

I was so sorry to get your letter last week that little Vollie wasn't any better but I am so hoping for better news next week. How disappointed Hylda must have been at you not being able to go to Dresden with her but I think you are quite right to stay and look after Vollie. There is no news for me to tell you from here. One does nothing but the same things day after day and sees nobody so that it is quite impossible to write an interesting letter. We have been having horrid windy weather, regular gales and at the same time it is hot. Then every evening a thick damp mist comes over everything. I'm sure it can't be healthy. St. Jack is coming down here next week for two or three days. I've just had a letter from him saying that he had been out for a reconnaissance and been fired at and two of his men had been killed. All they could do was to burn the farms near. I don't see how this sort of thing is ever going to end. Small sorties of Boers may go on like this for years & years and I can't make out how they are going to stop them. We have just heard that Buller is going home[6] but don't know what the reason is and what it means his giving up his command like this before his work is done. It does seem most extraordinary. However I suppose we shall hear soon. I suppose Jim has been very busy over his electioneering. I think he must have got in all right or I should have seen it in the papers as they put in all the seats we have lost. I wonder what you will do for the winter and if you will have to take Vollie abroad somewhere. Babbs is at Kimberley by now but I haven't heard from her since she arrived there. You will probably get a letter by this mail. This hotel is crammed full of children now and they make such a noise all day long. There is a father & mother & two children (this is the way they live out here) in the room next to me and they wake me up at five every morning. Most annoying. I'm really beginning to think I hate children. Fortunately there are two women in the hotel I know otherwise I couldn't stand it. All the other people are awful women.

Love to you all.

Isabel

Nottingham Road
Oct. 25th.

Dearest F.

I think my letters will just have to be "same as last week" and nothing more for there really is absolutely nothing to tell you. We can hardly ever go out of doors now as there is always a thick mist like a cloud so thick that you can hardly see a few yards in front of you and if you go out in it you get soaked through very soon. And they say it is like this all the summer. The Natal Carbineers are having a ball here to-night and people come from the farms for miles round riding and send their clothes by a kaffir and then ride back after the ball. Fancy people being keen enough to do that in this mist and rain. It is bad for fringes. My hair is always absolutely wet now! St. Jack hasn't been down here yet. He may come the day after tomorrow if he can get leave. We are all very excited and anxious to know why Buller has gone home in this sudden way. There was a rumour that he was to be made Commander-in-Chief as Lord Roberts refused as they wouldn't let him have a free hand but I don't think there is any truth in it. Everybody here thinks that things will go on just as they are now for another six months. You people in England fancy the war is over but it isn't a bit over. Every day there are a number of casualties in the paper and they add up tremendously. A couple of days ago we counted about a hundred killed and wounded & prisoners. It does make [me] feel so annoyed to think that they are all so unnecessary. I can't see how it is going to end until the Boers have no supplies left. It is rather amusing now to see how the different countries are climbing down about giving Kruger demonstrations on his arrival. They really are afraid of us after all. I think I shall come back to England next spring whatever happens as I don't think it would be good for me to stay out here longer. There doesn't seem to be much chance of my going to India. Unless they go very soon. I enclose Babbs' letter about her journey from here which she asked me to send and which I forgot to send by last mail. Lots of love to you all.

Yours affectionately,
Isabel

The Hotel
Nottingham Road
Nov. 9th

Dearest F.

I never got any letter at all from you by the last but I expect you were so busy over the election that you couldn't manage to write. Nothing of any interest has happened since I wrote last week. St. Jack writes that at last they have got an official order to say that they are to go to India as soon as they can be spared from S. Africa but when that will be goodness only knows. St. Jack says he doesn't see how they can possibly be spared just yet.

I am in great trouble again about my maid. She has been doing very well and I like her but unfortunately she is suffering from the horrid complaint called Piles & she is so dreadfully bad that the doctor says she must have an operation and so wouldn't be fit for work for some time so I don't think I can possibly take her to India especially as she is very delicate in several other ways and suffers from her liver. I don't know what on earth I'm to do as there isn't such a thing as another maid to be got here and I couldn't go in a troopship without one as there wouldn't be any stewardess and not another woman of any sort on hand. Isn't it annoying to be worried so. I do so wish now I had telegraphed to you for a maid but of course now there isn't time. Of course if I were going straight back to England it wouldn't matter! Wasn't it unlucky Babbs getting Influenza at Kimberley! It must quite have spoilt her visit there as she says she has never felt so ill in her life but she is going back there I fancy from Cape Town and may be able to have a good time then. She seems to like being there awfully and met a lot of men. Perhaps she may meet her fate at last!! I had such a nice long interesting letter from Johnnie the other day. He seems to be getting on all right. This hotel is crammed fuller than ever with Refugees and there are ten children now. Four babies, who yell all day and all night. One is called Redvers Buller and he yells loudest of all. It gets on ones nerves after a bit. It is just like living in a Crêche. Then there is an old lady in the room next to my sitting room who has two Parrots and they shriek all day. It's just like the Parrot House at the Zoo. The whole establishment here is just as good as a play, only it palls on one after a bit. The hotel is so full that they are now putting up partitions in the rooms & making them into two though they are already only like small dressing rooms. Then a father and mother and two children generally live in one room. There is an artist too among the crowd who is painting the battlefields but he is mostly drunk. Oh it is all too funny! It will be so strange to be among civilized people again! I got my Worth silk by last mail, many thanks for seeing about it. It was awfully sad poor Prince Christian Victor dying like that[7] wasn't it, we never even knew he was ill here. I do hope Miss Roberts[8] will get all right. I should think they would all go home as soon as she is better. I'm very glad St. Jack isn't at Pretoria. They say it is so dreadfully unhealthy there now. All the generals seem to be going home one by one now and yet the war is by no means over. At least it doesn't seem so to me out here. I suppose you really are in your new house now but I'll send this to Cadogan Square until I'm quite sure. Good bye. Love to everybody.

Yours affectionately,
Isabel C. Gore

The Hotel
Nottingham Road
Dec. 14th

Dearest F.

I was so glad to get a letter from you by last mail as I hadn't heard for two mails before that. I believe you must have written as you didn't say anything about not having done so. Thanks for the photos of the election but I do not think they are very good specimens. It is so funny to think that it is near Xmas again. I'm not looking forward to it at all. St. Jack says there is no chance of his coming down as Kitchener won't allow any leave of any sort now. I think he is preparing for his coup which they say is to come off in January. I don't mind what he does if he will only end the war quickly. They have gone and let De Wet[9] escape again which is too disgusting. I suppose it is so difficult because the Boers scatter themselves about when they are likely to be caught and then all collect together again afterwards. It does seem hopeless! I think Kitchener's reputation for severity is standing him in good stead now and is doing some good. But the authorities are stupid about some things. Now there is a most fascinating woman in this neighbourhood who is a paid Boer spy and she boasts that she can get round any man. She lets the Boers know when horses are being sent from Mooi River and then they catch the train and in many instances she has been known to give information of our movements. She was lunching here the other day with the Adjutant of Steineckers Horse. And yet can you believe it nothing is done to that woman. It does make me feel so cross. Mrs. King a friend of mine who is here is going away to Durban for Xmas and then afterwards she is going to board with a lady at Howick so I shall be left all alone. Dreadful prospect. There is a poor woman here who came from England less than a month ago to Durban with three little children and two of them have died in ten days of dysentry and the little baby she has brought up here has got it also. Isn't it dreadfully sad! I heard from Babbs the other day. She says she is going back to England the middle of January but I think that will be too soon for me as I must wait till after they have made this move that one hears so much about though how I shall exist here alone I don't know. The weather is fairly cool and we have the most dreadful thunderstorms nearly every afternoon. I have never seen such thunder & lightning before. Sometimes the damp heat is horrid. Just like an orchid house and then the next day will be quite cold. Rather trying. I shall be glad to get to a civilised country again where servants don't clean

215

their teeth with your toothbrush and brush their hair with your brushes. These are the sort of things the kaffir girls do here. Isn't it disgusting. Good bye. Love to you all.

Yours affectionately,
Isabel

1901

Nottingham Road
Jan. 18th

Dearest F.

I have just come back from Colenso where St. Jack & I have had a most interesting two days. I enjoyed it awfully. The only thing that rather spoilt it was the heat. It was something dreadful. The first day we started on ponies at about 9.30 and went to Harts Hill and didn't get back till 3 o'clock. We were in the grilling sun all the time and besides that there was a hot wind blowing so you can just imagine what the color of my face was like when we got back. And the thirst we had! I drank 8 cups of tea and was still thirsty. But it was worth it. I enjoyed seeing it with St. Jack so much. There were still a lot of remains of dead Boers lying about but I wouldn't go and look at them. We didn't go on to Peters but could see it well from Harts Hill. The next day we got up at 4.30 a.m. and rode up to the top of the Hlangwane from where we got an excellent view of the positions. Then of course we saw the place where Col. Long lost his guns and where Lord Roberts' son was killed. They are close to the town. I got back here in the middle of the night 1.30. in the pouring rain. Nobody to meet me though they knew I was coming. Nobody to carry my luggage to the hotel and when I asked the landlady if someone could fetch it she said in an insolent way "We can't send people to fetch things from the station at this time of night." So my maid & I had to go & carry them here ourselves. That is the sort of country this is! I was so cross! I would have stayed at Colenso for another night but I couldn't stand the heat & the mosquitoes. St. Jack went back to Volksrust the same night that I came back here. I am very glad I have been to Colenso as without seeing it one could have no possible idea of what Buller had to contend against and it seems a wonder that he ever got through at all. You never saw such a country! I came back in the train with a funny old couple who live at Rorkes Drift and had some interesting talks with them. The old man had been taken prisoner by the Boers. He seemed to think that the Boers could not hold out much longer and that the war would come to an end next month. I hope he'll turn out to be right! He was very much disgusted at the way the loyal people had been treated while the kin & families of the Boers were being fed and looked after.[10] I am glad to say that Ralph Gore is going on well so I hope he will get all right soon. I saw in the papers today that Capt. Glossop who is with the Imperial Light Horse has been severely wounded. It really is dreadful the way that people are still being killed and wounded. I haven't heard from Gertrude Ross since I wrote to her. I wonder how her husband is getting on. I must go to bed now. There is a moth the size of a bird in the room and it may sit on my hand at any moment. Love to you all.

Isabel

Nottingham Road
March 1st.

Dearest F.

I can't write you a very long letter today because I've got a headache. I've had my Rheumatism ever since I wrote last and it is only just better now. It got a bit better after I wrote and I got up but wasn't quite gone so I asked a doctor in the hotel to give me something for it & he insisted on my going back to bed again. He's a funny old thing! St. Jack said I was to tell you he couldn't write as he is out in command of a column about 800 men Mounted Infantry & Infantry. None of his own regiment and they have had a dreadful time as it has never stopped raining since they went out. They had no tents and had not taken off their wet clothes or boots for 8 days. Already 80 men had been sent in sick but fortunately St. Jack was very well when he last wrote. He is cooperating with French I believe. He said eleven Burghers had just come into his camp & surrendered. They had already surrendered to us before but were captured by Boers & so put into prison & so badly treated. They were starved & had no boots & were very bitter against the Boers. It really does look as if the end is not far off now. Wouldn't it be ripping if St. Jack could come back to England with me! I do so envy you having seen the Queens Funeral. I haven't got your letter about it yet. I'm afraid my mourning is of a very sketchy description. White frock black sash. Don't know what I shall do when it gets cold as I have no black clothes & one can't get anything made here. However I must scrape along somehow. There is no news of any sort to tell you & as I'm feeling rather sick you must be satisfied with this uninteresting letter.

Yours
Isabel

217

Nottingham Road
March 22nd

Dearest F.

You always say in all your letters that you have written to all the family out here so can't tell me anything. I think it is a bit hard on me. Do write to me first some day! St. Jack is down here again on three days leave. It is very short but I'm thankful for small mercies these times. He has had a terrible time taking a Convoy to Gen. French at Piet Retief and they suffered dreadful hardships from rain & hunger etc. but he was awfully well all the time. We have just seen in the papers that Botha has refused Kitcheners terms of Peace and are very much disgusted at the whole proceeding. Fancy our placing ourselves in such a position. Now I suppose they really will do what ought to have been done months ago and not spare those wretched Boers in any way. Two of St. Jack's men were killed the other day. The Convoy was attacked while crossing a River. What makes me so disgusted is that we are looking after all their wives and families housing & feeding them for nothing while our own soldiers wives & families are thrown upon the world. Nobody is looking after them. Now I suppose the war will go on for years and there is no chance whatever of St. Jack being able to get away with me. I'm dreadfully disappointed & don't feel in the least inclined to go by myself but I think I shall have to maybe. I shan't go till the beginning of May. I shall be in London for part of June & July and will get you to take rooms for me somewhere in Dover St. or one of those streets. It wouldn't be worthwhile taking a house. I wonder if shall still go to India or if the new C. in C. will alter all the arrangements. I heard from Babbs from the Cape. I wonder she isn't afraid of the plague as it seems to attack Europeans there! Good bye. Love to everybody.

Yours affectionately,
Isabel

Nottingham Road
April 12th.

Dearest F.

I'm still in a state of indecision about when I leave. They have not given me a very good cabin on the ''Norman'' so I'm trying for a transport again. There is one going on the 24th of this month but she is not a good boat. Probably a cattle boat & that wouldn't do and they don't know yet what is going after that. They never do know till a fortnight before which is annoying. I heard from St. Jack a couple of days ago & they have had an awful time again with this Convoy. Heavy rain & the roads in an awful state. We thought when they started that he would only have to go half the way to Piet Retief but he has now to go all the way so won't be back for some time & then I suspect he will have to start off at once for Pretoria so I shan't see him again. I feel awfully inclined to go to Pretoria instead of to England but I think I had better not as I have not been feeling very well lately & I think have been out here too long already. I haven't heard from Babbs lately so don't know what her plans are. I hope you will be able to get a maid for me. I want you to have her ready for me when I arrive if you can manage it. I prefer a French one if you hear of a good one but if not an English one will do, and I don't mind giving £35. Try Miss Symons 5 New Cavendish Street. She ought to give me another for nothing as I got the last from her and she was such a failure. You might say that she was a regular bad character, but she does have very good ones sometimes. I hope you'll be able to read this as I'm writing lying down. I'm so glad Maud Pennant is better and hope for still better news by next mail. I hear that the 8th Hussars are going to Volksrust so St. Jack may see Johnnie before he goes. I have nothing more to tell you. I'm afraid my letters must be very much alike.

Yours affectionately,
Isabel

BABBS VAN DER BYL

1900

Imperial Hotel
Saturday [July]

My dearest F.

Betts is writing to you today but I must just send you a few lines I think. I got your letter today sent on from Roodebloem. I am so awfully pleased to hear that the doctor thinks Volly really better, he must be very careful so as to keep all right now and not get a return again of his complaint. I have been trying to persuade Betts to go away some while, but she has got such comfortable rooms here that she doesn't like the idea much but I think I will be able to persuade her to go up to Howick next week anyhow for a short time, that is up rather in the hills and is very bracing. We have had some vile dust storms. I believe they go on all through August too which is rather sad, but the in between days are perfectly glorious just like Cannes when it is very fine. I do not think it is unhealthy here now, but I do think Betts would be better for a change as she has been here 5 months. I forgot to tell you in my other letters that Betts is so fearfully disgusted with Vintcent and the Adrian V.D.B. she hasn't a good word for them. She says she is terribly ashamed of them and that she considers them as good as rebels, she says she cant understand how I could think of coming out here now, and that she is so thankful her name is not Van der Byl. I don't think she likes people knowing that she was a Miss Van der Byl, she simply hates it! I think that was one reason she didn't want me to come out. I told her I didn't care a twopenny d. what anyone thought. I think our family is a jolly side better than a great many English ones who swagger so, and I failed to see that it was such a terrible thing to have a few relatives who sympathized with the Boers. I think she is making a mountain out of a mole hill, and its jolly unpleasant for me I can tell you!! I must say I am very disgusted with Vintcent, he has been defending some rebels again, and has had a lot of friction with Sir A. Milner[1] again which is very unpleasant, it has been in the Papers too, Betts said she was going to send the cutting so of course one cant feel proud of him. But I don't see how strangers are to know he is a relation of ours, and our freinds must know that all our relations are not Pro Boer. Of course it is natural for Betts to feel more hotly on the subject as her husband may be shot any day by these Boers but all the same I think shes behaving in rather a silly way. I was so sorry to hear about the dreadful time you had with Jo, it is so silly of her to think that we are trying to injure her, Hadgate & the trustees are the ones who will have to pay not her. As to Betts hating her I would just like to tell her that Betts has excellent cause for doing so. I really feel I have no pity for her when I remember how she treated her. I think it is too bad of her saying it was you that encouraged Anne to stay in England. I knew she would say that and everything Anne does will be put down to us, it really is too bad of her. What fun you will have at Henley staying with the Nuseleys, it is sure to be very cheery. I wish I could have seen Mrs. Hunter as Mary Queen of Scots. Good bye dear old girl, shed a tear sometimes when you think of me here so near my dreadful Boer relations! I hope Jim wont think of coming out. Betts could die in a fit at once.

Yours ever

Babbs

There is *no* chance of the War ever being over! I think Betts will have to go to England as she wont go near the Cape again she says.

5 Park Road

Oct. 29th   Kimberley

My dearest F.

I was so delighted to hear the good news about Arthur getting in for Henley and by such a big majority too. Fancy 2 brothers now in the House. I conclude that Jim got in, we have looked everywhere in the Paper but have not seen his name mentioned but he is sure to have got in. I can fancy how excited and mad the people must have been at Arthur getting in. I wish I could have been there to see all the excitement. You never mentioned Volly at all and I was so anxious to hear how he was as I had no letter from you by the last mail, however I am sure in this case that no news is good news. Thats why you forgot him. We had 2 days racing last week on Wednesday & Saturday. The first day I felt too seedy after the flu to enjoy it very much and Saturday was a perfect deluge, fortunately we were already in the Stand before the storm began. It was a wonderful sight, the whole course and felt was one sheet of water, they had to wait for ever so long before they could go on with the racing. I am still feeling rather feeble, it is wonderful how that disease pulls one

221

down. I began to think I would never feel strong again. Betts writes that several people in her Hotel have got dysentry, it makes one feel so anxious! she says it is so hot there too. I do wish the Regiment could get away but I dont see how they can so long as these gangs of Boers are marauding the country round. They are all round Kimberley and are continually having small fights. Col. Settle has been out for some time with a Column, today I see he had to abandon 2 maxims. I hope the old boy will come back before I go it would be nice to see him again. Sunday is rather a gay day here yesterday we had lots of young men to tea and a couple came to supper there is a nice band that plays in the garden opposite and its so nice sitting out on the stoep and hearing the music. They say Cecil Rhodes is coming back here so I hope I will really see him at last. We are going to make him give a dance when he's here. We have not been able to go to Magersfontein as there are too many Boers about it's a great bore! as it will be getting so hot I suppose I will stay on here at least another month. I do suppose I will leave the Cape hotel after Xmas now. As I still want to go and see Jim and perhaps I may do Pretoria. With best love.

Yours ever affectionately
Babbs

So glad Hylda likes D——.

5 Park Road

Dec. 31st   Kimberley

Dearest F.

Thanks so much for your letters. I got them within a few days of each other as the trains were stopped 4 days on account of the Boers, you must have been so excited reading in the Papers about Kimberley being cut off from Cape Town, it was really a sort of state of Siege, it was awful for the people in the mail train. They had to wait 4 days at De Aar, poor wretches musnt it have been beastly. On account of the delay of the mail we got our letters on Xmas day which was really rather nice. I am so delighted to hear about Eva's engagement. I hope she will be very happy. From what you say her fiancé sounds very nice. How delighted the Ward family will be. They were so proud of her they must be so pleased she is marrying well. Isnt [it] amusing about Brodrick. I would give anything to be in England to see him *look small*! I wonder which he will say the reason was he is sure to lie like anything. I liked hearing all about Hylda's clothes.

I think they ought to be very nice. I would give anything to see her dressed for her first ball. I am sure she will look sweet. What fun you must have had at Xmas, such a jolly party. We were very happy here too. Annie gave me a bit of shrapnel with Kimberley Siege on it, like the one I sent you. I wear it on my bracelet and it looks rather fine. I dont think Isabel will go home till St. Jack goes to India so I will have to find some one else to go with, as I dont think I will stay later than the middle of February. Do go on writing to me in case I do. Now that the peaches & grapes are coming on I feel I might stay and have a feast. The fruit is not very good here and very expensive.

I hear that Alice & family have gone to Southsea. There will be quite a large gathering of the family there. Its very hot here now, but on the whole its a cool summer they say and we get rain occasionally which is a good thing. Lots of love & happiness in the New Year.

Yours affectionately

Babbs

You never mentioned whether you saw Gertrude Ross. [2]

5 Park Road   1901
Kimberley

January 13th

Dearest F.

You must excuse pencil but I am writing out of doors. Fancy isn't it naughty of Betts its nearly a month since she last wrote to me. I have sent her a wire today but haven't heard yet. I hope she is all right. We have had it very hot the last week I wish it would rain then it would cool down a bit. There is going to be a dance in the open air on the Club Tennis Courts on the 25th of the month and Annie wants me to stay for it so I expect I will be here till the end of the month. I am enjoying the peaches awfully they are just coming in now, and melons too. I hope that Hylda enjoyed her balls, it does seem odd to bring out a girl at a masked ball, but as you say it would have been a pity for her to miss the fun. You must write and tell me a lot about them all as Hylda never will. Miss Lusen and I went and dined with the Budds a couple of nights ago, he is the son of old Mr. Budd you used to know. We had a very cheery party and we played roulette afterwards, ruinously high. We all started with £3 worth of counters, fortunately I only lost 30/–. The Provost Marshal here Capt. Ferguson is great fun we see a lot of him as he is a great pal of Annie's and we all tease him unmercifully. He is mad about racing and has heaps of ponies. There are not many nice men here which is rather sad. There are a great many passing through but one doesn't see them, as Will goes to the Club very little he doesn't get to know them. I have *just* got a letter from Betts, and am sorry to hear that St. Jack has been ill with a bad throat and he's got leave to go down to Nottingham Rd. The latter part I was glad to hear, but I feel rather anxious about him as he is evidently run down. She told me she had seen B.P.[3] for a few minutes on his way up, and that he was looking awfully well. I had an answer to my note to Miss B.P. yesterday. They were very pleased with the Cape and they say they hope to have B.P. with them again later on so I hope I will see him. Cant write more have so many letters to write. I was so glad to get a letter from Volly. I must send him a line.

Lots of love. Yours affectionately, Babbs.

Did you hear anything more why Brodricks engagement was off.

Roodebloem
March 13th

Dearest F.

I found a letter of yours waiting for me when I arrived last Saturday and I have just got another one today. I am so glad to hear Jim was able to get into the House of Lords he was very lucky! I am so awfully sorry to hear about Hugh Thaberley. I expect the girls and Eleanor are very miserable about it I must write to the latter. I hope she is better for her stay in Rome. I cant tell you how sorry I was to leave dear Kimberley. I had such a happy 5 months there, it is really too long to stay in a place one gets too settled down and its horrid leaving. There were really very few nice people there. The Hazels the people who chaperoned Gladys out were the nicest girls I really liked them very much. I came down with Mrs. Percy Budds sister Miss Blyth and there was an old friend of the Hopleys Mrs. Brown on the train who had a lovely hamper from the Club with every luxury so we did very well. At De Aar we met a nice man who is a barrister at Kimberley Mr. Bowen he came to dinner with us we had a great dinner champagne etc. Col Settle was at De Aar but I didn't see him as there had been a fight near there and he was very busy. We did not see any Boers! so sad! We had a fine armoured train with a maxim, I meant to take a photo of it but I didn't the first day and it didnt go further than De Aar our train was the 1st passenger one for 3 weeks so you can fancy how crowded it was. I do hope that this Conference that

Sir Alfred Milner is having at Pretoria will end in a settlement of some sort I think it looks rather hopeful. Fancy Frank Stone having come out I hear he has gone to Natal. I wonder if he will be near St. Jack. I heard the latter was mentioned in dispatches also Charlie Parmeter. I saw the B.P.s' yesterday. I believe they are very disappointed that people haven't made more fuss over them.

    Good bye lots of love.

           Yours affectionately

               Babbs

F.E. (ELLIE) RENDEL

Ellie Rendel served as a nurse with the Scottish Women's Hospitals in Russia and the Balkans during the First World War. She was a member of the Women's Suffrage Movement.

1916

> 7 Courtfield Road,
> South Kensington, S.W.
> 23.8.16

Dear Mother

You will probably think me quite mad when I tell you that I have decided to go to Russia for 6 months with the Scottish Women's Hospitals people.

We went to see the war pictures at the Scala on Monday night and as a result of that I felt it to be my duty to offer my services to Dr. Ingles. I never thought they would be accepted.

As a matter of fact she, or rather her deputy Dr. Chesney, jumped at the offer, as it appears that they are very short handed & find it exceedingly difficult to get people. The Russian government have asked for four units from this country. The British Red X & St. John's Ambulance are providing two & the S.W.H. the other two.

They say that they are going to sail on Wednesday next but I don't suppose they really will.

I hope you won't think it very foolish of me to go. It seems to me that there is no reason for me not to go and I haven't moved a little finger so far to help in any way.

I'm coming to Rickettswood on Saturday – if possible by the 2.5.

> Yours Ellie

P.S. I believe that Olive is going with the B. Red X lot under the wing of Mr. Berry! But don't say anything about this as she may not want it to be known.

H.M.S. XXX [deleted]
7.9.16

Dear Betty

This is a wild adventure I am on. It reminds me in some ways of the W.S. & W.C.C. & our camp life at Studland. So many of the women here have belonged to semi military organisations such as the Women's Reserve Corps etc in which they do a lot of saluting, that the military spirit has crept in, – much to the annoyance of the sisters who have already begun to rebel.

Dr. Inglis likes a great deal of deference paid to her as head of the unit, & she goes in for roll calls, cabin inspection etc. We have to stand to attention etc & at roll call she has given the order that we are to say "Here Ma'am".

Some of the unit are already rather upset by this & there are one or two grumblers. The officers i.e. the quasidoctors, matron & administrator are accused of being too much on their dignity etc. You can imagine the kind of thing. The secretary, Sanitary Inspector & myself feel secretly that our claims to authority have been a little overlooked, otherwise we loyally & wisely uphold the higher command. Anyway we have deck cabins to ourselves which is something. Some of the criticism is true I think. Just like Miss Gibbs & Streatfield etc some of our leaders have been bitten with the military craze & they love saluting, giving orders etc without having quite grappled with the essentials.

They rather like making us salute them for example without ever dreaming of returning the salute. However I think its all been rather a game to pass the time and make us forget submarines.

We have had a lovely journey so far – except for one day when it was rough. We have been close to Iceland & further north still yesterday it was so warm that we sat out on deck the whole afternoon. The sisters – As in military hospitals all the nurses are sisters here – are the oddest collection of old dugouts. Most of them apparently were private nurses & haven't been near a hospital for years. They look anything but smart. The average appearance of them resembles Miss Skinner. There is actually one old & toothless harridan who rouges shamelessly. The Assistant matron who is rather a bright spot told me that they had found it very difficult to get nurses. All the best ones have been snapped up long ago. These creatures will never have much authority over the orderlies. The orderlies are active intelligent educated specimens. The sisters are

227

essentially uneducated. Some of them go in for flirting openly with the ship's officers.

Yours Ellie

9.9.16. Arrived this morning early.

Camp B.
Roumania.
16.10.16

Dear Mother

Nothing much has happened since I last wrote but I am writing because there will be a chance of posting letters tomorrow in Constanza. We have no patients here so far because for the moment there is no fighting. We had an excitement two days ago when aeroplanes paid us a visit twice on one day & did their best to drop bombs on our camp. Luckily for us they made very poor shots and they were using rather small bombs. They dropped five on us but they all fell very wide of the mark. We have spent today feverishly painting our tents green & brown. We have also put up a large Red X flag. But no one seems to think they will pay much attention to it.

It was very exciting when the aeroplanes were here as they were fired at by our friends & there was a good deal of noise.

I am going to Constanza tomorrow with Miss Henderson. We are going to the Consul there & our letters will be given to him. The weather here is still lovely, and camping here is delightful after the hospital at Medjidia. The patients there were very dirty one of our orderlies caught 60 lice on herself one evening!

Olive is at Galatz. Two of her party came by train & motor to see us the other day. I have had no letters since the one from you dated Sept. 13th. Give my love to everyone yours Ellie.

Ismail
15.11.16

Dear Mother

Your two letters marked 6 & 7 have just arrived, also a parcel of chocolate.

Many thanks for the chocolate. It is very precious out here as it is very difficult stuff to get and is impossibly expensive. I was very much relieved to hear that my letters to you have arrived as I was beginning to fear that they were all lost on the way. I am afraid at least two have been lost: one I sent home by a member of the unit and at the last moment another person was sent and my letter was not given to her. The other letter I am afraid fell into the hands of the Bulgars.

My hair, which you ask after, is cut quite short. I had it done by the barber on the Huntspill and later Dr. Chesney insisted on trimming it. The result is that it stands up in front when I try to part it on one side. I am very glad I had it done as it would have been an intolerable bore during our retreat.

As for the 36 books you say I have borrowed I cant help thinking it is a gross libel. When next you write to Vincent tell him with my love that he is a pig not to write to me. I had a letter from Betty by the same mail as yours and as far as I can make out she is almost as much cut off from civilisation as we are.

We have just heard that we shall almost certainly go to a place called Tiraspol for a month or two. It is a small town about 30 miles this side of Odessa. The Serbians are still in reserve and are to be re-formed there. But plans are altered every other day. It will be rather dull I am afraid but I suppose the poor Serbs must have a rest after their hammering. There isn't very much for us to do as very few wounded were brought from the Dobrudja.

If you could send me some good maps of the Dobrudja and the rest of Rumania and Bulgaria I should be very grateful. Like an idiot I quite forgot to bring any with me and a few weeks ago a good map would have been really useful. Will you tell Aunt Rose that I got her letter and am most grateful for it. Also please tell her that I have heard nothing of the man in Odessa. Please thank Nurse also for her letter & tell her that I am writing to her. Give my love to everyone.

Yours Ellie

Ismail
28.11.16

Dear Mother

I got your 9th letter dated Oct. 29th to-day. Miss Henderson, our administrator, will be in London I suppose before this arrives and you will hear all the latest news of us from her. I believe she is going to lecture on our adventures in the Dobrudja but you must not believe quite all she says. She is very sentimental and is sure to pile on the agony.

I will do my best to look out for William Compton Lord Wrenbury's friend but I don't think it's very likely that we shall meet.

Do the London papers still boom Rumania I wonder. It seems incredible that they should. The fact is Rumania has behaved very badly and the Rumanian soldiers have run away on every possible occasion.

We are still in Ismail but we expect to go very soon now to a little town about 90 kilometres = about 60 miles from Odessa.

Everyone says that it is a hopeless place, very cold and dirty and destitute of provisions. This town is bad enough. There is no wood, no candles, very little petroleum, no milk. Fruit and vegetables are very expensive, sugar is not to be had, butter and eggs are very scarce. I wish we were not going so far from the front and all excitements. But we are attached to the 1st Serbian Lazarette & have to follow the army. The Serbs are going into reserve and so we have to go with them. This place is not on the railway & it is too difficult to get supplies.

We shall have to go in waggons for two days and then by train. It will probably take us ten days altogether.

Life here is rather monotonous just now. Our chief work is patching up soldiers who have been playing with bombs. There are four in our hospital now with their hands smashed up in this way.

Our amusements are (1) Getting letters, (2) Going for walks, (3) Tea on Sunday at the Café, & (4) Russian lessons from a Russian doctor. The other day we went to see some sports. There were about 2,000 Russian soldiers drawn up in a hollow square. In the middle of this sat the Colonel, his wife & family. We were also given chairs there. The soldiers were then ordered out & made to run races climb poles etc. It was all very solemn. Nobody clapped or cheered or even laughed. After the races the soldiers sang melancholy songs.

I had a letter from Betty by the same post as yours. She sounded almost as hard up for luxuries as if she were living in Bessarabia. Thank heavens we have been having warmer weather recently.

Give my love to all my family. Please tell anyone who expects letters from me that it is very difficult to get them posted. They can only go when some one goes to Galatz.

Yours Ellie

The Front   1917
19.4.17

Dear Betty

It is a long time now since I have had a letter from you. Your last one was dated Feb. 16th. We have been here now for a fortnight. We are about 8 miles behind the lines but I can't tell you where. This letter is going by the Russian military post & will be censored. We are in tents here. Very pleasant in fine weather, but it has been raining hard at intervals during the last few days & everything is damp & beastly. It has also been very cold & windy. We hope to open our hospital today or tomorrow. At first they asked us to start an epidemic hospital but now they say it is to be surgical for bad cases. I am very much disappointed as I wanted to see good typhus cases. The typhus is chiefly among the Rumanians who have been almost destroyed by this disease. We have been over two typhus hospitals here managed by Rumanians & it isn't very surprising that things are so bad. The smells & dirt were horrible. In one hospital the patients lay on the floor. In one room a man was dead. Until we went round no one had noticed it. In another room a man was dying. The patients lay very close together and not a window was open. There is only one girl in the town willing to look after typhus patients. Otherwise they only have aged old women (peasants) or decrepid old soldiers to look after them. They have nothing to eat but beans & soup. No milk, no eggs. But it is all due to laziness and incompetence & callousness on the part of the Rumanians. There is plenty of wood to make beds with. We bought 160 planks from the Rumanians to make beds for our patients. There is a certain amount of milk if you choose to pay for it & take the trouble to find it, and the Russians have plenty of eggs at ½ franc each. You can't imagine how dirty this little town is. It is filled with troops & hospitals and there is no attempt made at any kind of sanitation. The Rumanians spend their time abusing the Russians & playing cards. We have made friends with two French aviators here. They showed us over the aerodrome the other day and were very polite and kind. They hadn't a good word to say for the Rumanians. They said they were selfish cowards.

Thank heavens the sun is shining again.

Yours Ellie

P.S. I had a letter from Peggie the other day, the first for nearly five months, full of praises of Hilda! They are going to share a house & are evidently inseparable. It is a great bore because I shall never like her.

The Front
2.7.17

Dearest Mother

The game is up here & I am coming home as fast as possible. But at the best it will be a slow process. The Russian offensive after beginning well failed hopelessly in Galicia owing to want of discipline. Some of the regiments refused to fight & while their delegates were discussing the matter the Germans advanced. The result is that the offensive has come to an end all along the line. The fact is the Russian soldiers have had enough of it. All the officers say the same thing – there is absolutely no discipline, everyone does exactly what he likes. They moved us here two days ago. The main party came by night as the road isn't safe by day especially for a long trail of carts.

Miss Corbett & I drove over in the afternoon to find a camping ground & put up the tents. Nothing exciting happened but the day before when Dr. Chesney drove over to inspect the place a shell flew over her head & exploded fairly close to her. We thought our camp here was very safe from Geman shells as it is just under a cliff over which the shells come, aimed at some Russian batteries just opposite. Below is a map of our position.

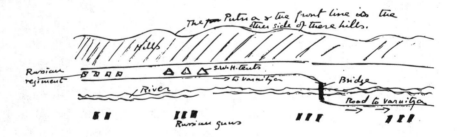

The very first morning we were here we were rather startled when a Russian shell lodged in our midst. Instead of going over the hills it fell in the middle of our camp. Luckily it didn't burst or it would have killed two or three of our Serbs who were sitting less than two feet away.

This is the most drearly hole we have been in yet. It is simply the bed of a river. There is no shade. It is burningly hot & there is nothing to do. Except for very desultory shelling & aeroplanes there is no fighting. Dr. C. saw the general today & he said there was no hope of anything happening. Dr. C. is motoring to Reni tomorrow to see Dr. Inglis & as soon as we can get our equipment away, we shall go.

I am sick of Russia & of Russians. The sooner we get home the better I shall be pleased. I'm afraid we shall be quite a month possibly more. Your last letter was June 7th. I suppose this Russian fiasco means another year of war. Everything is too beastly.

Yours Ellie

ELEONORA B. PEMBERTON

These letters were written to her parents in Buckinghamshire whilst serving as a V.A.D. (Voluntary Aid Detachment) in France. She worked at Boulogne from October 1914 to February 1915, then at the Gournay Red Cross Rest Station near Rouen between February and April 1915, a job which she did not find challenging enough, and was later at Abbeville between May 1915 and February 1916.

1914   c/o B.R.C.S.

Hotel de Paris
Boulogne s/m
November 8th 1914.

My dearest little Mum,

    Thank you ever so much for your lovely long letter of Nov 4th which arrived the day I wrote last. The cigarettes also came, also the Formamint which I am so glad to have and a parcel of 3 hot water bottles from Lilian! It is most sweet of her and they will be most acceptable at one of the hospitals; that parcel of bed socks would be very welcome too if you liked to send them straight here. Letters addressed here only require 1d stamp.

    Mrs Furse is going over today and returning Tuesday so she will post this. I am glad my various communications have turned up, but they seem to be a bit erratic. Everything has to pass the Censor, except what we can get people to take over and I shall be curious to hear whether he stamps anything out or keeps back letters at all.

    How splendid of the servants to contribute 19/– I *do* think it is good of them and it could not be devoted to a better purpose. Such *heaps* of accomodation is wanted for the poor wounded and even with it all they must suffer so much that one feels no effort is too great to make. The hospitals here are packed to overflowing, beds along the passages, on the landings, & mattresses even on the floor. A lot of cases have been cleared out to England or the convalescent homes at Rouen but a big batch is expected down from the Field Hospitals tomorrow.

    It is terrible, but I believe inevitable, that in every way the wounded are looked upon by the transport officials as – well, to put it brutally – a bother. Their work is done, they are no more use, they are only cumbering the line and the ships which are wanted so badly to send up more fighting men, more stores, more ammunition & to feed that most voracious of monsters, an army in the field.

A few days ago we received a message that 700 men were leaving the hospitals here and would we feed them between 4 & 7. Well, they arrived in ambulances, trucks, omnibuses and every other kind of conveyance, and were herded into the train about 4.30; there were only quite a few who were obliged to lie down – for the most part they were packed 8 in a carriage – they had not the *least* idea where they were going to and it apparently did not occur to the authorities to attempt to enlighten them. They were all 'on the mend' it is true but there was many an empty sleeve and not one but was bandaged in one place or another. As a matter of fact they were going to Rouen, but how long, in these days of congested lines, it would take them to get there goodness only knows. They did not finally get off till 8 and would probably travel most of the night sitting bolt upright with not a rug or an air cushion between them: what a journey! And *we* almost think ourselves badly treated if we do not have sleepers going through Switzerland! It is really amazing what the human frame *can* endure, and this particular case is not to be compared with those gruesome journeys down from the firing line when, on arrival, living and dead are found sitting side by side because there is no room for anything else.

Last Sunday Craster & I had some time off in the afternoon so we walked up to the top of the town, past the Cathedral, & through the old walls to the cemetery. It was All Saints Day and as you know this and All Souls are great days in France. The place was looking really beautiful – masses and masses of flowers everywhere, all the graves looking so neat and well cared for, and in the corner which, alas, is growing all too fast, set apart for English soldiers who die in the hospitals here, were really beautiful flowers, wreaths, poems and evidences of the kindliest feeling on the part of the French people. There are no names as yet, only numbers and some are buried in a big grave together. Some have lost their identification disc by the time they get to the hospital and then the only thing to do is to photograph them after death. Whether the poor wife or mother will ever see this and learn the fate of her dear one seems problematical, and I fear that many many of the "missing" will remain so for ever.

The longer I am here, the more sorry I am for the poor Tommies' home people. Officers have so many more means of communicating with them and setting their minds at rest; they can tip orderlies to telegraph for them – often their wives can come out or friends are asked to look them up; but Tommy is just one of the herd; he has neither pens, ink nor paper, even if he feels well enough to write and as many of them have said when I have asked them – "I'm not much good at writing, Sister – *you* write for me". Almost every one I have asked has preferred to have it done for him and has not even been willing, or I suppose able, to dictate his own letter, but has preferred a stranger like myself to say whatever they chose! It seems strange, doesn't it? but I suppose it is a different level of education. In most cases they had hardly anything in the way of *news* to suggest and yet when one persevered one could drag quite an interesting story of personal exploits out of them. One Scotch boy (who talked so broad that I could hardly understand him!) commissioned me to write to his sweetheart, a barmaid at Lyndhurst, and was prepared to say nothing except that he was wounded and hoped she would write. A little probing, however, elicited details which would interest her immensely. He said that he was attached to the cyclist corps of (I think, but I muddle them up rather!) the Scots Guards. At 1 am they received the order to advance upon a certain German position: it was pitch dark as they pedalled rapidly along, eyes & ears alert for an alarm which might mean their last moment. Arrived within *20 yards* of the Germans, they left their machines by the road side and crawled with fixed bayonets nearer and nearer till suddenly, the word "charge" was given & they were there, right on top of the Germans thrusting and stabbing in the dark at a foe they could only see when a gun was fired. It was a weird sensation, he said, but for him it did not last long as he was shot at close range by the friend of a man into whom he had just stuck his bayonet, and after that he knew no more. He was very bad and in great pain when he first came into hospital but now he is better.

When I was up at the Casino the other day the Sister showed me a case of Tetanus, the only one they had. He was not *very* bad & they had some hopes of him recovering. Sir Almroth Wright is here and he had injected the anti-toxin and the man's leg had been opened right up and gauze kept wet with sea water threaded through it and fresh sea water was constantly being added. Isn't that interesting. I must try and go and hear how it succeeds.

I went to see Major Phipps on Friday and found him very cheery and hoping to go home on Saturday. He had a new son aged 10 days waiting to greet him at Woolwich. He is a nice looking man and reminds me of his father, his wound was just below the lung which had been slightly touched so he will have to be careful. He said that Major Maloney was also in the Hospital but that his wife was here so I did not go to see him – there is not much time really.

A few nights ago we had come back from the station and started dinner when a message came from the Quartermaster that Preston – who drives our motor ambulance – and I were to go off at once to an outlying station to fetch three men with fever and take them to any hospital wh. could find room for them. Off we went in the dark, hunted up the R.T.O. office (wh. had been moved since I had last been there) and were told that the train was just coming in. It contained those of the British troops from India who had not been well enough to go up to the front with the rest of their regiments. They had been in hospital at Havre or Rouen or somewhere & were now going up, but these three had developed fever and were to be again left. We waited in our "bus" having got it as comfortable as possible & presently three chattering ague-stricken wretches were delivered over to us, and Preston & I started off with them. She drove of course & I sat inside with them clutching on to the worst who rolled and swayed with every jolt of the car. We had been told that they could all sit up so had not taken any stretchers, only blankets. Luckily the Allied Forces B.H. was able to take all three so we unpacked patients, rifles, kit and everything & handed them over.

There is a great stir in the port today, cruisers & torpedo boats in. I wonder if Lord K. has come over again. Last Sunday M. Fallières came down to meet him and they went right out to the front. An armoured train is lying in a siding close to us – such a fantastic "cubist" affair, painted in dabs every colour of the rainbow. The German shells are similarly painted and it is said that the colours fade into the background & look like trees!

Well, dearest, I must stop. Please give my love to Cousin Katie & as Mrs Furse will be coming out on Tuesday you might write to Beaufort St. this time. Heaps of love to Dad & your little self

from your loving Nora.

P.S. What has been wrong with my Robert's foot? I should so much like to see the snap shots.

1915

c/o Major Meadows,
No 5 Stationary Hosp. B Section

May 1st 1915

L. of C.   B.E.F.

My dearest Mum and Dad,

A perfect whirlwind has swept over me since I last wrote! Weren't you surprised to get my wire? I wonder whenever I shall get your letters. Once they start coming I think I ought to get them quicker as it is a more direct line.

On Wednesday at 2 pm I was very happily doing the ward washing in the wash house at the hospital when the Quartermaster called me in and read out a wire from the Commandant 'Send Pemberton – tomorrow morning Thursday to take charge of new Rest Station. Crowdy'. Words failed us all! as it had never entered our heads that we should be separated – only that we should move as a unit. It was heartrending as I was so *awfully* happy there, but you can't argue with the British Army authorities nor your Commandant speaking for them. Also, there was a certain satisfaction in the promotion and the fact that I had been chosen to run & work up a brand new Rest Station.

So you behold me swanking as 'Officer-in-charge' and finding it quite difficult to issue orders after having only obeyed them for 7 months nearly! I have three members working with me and four orderlies and it is going to be a pretty big thing just on the same lines as Boulogne but with many more dressings to do. Improvised trains are coming through now with no sisters on board & we give them cocoa & serve out Army rations – bread & bully beef or tinned boiled mutton. It is just midnight and 2 of us have just come back to bed leaving two down there in case they are wanted: they will then sleep by day. We have just fed a train of 755 and had quite a lot in for dressings.

Our installation consists of a large piece of the platform in the goods yard canvased off & we have now got to make that look like a casualty dep. There is also a French Red X station & we each feed our own wounded. So sleepy. Love

Nora

E.B.P.
V.A.D. Rest Station,
c/o Major Meadows,
No 5 Stationary Hosp. B Section
L. of C. B.E.F.

May 3rd 1915

My dearest Dad,

I was simply *delighted* to get your letter this morning and so surprised as I was quite expecting to be weeks without news of you!

It is very odd the way we are not allowed to say where we are but yet if we telegraph it appears! Anyhow I am glad you know where I am so that you will not be uneasy. You will also, I hope, have received a few lines from me as I wrote – I think – on Saturday – just hurriedly.

Well, now you want to know more about it all don't you! Your surmises as to being on the direct line are quite correct & that is what we have been sent here for. General Wodehouse applied for us and we are directly under the R.A.M.C. It was found that in that last rush so many non-ambulance i.e. improvised train loads of wounded came through on their way to the Base and naturally they were neither fed on board nor were any dressings done. Also many were too bad to take any further and had to be evacuated here. A rest & dressing station was obviously needed so, a few weeks ago, the B.R.C.S. and the R.A.M.C. started one between them, the former doing the feeding & the latter the dressings in each case Sisters & orderlies doing it. Now they have handed it all over to me and my heart is spending its time alternately filtering through the holes in the soles of my shoes at the enormity of the responsibility and bounding high in the air with the pride of position.

I do not mean that we shall have to do the dressings unaided, one or two M.O.'s will always (at least I hope so) come down from the No 5 Sta. H. and up till now a Sister has come down too, but later she will not come and anyway they only come when the train comes and we have to get every single thing ready beforehand and of course clear up afterwards.

At present the rush seems to have quieted down, and the last improvised train came in the night before last when, as I think I told you, we cocoa-ed and rationed it in just under the hour. We are very glad of a quiet time as it enables us to get straight and fixed up thoroughly and also we have all been having a pretty strenuous time lately, they at Boulogne and I at —— so that a bit of a rest is most acceptable. After being up for about 2 months at 6.30 and having breakfast at 7.30 it feels almost sybaritish not to come down till 8 o'clock!

For the last four days we have been doing day and night shifts, the latter 6.30 p.m. to 8.30 a.m. and the former 8.30 a.m. till whatever time they were wanted. The first three days it was 12 midnight or after but yesterday no train came in so we were able to go off comfortably at 8.30 and had a glorious night!

Now I have altered the shift times and propose that we should work 12.30 – 12.30 so that each shift will get part of the day up, and part of the night in bed. Of course when any train is announced the other two have to be summoned – even dragged from their beds as we were on Friday night as we have to have the whole staff or we could not manage.

The party consists of Barber F. a jolly, cheery party of 42 who is an a.1. carpenter, Greg aged 23, very capable & done quite a lot of hospital work and Saunders, a new member come out since I left Boulogne. She is also 23 and looks young, reminds me rather of Guy Handcock in being small & bright though she has Dorothy's colouring. Greg looks much older.

At present Barber and Greg are on by night and we by day but now we are changing we are staying on till 12.30 a.m. and then they come on & we go to bed. I think it will work very well as it will really enable me to be down here all day which is rather necessary when one is in charge, particularly at the beginning. I shall come down about 9.30 or 10 and as Barber & Greg will also be here it will leave me free to dash out & do any necessary shoppings which is not possible when only Saunders is on as she is too young to be left quite alone in case any cases are brought in.

If they are too bad to go any further (even on Ambulance trains) they are brought in here till an ambulance can be obtained from the Hospital. Two were brought in on Saturday and one has since died.

General Wodehouse came in to see us yesterday afternoon and was very amiable. He said this was going to be a very big centre & that we should get lots of work although it might not come immediately if there was a lull in the fighting. He seemed quite pleased at what few improvements we had already made but I assured him that we were going to make many more!

Our installation consists of a large piece of the platform in the goods shed which has been screened off with canvas. It was all sagging & looking most untidy when we came, but is now fixed to horizontal battens which make a very neat job of it. We have also a small 'cabine' with glass windows all round wh. sits by itself a little further off on the platform & this we can lock up & keep all our goods & chattels in. It has a tiny stove & last night the others lit it & were quite comfortable. We are billeted at the

Hotel de la Gare wh. is only two minutes walk and so most convenient and the orderlies are in a tent not far from the station.

It is quite the smuttiest place I have ever struck! beats even Boulogne hollow and we look as though we never washed! After the pretty country that I have just come from the smutty town seems very nasty! No chance of leave now, alas, my very dears, unless, like the Base details I am sent down as 'unfit for duty'!!

I was terribly shocked and grieved to hear of poor Mr Gordon's death. If you have an opportunity do tell Mrs Gordon how *deeply* I sympathise with her. He was as you say one of the kindest men alive and such a good neighbour. He will be very much missed.

Has Audrey been ill? I was so sorry to hear of her being in bed, she doesn't seem to be over strong now.

How perfectly lovely the primroses must look & will look in the garden, but what a business you must have had planting them. I hope I may be there to see them next spring.

I do hope my parcel will turn up all right – I want the things so much more here than I did there as we have no tea provided or night meal on night duty and there, in a house, cooking for ourselves we really had everything we could want. I am writing to ask them to take out the games – the men will simply love them – and send on the food stuffs!

Well, little dear, I must stop & so goodnight. It is 10 o'clock and I am getting sleepy. I don't like a hotel bedroom after sleeping for two months in one that I cleaned every morning myself & knew to be clean in the extreme!

Ever so much love to you both and to Saunders,
Your loving daughter
Eleonora B. Pemberton
O/C V.A.D. Dressing Station!!

M.G. (MINNIE) FOSTER

These letters were written to her family whilst serving as a nurse in the Territorial Force Nursing Service at the 21st Stationary Hospital on the Salonika front, between September 1916 and April 1918.

1917   [undated]

My dear Mum.

Many thanks for your kind & welcome letters. Since receiving them, Ive been on the sick – thought it was malaria at first, but pleased to say it was nothing so exciting at that, I've still got a very nasty cold which I cannot get rid of. I think I caught cold the first night I was here, I had to sleep on the floor as my kit had not arrived. Still, I must remember Im on "Active Service". I often wonder if I shall ever see England again, quite a lot of people finish up out here – its not at all a healthy country. If I was only good at writing letters I could tell you such heaps of things. I saw a Greek Funeral the other day – 'twas interesting, the bodies are put in a sort of case fully dressed, also sitting bolt upright, the Priests walk in front carrying nuts & cake on plates covered over with muslin. I did laugh when I saw it, thought it was some play, fancy sitting up with collar & tie on after one is dead. The day before Xmas I went to get evergreens, we got into some place where the monks used to live, since the war they have discarded it & the monastery still stands, so I went in & stole a Cup & Saucer, the only thing I could bring away with out being seen, as I was squashed in the ambulance amongst the evergreen. Was very much afraid of it being broken – but no harm as come to it at present. Wish I could tell you more of the life, for one thing I do my own washing, which is rather trying having no convenience, we have to kneel on the floor to iron unless we can get a box which I am now fortunate to possess, have got print to cover it & it looks nice like a proper dressing table. We fetch all our own water, which is heavy & tiresome in wet weather the soil being so slippery. I'm nearly always on the ground as you can well imagine. What colour my things will be in time, remains to be seen, you'd go mad if you saw how we dry them. Windy nights we are nearly blown out of bed. Im afraid I shall not like living in proper houses again. I wonder if I told you about our mess in other words the dining room (in the army its called The Mess). We dont have table cloths just white oil cloth & all enamel things, no cups only mugs with out handles. We pay so much a month out of our salary into the mess to buy ourselves vegetables & butter now & again as that is not included in our rations.

On the whole we had a very good Xmas especially for Camp life, its wonderful what can be done (in the way of decorations) with colored paper & evergreens. The day was perfect – we had all the tent sides up & although the patients had potatoes boiled in their skin, they enjoyed themselves & was more than delighted to be in hospital instead of the trenches. Poor bounders the hardships they endure is dreadful, at times, especially in the extreme heat & cold which this country is noted for – extrems.

Im sure its impossible for you to imagine what ground these motor transports get over. Its nothing to be bumpted two or three yds up in the air (sometimes I think Im never coming down again) through the holes in the tracks – talk about *wild* country, wild dogs, & every thing creepy in creation. What an experience & what a lot I shall have to tell you, *if* I ever see you again. Its strange to see the Turkish women with their faces covered – in fact we see all nationalities, when we go into Town its like going to the circus. England is a lovely spot after all. Except for the free life, this is a dreadful place. When we are off duty there is nothing to do. We are just confined to our Camps. There is talent here & its put to use, for instance they get up plays etc. The dresses that are made out of nothing practically is marvellous – just use muslin & mosquito netting & ordinary paint, the effect is wonderful. One of the men (for one of the sketches) had on a suit of Armour made out of petrol tins, I could scarcely believe it, but seeings believing is'nt it? Please tell Gwen & Lin I'll write to them both in a few days. I must thank you for the cards you sent. Its nice to hear from home. Also thank Rosie for her nice letter.

Must be closing as time is flying. The posts are not regular. I think if I dropped you at least a P.C. once a week we should know where we are more, especially if you did the same.

I have not received Gwen's films. *6th January*. Can you get me a pair of grey woollen gloves size 6, nice thick ones to wear on duty don't trouble about the price I'll pay for them. Wrap them in paper then sew them up in any sort of calico with my name in rather big letters Sister

M.G. Foster *T.F.N.S.* 21st. Stationary Hospital Salonika Forces.
My love to all. Dont worry at present Im alright
Your loving Sister

Minnie

14.2.17

Darling Gwen.

Just a note in answer to yours & Masters, I did write to you all last time I think. Cannot understand why you dont get my letters oftener than you do. Lin wrote last time. I wonder why she couldn't manage to send me a line this time, she would get quick used to scribbling a line to her heroic Auntie in time, & it would'nt be so irksome. At any rate thank you for writing so regularly I always expect a letter from some one at home when ever the mail comes in. What would you think at home if you went out for a walk & came across a few human skulls – its rather weird.

We are in a hot bed of disease & can hardly be wondered at when you think of how little they look after things here. Theres very little respect payed to the dead. The birds are at the bodies almost as soon as they are dead, or rather buried. They are only put in the earth about 3 ft deep one can hardly wonder at the birds & animals but to me it seems awful, Im rather full of it today as I've been out & seen a few things which rather disgusts one. Im sending a bag to Lin for her birthday. Its all hand made & done in the Greek villages by anyone old & young alike; the white is even woven by hand – they are fearfully expensive, nearly cost as much as the brown bag I bought. Im only telling so that you can value it more.

I'll send one to you later if you would care for one. Theres very little in the way of curiosities this way. We dont get into Salonika very often. Its most interesting to see the colours in dress – but I'd rather have good old England. If you are successfull in getting the gloves I asked you for, let me know the price & I'll send on the cash. Another thing could you get me two or three small tins of *Cherry Blossom Boot Polish Black* together with some Dacytlus scent its 2/– a bottle, its made by the Coligate people. Just pack it in a box & cover the whole with calico sew up the box with calico or something old, & print my name on, it will come alright. Sister M.G. Foster, 21st. Stationary Hospital Salonika Forces. Just finished my meal of Bully Beef & Dog Biscuits. The weather is simply awful, cold as charity & only oil stoves for heating. Send as soon as possible, by return if you can as its ages before it gets here. Much love to all as ever your loving Auntie

Monica.

Fancy me having a real grown up neice.

Dont think for one minute everything you see in the papers about Salonika is true. Its not all gold that glitters you know.

20.11.17

My dear Ones.

I suppose you had my letter telling you all about my latest experience.

I expect you have also had a notice from the War Office, stating that I had been admitted to hospital, "Suffering from Shock After imersion into Water".

What a time I've had to be sure, only in hospital 5 weeks, glad to say Im very much better. I do hope you will write to the boy who saved me. I think he is getting the human medal.

In my last letter I told you how you all seemed to come before me when I went down the second time.

The only thought I seemed to have was for you all at home & I had an idea my body would never be recovered.

There were 4 bodies found the morning after the storms, just about where I went in, dreadful to think of is'nt it.

My great trouble is I cannot sleep, I always think Im going under water when I try to get sleep. Please write to the boy who saved me, his name is

Pte Willis
27th R.E.s
Salonika Force.

You might just mention to thank any of them who were kind to me the night of Oct 13th there were a lot who did things for me.

That will be an experience to relate when I come home. Here's another Xmas close on us & I did think I was coming home for this one. We seem farther away than ever this year.

What an age since I heard from you. I had one letter from Gwen while I was in hospital & thats all lately.

Perhaps you have all gone down. Im longing to see you all again. What hopes!! I sincerely hope you will have a very happy Xmas.

245

I did want to send the girls some cash, but Im afraid of it going down, but I'll try later on, for Xmas presents. Am enclosing a P.C. of the firs. Did you get the other one I sent you, quite a large one. Again wish you all a very happy Xmas.

With love to all,

Yours lovingly,
Minnie.

KATHLEEN (D'OLIER)
COURTNEY

The daughter of Major D.C. Courtney of Milltown, Co. Dublin and Alice Margaret Mann, Kathleen Courtney (1878–1974) read modern languages at Lady Margaret Hall, Oxford. A keen suffragette, she was Honorary Secretary of the Oxford branch of the National Union of Women's Suffrage Societies from 1911 to 1914. She attended the Women's Congress at The Hague in 1915 and was one of the founders of the International League for Peace, chairing its British Section for 10 years. During the First World War she undertook relief work with Serbian refugees, and later worked with the Society of Friends in Austria, Poland and Greece. In 1928 she became a member of the Executive Committee of the British League of Nations Union, becoming its Vice-Chairman in 1939. During the Second World War she twice toured the United States, giving lectures on behalf of the Ministry of Information, and in 1945 was in San Francisco for the drawing up of the United Nations Charter. She became Vice-Chairman of the British branch of the United Nations Association in 1945 and in 1949 took the posts of Chairman and joint-President, retiring as Chairman in 1951. She was awarded a CBE in 1946 and the DBE in 1952.

Salonika . . . Jan. 7/1915   **1915**
Address: c/o L. Behrens Esq.
Hotel Continental.

So many days have passed since I last wrote that I think I had better write a sort of diary, which, if dull, will at least give you some idea of what we are doing and how we are living.

Monday Jan. 3/. We spent most of the day getting ourselves and luggage ashore. Even then the stores, with the exception of one packet, got left behind and we have since heard that they have all gone to a hospital to which other things were consigned. We hope to retrieve them shortly as we really want them rather badly. The hospital ships anchor rather a long way from the quays; there are very few boats to be had and in rough weather it is quite difficult to manage the journey without getting pretty wet. A room containing four beds had been engaged for us at the Hotel Amaricani; the charge was 20 francs for a night, and breakfast with rather nasty bread and wretched tea cost 9 francs for the four of us. It is some distance from the camp so we spent the evening looking for rooms in a more convenient place. We had an address given to us at the camp and were lucky in finding two rooms each with two beds quite close to each other and only about ten minutes walk from the camp. One of them has a sort of little sitting-room attached to it which is extremely convenient for breakfast and other meals when necessary. The most absurd scene was witnessed over the taking of the rooms; the whole family including grandmother and baby assembled; marmalade was handed round which we ate out of a spoon, and we then firmly refused to take the rooms for more than a fortnight and demurred to paying the whole rent in advance. They finally agreed to the fortnight and we agreed to paying in advance. The price is fifty francs each room for a fortnight. Of course it is absurd for these small rooms, but as it only works out at ten shillings a week it's not really expensive. I am in the room with the ante-chamber and we are really very comfortable. Our landlady looks after us very well in the way of keeping things clean and tidy and does all the washing up. Also they wash our clothes for us and return them in one day. Of course it is not very comfortable to have only one washstand and it's a bore to have to boil yourself every drop of hot water you use, but these things don't really matter and the primus stove (which H. gave me) has come out extremely handy for the water. We always have breakfast in our room and sometimes other meals; a meat meal is now provided at the camp at midday and we often find it cheaper and more comfortable to have our other food here rather than at the crowded restaurants. Bread costs sixpence or sevenpence halfpenny for a moderate sized loaf and butter is not to be had at all, but we have plenty in our store – otherwise I don't think the food expensive; you can get an enormous plate of macaroni cheese for 40 and a piece of bread for 10. Tea, coffee, and in fact all other drinks except vin ordinaire are prohibitive, but these we can quite well make at home and ideal milk is excellent. Altogether I think I may say that except for sharing a room we are living very comfortably.

TUESDAY JAN. 4/

We started work at the camp. It must be said that the whole thing is not exactly well organized, but it is certainly being worked under difficulties. There is a mixed Russian, Serbian and British control, and no one seems to be absolutely and finally responsible. The object of the camp is supposed to be to collect together all the Serbian refugees from this district and send them to Corsica where a colony is to be started. The camp is thus quite a temporary affair and of course its inhabitants are constantly changing; new ones come in from the surrounding country and others go away. It's very difficult to maintain any sort of order or discipline. The people are housed in large tents which hold fifty at a pinch, but very few are quite full; they are provided with beds, as far as possible also mattresses, or failing them sacks and hay and blankets. They generally have any amount of luggage of their own as well, and I think that for this kind of thing they are fairly comfortable. The tents are warmed by stoves and are hot, not to say fuggy, and the people are for ever cooking various dishes with which they supplement the food provided. There is a place for women and children to bath and also a place for clothes washing, but hot water has to be scooped out of big cauldrons which stand over a fire. At present I don't think there are more than about 500 people in the camp. My job is to look after half the tents, and see that the right people have beds, & give them tickets for clothes and try to get them to make ready with passports & for Corsica. This is a pretty endless job as you can scarcely let people out of your sight without their escaping and many of them are quite helpless. Besides which one is continually being interrupted to deal with or discuss problems which arise. The people are a mixed lot, some of them the most awful looking ruffians, but for the most part I fancy minor officials from Macedonia who have fled to escape the vengeance of the Bulgarian population they have been oppressing! It's a rather disheartening job in a way as it's really impossible to get the camp properly organised and not worth while as it's only temporary. It will be more interesting and more satisfactory when we get to Corsica if we ever do!

On Tuesday afternoon we packed our possessions at the American Hotel and sorted out what we should want here so as to bring as little as possible. Of course lots of things I have got will not be wanted at all. I could have saved several pounds on boots and a good deal on other clothes which I shall scarcely wear. It's cold here in the morning and evening and very chilly at night, but quite hot in the middle of the day when the sun is shining. Even at its coldest it is not so cold as in England; for instance I am sitting now in the ante-room with no means of warming it, and though I am cold it is not intolerable.

249

WEDNESDAY

Spent the whole day at the camp.

THURSDAY

Whole day at the camp. Largely employed in trying to get the women and children to go and get washed.

FRIDAY

Serbian Christmas Day. Spent the morning at the camp. In the afternoon there seemed nothing particular to do as the people were all feasting and amusing themselves. We went into the town and climbed up to the citadel at the top to see the view. Salonika is the queerest place; the town proper has wall all round it and at the top pretty high up the hill is the old citadel with a wonderful thick wall round it. We are away outside the town itself, about a mile to the east or perhaps less. The camp which is attached to a new Russian Hospital is fairly high and the streets in which are our rooms are on about the same level. We should be quiet but for the fact that cocks crow all night, and that sometimes the people next door make themselves heard. Last night being Christmas, they sang songs till about midnight.

SATURDAY I had hoped to have a quiet evening and write to you yesterday, but I went back to the camp in the evening and spent ages looking for a sick baby which was to have special food, the number of whose tent the doctor had forgotten. The baby had to be found as it was starving, and despair seized me when every tent refused to admit that it possessed a baby of eight months old, which was all I knew about it. These people are I believe mostly thieves and liars, but one can't help liking them all the same. They are very quick on the uptake, and manage to understand my extraordinary Serbian in a surprising way. Sometimes I take an interpreter, an Austrian prisoner who talks German, but as he and the refugees generally engage in conversation I generally prefer to go by myself. He is really one of the nicest people in the camp and talks to me of the tents which we visit as "our" tents, the others being quite outside the pale, and not to be considered. The languages are an awful muddle; one has to talk German to some and French to others. Italian is the only means of communicating with our landlady as she speaks a little and I am always struggling with Serbian with the refugees. Fortunately I haven't attempted modern Greek; as it is I find myself talking a mixture of French and German to the interpreters and officials and of Serbian and Italian to the refugees. I would give a good deal to speak Serbian fluently and am thankful for the little I have learnt. I should like to have some lessons, but there is no time here, indeed this is the first evening I have really had time to write.

SATURDAY JAN. 8/ (to-day)

We are having the most lovely weather; bright sun and clear nights, very cold morning and evening and warm in the middle of the day. I find this climate invigorating and feel very well. I am getting chilblains on my hands, but otherwise am not suffering.

No letters have come since our arrival; one Messageries boat has been torpedoed and we heard that the mails on another had got burnt so I am afraid we have lost a number of letters. We shall probably be going to Corsica soon, but as the date is quite uncertain we can't fix anything. I shall wire as soon as I have anything definite to say. It seems far more than a week since we left Mudros Harbour, I feel as though I had been in the camp for years. The whole thing is rather disappointing; I don't think we are essential here as things have turned out and it is rather uninteresting to stay at Salonika and not to be able to see anything of the interior.

The excitements here consist of enemy aeroplanes dropping bombs; this has been done almost every day lately, but so far nothing has been hit of any importance. I took a photograph to-day of the whole camp pointing skywards, but afterwards spoilt it by taking another on top of it.

Hotel Cyrnos. 1916
Bastia.

Feb. 17. 1916

My dear Mamma,

A boat leaves for Nice this evening & I am resolved to get a letter off even if it is only a short one. I have been horribly busy since I last wrote & have had no time at all for writing, but I hope to send you a long letter on Sunday with a full account of the work here. We have now between 1500 – 2000 Serbs at Bastia, & I am principally occupied in the following ways. 1). Taking a house & equipping it as a hospital. 2) Taking houses & furnishing them for the women & children so that they can be removed from the barracks where they now are. 3) Trying to arrange for the installation of a proper place for the washing of clothes & for baths. 4) Helping in the distribution of clothes or rather trying to organize it. 5) Generally running about trying to find out what is wanted & supplying it if possible. Our party here now consists of Miss White whom I am

251

delighted to have, & a Mr Coventry who arrived quite without warning rather to my annoyance. However I think he can be made quite useful. The tower of strength here has been a Swiss who came about three days after the first lot of refugees & who has worked with me in the clothes department & in the washhouse question. I don't know how we should have got on without him. He has really organized the clothing on a satisfactory basis. The French people here are awfully nice, & work splendidly, but they are not organizers. We are having rather horrid weather. Bastia has a wind called the Libeccio, the tales of which I did not believe, but I now know that they are true. It swirls about in extraordinarily fierce gusts which break windows, throw people down in the street & worse than all envelope everything in a cloud of blinding suffocating dust. We have had it on & off; more or less violent for three days & I don't wonder that Bastia is not frequented for its climate! Thank you very much for your letter of Feb. 11th received this morning. I have also received letters from Salonika & two from D. as well as one from R. telling of her plans.

I have to finish this at once so must stop in a hurry. I am very well indeed but have a sort of cold in the head caused by the appalling dust, otherwise this climate agrees with me. I had breakfast at 7.15 this morning & am not tired in the evening. Miss White says she feels ever so much better than at Ajaccio.

Much love to all,

your affect. daughter
Kathleen

NANCY BOSANQUET

Nancy Bosanquet was aged between 22 and 23 when she wrote to her parents in Kensington about her experiences as an ambulance driver during the Cardiff blitz.

A. A. G.B.   1941
68 Park Place
Cardiff

2.111.41.

My dear Mummie

I have been having a pretty busy time lately so I will tell you all about it now while I have time.

It all started on the night of Swansea's first blitz. One of our cars was called out at 12.30 at night to take blood & the transfusion doctor there – another to take nurses – and at 3.30 Queen & I went to Newport to pick up an X-Ray apparatus to take there – that alas was no use as it was far too tall to go into our ambulance so they had to commandeer an army lorry while we trailed sleepily home.

The second night two of our cars were called out at 4.0 a.m. & by the time they got to Swansea were hardly wanted.

The third night was my turn on one of the cars & at 9.15 the message came through to stand by at the transfusion-centre. I went there, & then on to pick up the doctor – a pathologist who is his deputy – a sister & two nurses. They had a message that Swansea was having a bad time so they decided not to wait till a message came through for them, & at 10.30 we set off. By the time we got to Neath we could see the light of a terrific fire in the sky and the road was a stream of fire-engines – coming from as far as Reading & Swindon – and guns & cars, all going in the same direction. It was fun driving my party as the police were looking out for me & I had orders to ignore red lights so I willed them all to turn red as I approached so that I could importantly shoot over.

We got to Swansea eventually about an hour before the all clear, with searchlights waving about the sky & everyone much harassed. Driving was not easy as we had only side-lights, the night was dark, and the fire ahead blinded one. It was also very difficult to find our way about because of constant detours round unexploded bombs. We went first to Cefn-Coed hospital about two miles outside Swansea where all was fairly quiet but a number of the casualties had been taken. It is really a mental hospital with one wing turned into an emergency hospital, & quite full of casualties, – a depressing place, with a long dark stone passage along one side, and endless large & small wards, each block exactly alike so that I continually lost my way.

I pottered about for about an hour till the doctor, sister & one nurse were to be taken to the other two Swansea hospitals, and then I drove them – first to Towy Lodge, past blazing buildings, and bomb craters, using only my sidelights as the whole place was lit up by the fires. We waited a short time there while homeless people filed into the hospital as being the only place they could go, – and then on to the Swansea General Hosp. – The way there was down a fairly narrow street flanked on one side by the technical college which was all on fire, with shooting flames and glowing pieces flying about the air. – I rather expected to detour this but I was told to drive straight on, so I wound up my window, & drove past – between the firemen & the fire. – But we didn't get soaked with water as the water had given out – in streets on fire I only saw one small hose being used, and the firemen were just standing about their yards of hoses. They had some nasty rescue jobs. – I heard of one husband and wife who were pinned into their bed by debris. Firemen worked for hours & in another ten minutes might have released them – when the gas caught fire – & the man begged them not to leave them as the firemen all fled for their lives. That fireman was still having nightmares I think.

After Swansea General – we went back to Cefn-Coed – where they had the worst casualties, and for the rest of the night I tramped round the wards giving a hand here & there, getting tea & water for patients & nurses, tucking in the restless, and meeting Charlie. – That was a funny affair. I went along a dark stone passage to the "pay-a-penny" at the end and opposite it, in a tiny private ward, I saw Charlie getting out of bed – a thin elderly man, head bound up, limbs as thin and white as sticks, and one leg amputated just below the knees. I don't know why that should have nauseated me so but it needed all my courage to go and tuck him in & talk him quiet, while he gabbled incoherently at me. – Whenever I went that way he was getting out of bed – once getting out of his pyjamas, and I would fly to a nurse and say "Charlie's out of bed again." Apparently he was a paper seller who had been buried under debris and under the impression that he was at home.

At four some of the nurses went off duty as they were coming on again at 7.30 and the other driver (who had brought a surgical team from Cardiff), a red-headed young soldier actually also a patient, and myself, found ourselves in charge of a large ward and some small ones, with most of the patients in the large ward wanting attention and none of us feeling at all sure of ourselves.

I found myself not so much affected by the sights, which were pretty horrible, as the sound. There was one child who was delirious & called out to his brother, another who screamed for her mother in her sleep, – one woman who mooed like a cow the entire night, and a lad with a broken shoulder-blade who groaned all the time in great pain, etc: Numbers of them had had hardly any treatment at all. The screaming child's face was black & bloody on one side – & her pillow soaked in blood, & the man next door to her had a bloody lint across his eyes. The latest patients seemed to have oddly black faces. etc: etc: but the sounds I heard haunted me for days, and the stench of unwashed patients, – some because they were that type & some because they were sweating with pain. One old man had several blood transfusions but when I last saw him I could hear the rattle of his breathing in his throat & he died before morning. There were a number of amputations & for that sort of operation I believe blood transfusions are most useful – they restore a very shocked patient to a state in which it is safe to operate on him.

We finally drove back here about 10.0 – most of my cargo asleep, and then I got back to headquarters again after a sleepy lunch with the two doctors.

That day I spent recovering while the rest evacuated the General Hospital which was surrounded by unexploded bombs, and the following day we evacuated patients from Cefn-Coed to the Caerphilly Miners Hospital, which is one of the best, cleanest, brightest & most efficiently run hospitals I have yet seen.

The day after that I took blankets to Camarthen which I enjoyed, & then on Wednesday I hitch-hiked down to Barnstaple to see M. F. married. That was great fun – the journey I meant then. It took me eleven hours because I foolishly went round by Minehead. I got lifts on innumerable cars – including three travellers, & about four army vehicles, – one with scarcely any windscreens & *fearfully* cold, & then I almost got stranded at Minehead because there was no traffic & it was already dusk. However, by great good fortune I got a lift to Lynton, where I threw myself on the mercy of the army stationed there & said had they got anything going to Barnstaple, because I was stranded? & the MT sergeant said No – but I could go on the rations truck at 7.0 am next morning, so I retired disconsolate prepared to stay the night there. Outside I got chatting to a private who said he thought he could smuggle me to B on the back of a motor-bike. Just as that was being nicely arranged out came the MT sergeant again at which I lied glibly that I was just arranging where to stay the night – & then we got talking & he advised me to get to Lynmouth & see if there was any traffic there & said he would take me the mile there – "If I would go round the corner while he brought round the motor-bike where his men couldn't see"!! – So I went round the corner & he appeared – not on a m-b but in a truck which an officer had been going out in (!) & finally decided to take me nine miles on my way to Blackmoor Gate where we had a drink & found a man going to Barnstaple – who was knocking back drinks far too quickly but we decided I must take what I could get. Actually he was maudlin tight by the time we left & *frightfully* funny. He assured me that he had a wife & three kids at home & I need fear nothing – & called me "Old Girl" – & was dreadfully depressed about his work – over & over about the same things, & apparently fell in love with my voice because it was so practical (!) & finally got awfully worried when I wanted to go to a hotel to telephone to the people I was staying with because he thought I was "In Trouble" & offered me to stay with him & his wife & three kids.

The wedding was v. pretty & went off well, & I liked the bridegroom immensely. They have apparently known each other for some time.

I hitched home on Friday – less eventfully, but twice with the same man, who had stopped for business in Taunton & took me a sort of Cook's tour of the worser parts of Bristol, – which is quite shatteringly awful.

When I got home I found that Cardiff had been blitzed on Wednesday night – that we had lost several window-panes, & that half the University College Union just down the road had gone.

Since then life has been uneventful – at last, & I can rest & do my washing & all that.

With v. much love.

Nancy.

Tues

We are still O.K. here after last night's blitz – which was *terrific*. I was in the centre of a lot of it & will write again when we are less busy. N.

D. F. (DOLL) RATCLIFF

These letters were written to Captain C. J. Ratcliff by his wife during 1940. Some letters were written whilst working with the YMCA in France, helping to run a canteen for the British Expeditionary Force before Dunkirk, others whilst working in London during the height of the Battle of Britain.

Y.M.C.A.   1940
c/o Town Major
A.P.O. S15
B.E.F.
Friday April 19th.

My dear Jack,

Well here I am, and as far as I can see at present I have fallen on my feet. We arrived in time for lunch today and found this is a new canteen only opened yesterday. This is a very large town but we are in the nicest part. The canteen is just out of the Cathedral square and we are living in a hotel about 5 minutes walk away by the bridge and overlooking the river. My room gets all the sun and I see all the shipping on the river which I love. I have hot and cold water in my room. Mrs. Meiklejohn is next to me and Miss Baring and Miss Vivian Smith who runs this canteen, also live here. They both seem very nice. Now about the journey. We went on board at Newhaven at 7.45 pm. and had dinner. We then took a private cabin between us as we were told we should not sail for hours, not till Admiralty orders came through. It was a very small French boat and the 1st. class was very empty. We did not sail till 6 this morning and it was *frightfully* rough. I was not sick thanks to my stuff but felt pretty rotten. I did not get up till after 9 just before we got in. Everything was easy for us being in uniform. All the officials hurried us through everywhere. There were some British officers on board, and one, a major attached himself to us and when we landed took us off to breakfast. It was a lovely summer morning and we had breakfast in the sun *outside* a café. I did enjoy it. At 10.45 we went off in a little train like the Toddington one stopping at every village. It is a very pretty country between Dieppe and here, just like Herefordshire, wooded valleys and orchards full of primroses and daffodils. The boulevard outside this hotel which runs along by the river is most gay in the evening with *all* sorts in great numbers. I can not tell you more, and they seem very pleased to see us. Have just got back from Dinner in a café and I am dropping with sleep. I start work at 9.30 tomorrow morning. Very many thanks for your greetings telegram.

Best love
Doll

Y.M.C.A.
c/o Town Major
A.P.O. S15
B.E.F.
April 26th.

My dear Jack

Got your letter two days ago and I expect Mamma showed you the one I wrote her. Since then we have had an air raid. They only dropped impertinent leaflets but the firing from here was terrific for about an hour. It was at 2 am. Of course I looked out of the window and the 'flaming onions' were lovely, just like enormous fireworks. 'L'alèrte' went again last night but nothing happened. No one takes much notice! I am allowed to tell you this as it is over and no damage done.

Thank goodness we have been given permission to censor our own letters, up till now Mc.Arthur the head Y.M. man was doing it and we all hate him and disliked the idea of him reading our letters very much. Mrs. Meiklejohn and I get on very well indeed, we both find Miss Vivian Smith a bit too intense for us but she is very just and considers our comfort. Olivia Baring is no good as a worker, I shall be glad when she goes. Three more should then come out here which will make six women in all which will then give us one day off a week and one shift off each day and two on. Monday and Tuesday appear to be our only slack evenings every other is terrific from 5 to 9.30, it works up to a climax on Saturdays and Sundays.

Of course I can tell you no details at all about our 'clients'!! We had a real heat wave the first four days we were here, quite like summer, now it has been raining on and off for the last three days. The plane trees under my window are almost in full leaf. Daisy Meiklejohn and I climbed to the top of one of the Cathedral towers the other day. The view from the top is wonderful. Give Picot a very big kiss from me, I hope she enjoyed her visit to Southam. Tell her I saw a long haired Griffon here yesterday.

Best love from

Doll

Y.M.C.A.
Ruen Sub Area
B.E.F.
France
May 8th

My dear Jack

Please note my change of address. I was very glad to hear that Jim was safe but I can hardly believe he is in Moscow! How was Dick? I suppose Picot was delighted to see him. The weather has been lovely since Sunday and everyone's feeling more cheerful, especially as we are now working on our proper shifts with a full staff so life has ceased to be a treadmill. The two Harrison girls arrived out last Friday, they turn out to be neices of Mrs. Reynolds at Comdron! Do tell her if you see her in Winchcombe. Friday, Saturday and Sunday evenings will always be rather a nightmare but if one is not tired before one starts one can bear it. Last Saturday we broke all records for canteens in France by taking over 13000 francs in the day! Another thing, the men's side is going to be better run. It has been awful till now and we are continually let down by them over shortages of stores and small change. There was no proper organisation and serveral were talking of leaving because they could not stand the muddle. Then, fortunately, the man who was the trouble was found drunk in a café so he has got the sack and everyone is more cheerful, and no one is leaving. Our side is so beautifully run by Vere Vivian Smith it was sickening having the men let us down like that. I have every Wednesday off now and today I am going to Dieppe by car with a very nice English girl who is married to a French officer here, she helps at the Canteen. It is a lovely morning and I am looking forward to it very much. Monday after 4.30 Daisy Meiklejohn and I took the train up to Bon Secour, which is like Cleeve Hill is to Cheltenham. The view was lovely, one can see the Seine winding away for miles. We walked down as it would be as far as Prestbury and took the train back.

This is a marvellous place for wild lillies of the valley, they grow in all the woods and they sell them in masses in the streets.

Best love from
Doll

Y.M.C.A.
Ruen Sub Area
B.E.F.
May 13th.

My dear Jack,

Everything has altered since I last wrote. I must say I am glad I was here on Friday. The excitement was intense over the Dutch invasion and the French thoroughly worked up.

We started the day with an air raid at 4.15 a.m. before we knew about Holland but the b——s were driven off. Our French gunner forgot himself in the excitement of the moment and fired off a '75' which took off the back side of a house in one of the suburbs!! Since then we have had constant 'alèrtes' but nothing happens, we are sick of the sound of sirens. The whole feeling here is differant now. What a good thing we did not send more troops to Norway. Ever since I came out I had a feeling that something was being expected here. I am very sorry about Chamberlain but it had to be after what Sir Roger Keyes said of the Tronjheim débacle and he made a great mistake in his speech appealing to his *friends*. Of course the socialists jumped on it. One can not consider personal friendships when the whole existance of the nation is hanging in the balance. I think the French are very sorry, they adored Chamberlain. I am so thankful that Dick is safely at home now.

I had a lovely day out last Wednesday with Priccilla Daynell, it was a perfect day and we sat on the beach at Dieppe most of the afternoon. The country was looking lovely, apple orchards in full bloom and beech trees looking lovely. Daisy Meiklejohn went out to some woods near for her day out and came back with masses of wild lillies-of-the-valley, we have all got some in our rooms.

Best love
Doll
I hope you are not worrying about me. I shall be alright

Y.M.C.A.
Ruen Sub Area
B.E.F.
May 16th

My dear Jack,

Please note change of address, and postage to B.E.F. is still 1½d. Many thanks for the photographs which I was very pleased to get, the garden looks lovely. The wonderful weather broke here yesterday with a thunderstorm. I hope you will have heard by now that I am alright, but all letters were held up at the time of the invasion. I am so sorry you feel lonely but it is not all 'fun' here I assure but it is no use thinking about that sort of thing when our whole existance is hanging in the balance as it is now.

Are you going to join the local volunteers for looking out for parachutists? I assure you it is a *real danger*. It is pathetic to see the Belgian refugees pouring in here, the better off ones in cars with their bedding tied on the top and the car bursting with people and things. There is generally a 'poppet' with them too. Tell Picot how lucky she is! The poorer ones who come by train have all had the compartments machine gunned by those devils when they left.

We have constant 'alèrtes' but nothing has happened.

Could you possibly send me £5 in a note of the 10 you owe me now? I am rather short, and send the other £5 the end of the month. If you could add a little to it then I should be most grateful as I am keeping myself entirely. Send it in a registered envelope. You can send up to £10 at a time I think. I really must have £5 now. I do not want anything sent on with a halfpenny stamp. I went to a real old Norman farm with Priccilla the other day, such nice people, her husband was billetted with them at the beginning of the war. Much more simple than our farmers but charming. The house was very like the Worcestershire farms.

How dreadful about Jim. Do tell Monica how I feel for her. Do they think at Southam that it is fun to be a prisoner with the Bosch!!!!

Best love
Doll

Y.M.C.A.
A.P.O. S18
B.E.F.
May 22nd.

My dear Jack,

I am very sorry I can not wire you to say I am alright, but it is quite impossible to send private wires at the moment.

Well, you have seen all about the German advance in the papers so I can tell you that the Y.M.C.A. were evacuated from Ruen yesterday at three hours notice! I was not surprised as the last 48 hours there had been pretty beastly. We all, 8 women and 8 men left with one suitcase a peice in the Y.M.C.A. stores lorry. If it had not been so tragic it would have been very funny! I hope we shall see our other suitcases some day but I don't know. We left at 3 p.m. and drove 200 miles south west with only two short stops, to a sea port where we are now, arrived here 11.30 p.m. very tired indeed but all cheerful. The first ten miles we crawled along in a procession of refugees but after that got on well through lovely country. We thought we might be shipped straight on board for England, however the Y.M.C.A. here need helpers badly so Vere Vivian Smith is staying here and keeping me, Daisy Meiklejohn and Olivia. The other four go home as soon as there is a boat. If they go soon I will get them to wire you when they land. Better let Dick and Lance know I am alright and note my new address. I want money badly, please send the £10 in £5 notes at once. I could not even get to the bank at Ruen before we left, people were fighting to get money out. I have practically nothing. Lance's address is Reed's Cottage, Brockenhurst, Hants. Tell Dick this place is very *windy*, he will know what I mean, so will you! Too tired to write any more now.

Love
Doll

15 Clarges Street
W.1.
Sept. 10th.

My dear Jack,

The last three nights have been absolute hell! We are bombed from about 8.30 p.m. to 5.30 a.m. every night and I have not had more than 2 or 3 hours sleep on either night. I sleep in the afternoon whenever I can but I would just give anything for a quiet night in the country, but having taken on this job I can not back out of it now on account of danger, can I? *Everyone* is tired out, they say the firemen, A.R.P. and ambulance drivers are beyond praise. The hospitals are packed with casualties and the damage all along the river has been very great. An ambulance driver at my club told me the scenes in Battersea and Wandsworth were pitiable the other night, so many children were killed. In the west end there has been a bomb through Harrods, the Natural History Museum. Two quite close to Kathleen's in Chelsea, alot round Victoria and one in Green Park. Added to the crashing of the bombs, the Hyde Park guns make a terrible noise too. I started at Liverpool Street station at 8 a.m. this morning having only slept since 5.30 and up again at 7. I had to walk the last mile as the bus had to stop owing to fire engines and hose pipes across the streets. The Bank of England had been hit but not much damage done. However I now find I can get there by tube which will be much better. They say now that all leave is stopped as an invasion is expected. It really is just my luck for this to start when I get comfortably settled with a job here. However don't worry, I shall no doubt survive it! If only one could sleep. I find that Mrs. Trefor James is working at Liverpool Street, I ran into her today just as I was coming off duty. The shifts are only four hours, so it is easy after what I have been doing. Tell Picot that she must not dream of coming up here, it would never do, much as I should like her companionship. Now the weather has changed and it has been raining today it may make things better.

Best love
Doll

15 Clarges Street
W.1.
Sept. 13th.

My dear Jack,

I am leaving here tomorrow, Saturday and go to live with Vere Vivian Smith at 9 Hill Street, W.1. We both think it will be much better for us. It is really too nerve wracking to be alone at night. The first night I had alone here nearly finished me, the next night I slept at Vere's and the next with George, both of us on camp beds in the dining room! The windows of the house next door to him were smashed that night by the bomb in Rotten Row, we thought our last moment had come!! However, everyone has fresh hope since the big guns have started for although the noise is *terrific* and the houses shake it gives one a feeling of confidence, and the devils did not get through in masses the last two nights. Anything is better than those screaming bombs all round one. One waits absolutely rigid in bed for them to burst. Anyway I have had more sleep the last two nights and feel much better. Poor Kathleen Graham was terribly shaken on Wednesday, she had had three nights out with her ambulance amongst the most awful horrors. The worst shambles was outside the Cinema in the Vauxhall Bridge road on the first night, now of course all Cinemas are closed. To make matters worse they were wading about in the dark in a sea of broken glass from Victoria station roof. These day raids are not so bad, but you have no idea of the disorganisation they cause. If one starts when one is in the tube one has to stay there or if in a bus it very likely stops and one has to take cover where one can. The behaviour of all the people is wonderful. We are very busy at Liverpool Street. I am having tomorrow off, I really feel I need a day's rest. Dick is coming to tea with me this afternoon. I hear that Picot stayed at the Taylors with him!

Best love
Doll

9 Hill Street
W.1.
Sept. 17th.

My dear Jack,

I am coming for the week end on Friday arriving Evesham 7.20, I hope you will be able to meet me. Dick may be coming too. I just want to sleep and sleep over the week end. We have had two very bad nights again. Last night about 10.30 I thought we were hit. Things had got so bad that we were just dossing down for the night in the hall when suddenly there was the sickening swish of a bomb quite close, we flung ourselves down flat, the fat housemaid on the top of me! there was a deafening crash and three of our windows fell in the street. Actually the bomb passed this house and fell in Berkeley square, there is not one window in the whole square left intact! Now we have had our beds put down in the dining room, it is the safest place. Reggie has just been in to see me, he says half the people at home do not realise the horrors we are going through. I will sleep in the spare room, it so much warmer.

I *am* looking forward to getting home.

Best love

Doll

9 Hill Street
W.1.
Oct. 13th.

My dear Jack,

Actually the last two night have been better, the 'all clear' has gone between 8 and 3 a.m. but alot of damage was done this last week and some in the day time too as there was rather a low mist in the mornings. We had a narrow escape on Wednesday evening about 9.15, one of the houses opposite to us was hit, not more than 30 yds. away! For a minute we thought it was us, I shall never forget the look of horror on Vere's face! it quite pulled me together! The whole house swayed and the wall seemed to crack and some plaster fell, but apart from the front door dropping so that we could hardly open it no real damage was done. Anyway I shall never worry again when I hear the swish of a bomb as when they are almost on you, you hear no swish, nothing till the terrific explosion, it is when they are passing you that you hear the swish. One end of Piccadilly was closed for 24 hours for a time bomb just outside the Ritz but they were able to put it out of action and take it away. Lance and Daphne were up for two nights, they complained very much of the noise of the barrage. I shall be home Friday. I am going to enquire about the Black and White buses as it would be far cheaper and more comfortable for me to come to Cheltenham that way than that crowded train. I will write Tuesday when I have been to their office.

Best love

Doll

E. (HETTY) SPEAR

These letters are not dated, but were probably written between 1940 and 1944, whilst living and working as a bus conductress in Bristol, to her husband, a gunner NCO with 208 Battery, 70th Light Anti-Aircraft Regiment, RA.

129 Broadfield Rd.

Monday Morning.

My Dear Gilb

I cabled you a letter on Saturday on my way to work, thinking, that perhaps you were short of cash, or something, I expect you received it the same time as I, yours this morning. Oh! my dear, was ever a letter more welcome, & to know you were alright too, I could have cried with joy.

You say about your parcel. I am so sorry to have made you so dissapointed, but darling you've no Idea what little time I have, life Is'nt like it was when there was'nt such a thing as a Blitz, you see we have such a lot to do to get ready, the shelter has to be prepared every day whether they come or not, you never know what's going to happen. we pack our clothes each night as a ritual, so many people have woke to find themselves with nothing but what they've been wearing. & now that the gas scare has started there is all that too, I mean food & water & first aid & umpteen things I can tell you my dear, with my job, & the house to keep straight, its a big thing. however, I am sending this with the watch & helmet, so you really will get it as soon as the GPO. thinks fit, I hope you wont think the helmet small, but mother said it's got to be like that to fit & of course it stretches a lot. by the way, are you dissapointed that I hav'nt sent a food parcel lately. you see darling I thought the money might be better for you, & Its so difficult to get anything to make cakes, & cheese is almost rationed, besides with the money you can get what you like when you like. anyhow if you particularly want anything made, do say so & Ill try very hard to do it.

I went with Pauline to Winford to see Albert yesterday. I quite enjoyed a day out, if It had'nt been such an unhappy errand. We found him very much the same. but It's so terribly brave, he even tried to hum a tune once or twice. & he must be bearing frightful pain. I do think though, that now he's lasted this long. he'll pull through.

Im very glad you heard from your Mum, & Dorothy it's nice I know to get letters, when you're away from home. You'll know I spoke to you about Pauline being evacuated, well I'm sorry to say she cant go. a child must be five on February 1st. Im so frightened of this gas business. I did think that if she was away with the school, they would be so much better if that came, I mean people trained for that sort of thing is much more proficient with kiddies than a Mother. of course Sheila is alright, but I think Mais is afraid of parting the two, still we're going to talk it over with George tonight, so we shall be able to decide.

Oh! how wonderful of you to remember the 12th. its very sweet of you to say you will send me something. but I don't know how you can without cash. besides there is'nt anything I want (only you) unless you could see a little cross for my neck, but not unless you can get one for a couple of bob.

I was terribly bucked to read of your promotion, how wonderful. You must have worked very hard, it made me very very happy though & proud of you. I always knew there was a lot more in you than most people think. Keep it up Sweetheart. Well I really must stop now because I have to go to work soon. So cheerio once more & do please try to come home if you can. all my love & thoughts, my dearest & God keep you safe.

Mummy & Pauline XXX

Socks following

My Dear Gilb

This is just to let you know that we are all alive *thank God*. I know you will have heard of what happened here Sunday night, & will be wondering all sorts of things, I know it was only the Good God that gave me my life to get back to Mum & Pauline. I was on a St. Annes Bus when it started & coming along the cut a big garage was struck by an H.E. just as our bus reached it, you can imagine what the bus was like afterwards, I was taken to the BGH & kept there until 6 a.m. next morning only suffering from shock, but my only fear was, how can I get home, when the casualties were brought in & I heard them say Melvin Square I nearly

267

went mad. I walked around the stretchers to see if my own was there but could see no-one. however when I was allowed to go home, I found Mum & Pauline huddled in the food cuboard, & Mum as near death as ever she'll be, with fright & cold the gas, light, (some water in places gone), however I quickly made a fire & somehow after a hot cup of tea got her into bed. what hurt me more than any thing was not a soul either side looked to see if she was alright, anyhow George has made us come round here & again last night & tonight we have had to get in the shelter.

[Extant MS ends.]

Saturday
129 Broadfield

My Dear Gilb

once again a few lines to you in answer to yours, well my darling *I am so glad* to know you are feeling A1, thats the main thing if you are fit, you are able to battle with things so much easier. Oh darling Ive such a lot to tell you, but I just feel too sick at heart to start. anyhow, I hav'nt started work, – dont know if I shall ever go again, you know we are still here, & Mais is at work, well I look after every body all day, so that knocks my going back into bits, I buy all our own food & pay my own rent, the only thing I save is coal, as we have no gas or light to buy (there not being any) but you dont want me to tell you what living here means. (you know), Mais wont give up her job & I cant leave Mother, so there you are. anyhow I feel pretty hopeless at the moment.

We had another Blitz here on Tuesday, & another last night, so with the first Sunday as well, you can imagine what Bristol is like. Last night they got the Power Station, & G.P.O. you can tell what havoc that caused without all the other terrible things. Oh my dear you've no Idea how awful it is, to lie hours listening to the screaming bombs & Guns, & houses collapsing & burning, its just Hell, Pauline was awake last night through it all, I thought I should go crazy, & God above how I longed for you, you know, Gilb without your own man you feel sort of lost, I dont mind dying but I do want to be with you, it would'nt matter much would it if we were together, Bristol is full of R.E.s pulling down the buildings that are just hanging & helping generally. they are blowing up Victoria St & the main places, because its all so dangerous as it is. Oh! Georgie Brewers is gone, Robinsons, Mardens, Rowland & Adams, & numerous others I cant mention. I dont know if we shall get another but if we do there wont be much to hurt, only people.

I have not had any compen yet apparently. now its sick pay I get & when I'll get that I dont know, you know what a lot of red tape there is to it.

No I havnt heard anything any good from your letter to the Company only that they could do nothing & you could if you wished refer it to your Company Officer. but I dont think I should bother if I were you.

Mother thought if Mais gave me the Money she gave Vi Barrett for looking after Sheila, as I have had her all this time, & with my Sick Pay, I could manage alright, but you know what Mais is for paying. She just opens her purse & shuts it again, & I dont feel Im playing the game by you, to sit down & do nothing, when I could be earning your wages. at the moment I'm compelled to, I really do feel ill, but I know its the fact that people are taking advantage of me, & they know I hav'nt got you. that pulls me back from getting well.

I should have answered your letter before, but I've been hoping that I could get another parcel made up for you, but I'll just send these cigs & try the Parcel in a day or two, & perhaps its just as well if you are being moved. You dont say much about your food. is it any better, or is it that you are getting used to it.

You say you've had a nasty tooth out, well, I know its unpleasant, but its just as well if it was a bad un. Ive had toothache on & off, Im afraid when mine start coming out it will mean the lot.

I expect you enjoy your games of football, I heard a Soldier say this week that one wants to come to Bristol to realise there's a War on, & Im sure its true.

Young Bill Green is *very ill* his arms are full of holes, that cant be stitched because they found after the first try, that the flesh broke away its not like a straight cut. So God knows if he'll get over it, poor kid. The Doctors say they are doing all thats possible, so it does'nt sound too good.

I will send your vest on as soon as I can get something to go inside, so let me have your new address quickly if you have moved.

Freemans have asked for particulars of Mrs. Lethbridge will you tell me who she is, when you write.

Thank you darling for saying such lovely things to me in your letter, its such a blessed feeling to know that you love me like you do. would you have been terribly shocked to have found me in Cornwall last week. I was so terribly frightened after Tuesdays blitz that I almost packed a case & took Pauline to the Station. It was only the fact that you might think me a nuisance that stopped me. The Soldier at the end of the Rd was talking to me yesterday, & I was telling him about you, & his advice was get right out of it if you have a chance, Ive said before I dont care about me, but when Pauline clings to me terrified I do so wish there was somewhere to run away. I know Darling, God is taking care of us, & I do pray so hard for *Courage* but sometimes I get so hopeless & wonder when it will end, & will I see you again, Oh! there I go again being a misery, & I dont want to make you unhappy. It must be bad enough for you to be there, & know all this is going on, & not be able to get near us. perhaps something will happen to change all this, well my sweetheart I wont say any more now, only I love you terribly & God bless you & lets meet again Pauline & Sheila are Shrieking outside Roll out the Barrel. Oh! I hav'nt told you the News. we had a nose cap of a shell through our own roof on Tuesday, it fell right where you sleep & split your table in two. I was thankfull it didnt go through the living room; you shall see it when you come home Im saving it as a Momento (what a weight).

Well darling cheerio once more & God bless you always.

heaps of love

Hetty
Pauline
XXX

LUCIA LAWSON

These letters were written to her family during service in the ATS (Auxiliary Territorial Service). She eventually became a Company Sergeant Major and went to Paris in 1944 to work in the public relations office of the Allied Expeditionary Force.

W/219676 Private Lawson L,   1942
No 4 Platoon A Coy,
No 7 A.T.S. Training Centre,
11.9.42   Guildford,
Surrey.

Darling Mummy,

Well, well, well!! here is my history up to date. I arrived at Waterloo at 9.45 having never expected to get a taxi & having got one very easily. (Before I go on I must tell you that my writing will be awful because I am writing lying on my bed with a very stiff arm from inoculation) we then waited for three quarters of an hour before anything happened, but that time was not wasted as I found a friend, a sweet girl who talks the same language & is married and her husband missing in Singapore, I take my hat off to her, as she is 29, & that is hardly the age to start careering round a barrack square. Eventually a Sergeant arrived checked us in & moved us in some sort of order onto the platform where we wasted another twenty minutes & then got into a train. Brenda & I sticking together of course. We arrived at Guildford at 12.15 p.m. & were piled into lorries many too many of us & we sat on our cases on the floor. We drove about two miles & were let into a high barbed wire surround with sentries at every gate! we then got checked in *again* & were given a mug, knife, fork & spoon. From there we were marched to lunch, we had roast beef, yorkshire pud, veg, stewed pears & custard. The dining room is enormous & holds our entire company & our N.C.Os. We then rose & marched (in future the abbreviation of marched is M. because it seems to be the only [way] we move about) back to our luggage; and then M

271

to medical inspection. Nits etc! very jolly, several of the noble members of my platoon owned the little beasts! we then M to collect luggage, got same & M to our hut, which we just managed to reach as it was about a mile away. Brenda & I got beds next door – they are quite nice huts holding 24 of us. We left our luggage & went to the QM's stores where we were entirely fitted out & I look AWFUL!! but alas it is not because the clothes don't fit because they fit beautifully. We then M to tea & *walked* back, from thence we M to the Gym & gave in our ration books etc *walked* back to the hut & we were finished officially for the day. Brenda & I went out to the N.A.A.F.I. & bought some boot polish etc & then went back to bed, where I had a bath in pitch blackness as I couldn't find a light & went to bed lights out at 10.15 & I cried myself to sleep purely from tiredness & self pity!

Woke up in the morning at 6 a.m. having slept *very* badly and got up feeling considerably better. We barracked our beds, visited ablutions to wash & swept & garnished our hut & went to breakfast at 7.30 a.m. M back to hut collected a blanket & went to various short talks by the C.O. a charming person called Mrs. Gill. We went to the cinema! a film made to encourage us to do Ack-ack! but didn't anyway where I'm concerned. We then had half an hour's break & a cup of tea in the N.A.A.F.I. & went to be inoculated where everybody passed out like flies except Brenda and self & about 100! others. We then had lunch & now have the rest of the week-end off but of course C-B. & so I can't telephone.

The girls on the whole are O.K. but there are a few shocking types which no amount of mixing with, could possibly win them over to liking us.

Now here are the things I want *please*. A pair of pyjamas, preferably a warmish pair but not the very thick ones as we weren't issued with any. Some cleaning rags *important* & a duster. Could you possibly send them in a large box even if they do rattle as I must send back some things. This is urgent & so could you send them off quick. I will write again tomorrow & let you have some more news.

Lots of love to Daddy & Hugh & tell Daddy that as far as I can see promotion is non-existent & I shall be a Private for the rest of my natural life!

Love & kisses
Lucia

W/219676 Private Lawson L,
No 4 Platoon A Coy,
No 7 A.T.S. Training Centre,
Guildford,
Surrey.

Sept. 14th

Darling Mummy,

I'm sorry I didn't write yesterday but I've never known anything like the cleaning that goes on buttons, shoes, & goodness knows what else. I am beginning to enjoy it though, if only it wasn't for three or four members of our platoon who are doing their best to make life hell for us, the trouble is there are three of us who are quite good at drill & try pretty hard & on the whole of course we are keen to get on, but those few make the most filthy remarks & use the worst language I've ever heard, about us, & really it isn't much fun, especially as you know I hate having nasty things said about me. It isn't because we are uppish, we do try our hardest to mix with them but it simply doesn't work. The others we get on with very well under the circumstances & are really quite sweet. But those four are terrible almost unbearable, I suppose it has got to be put up with & I *suppose* a month isn't long! What I am dreading is becoming an N.C.O. & staying as such for the rest of my natural days, but I don't expect at the present rate of going I shall ever reach that exalted rank.

We are a bit fed up because we haven't had our pay books yet & so haven't been able to get out of the camp but we shall tomorrow & so I will try & ring you up.

I'm afraid there isn't nearly as much time for writing letters as I thought, owing to this awful spit & polish, but we find time in the evenings all right at the moment.

Are you sending my sweet ration card on, because I must have it soon as Sergeant has asked for it. We have been very lucky with our N.C.Os & they are all strict but very sweet & human, one especially who is a canadian & was six months in the star demonstration platoon touring the country.

Lights out are just going & so I must stop, but I will try & ring you up tomorrow.

Lots of love & kisses
Lucia

W/219676 Private Lawson L,
No 4 Platoon, A. Coy,
No 7 A.T.S.T.C.
Guildford,
Surrey.

Darling Mummy,

Here I am back at work again after a very brief visit into civilian life, and I did hate them all!! Ronnie was very well & we had great fun, but lunch at Claridges in uniform was a little hard, I tried telling myself how much superior I was to all the be-foxed, be-minked, be-scented & altogether pretty be-stinking & I think it worked. I saw quite a lot of the "good time" girls & did some wonderful propaganda for the A.T.S.

Life here now is really very good & even if we do have occasional rows. Last night I came back in the train with Ann & five moderately drunk Canadians & one very drunk sailor who gave a short but to the point speech on Lady Astor!

I am just off to a dance at Sloughton Barracks which belongs to the Queens with some of the East (as opposed to the west) end of our barrack room & I've no idea what it will be like, but we are all in cracking form having been on a route march in the pouring rain & sung all the way. This morning I got down to winning the war by scrubbing the floor of the cookhouse!

See you in about a fortnight.

Lots of love & XXX
Lucia

L/Cpl Lawson W/219676
A. Coy, No 3 Platoon
No 7 A.T.S.T.C.

Darling Mummy,

Oh what work! I've never worked so hard in my life, & I trust never quite so hard again. My whole time is spent doubling from one place to another in search of a recruit, or else marching the platoon backwards & forwards from lectures or P.T. This evening is the first evening I've had a moment in which to write at all! I answer inumerable questions to which I've only just learnt the answer myself. But it is the *greatest* fun in the world. The people are sweet I have to work with, we giggle hopelessly & great deal of the time, & I have found a real friend in the shape of my fellow L/Cpl Philippa Sawers. Until yesterday we were sleeping in a barrack room, but we have now been kicked out (not from lack of competence but lack of beds) into an N.C.O's bunk, which is a small but cosy box for two people & Philippa & I are in it together, which is I fear too good to last, but I have hopes that it will see us out the intake & then we go on Cadre.

I see I have put no paragraphs at all in this letter but I haven't got time to! we are just off to see a film in the lower gym then to a party in the Corporal's bar at N.A.A.F.I. tomorrow night we go to a dance at the neighbouring barracks.

Tell Daddy that there is a girl here on this intake but not in my platoon who is writing her story of training in the A.T.S. for the Daily Mirror, I think it ought to be checked up on because I'm not sure that all the girl says is true! her name is Sykes & she is being photographed at work which I feel sure she isn't doing but may be that is being difficult.

Must fly to the film, will ring you up Sunday if I can get a pass to London, they are all being stopped.

Love & kisses

Lucia

W/219676 L/Cpl Lawson,   1943

A. Coy,

No 7 A.T.S.T.C.

Guildford

January 13th 1943

Darling Mummy,

Bad news I fear – I have failed my board which seems a pity. I suppose they don't think I'm the right type to make an officer! I didn't really want a commission but I must admit I feel a bit of a failure. Still having seen the majority of women who are made officers, I'm not at all sure that it isn't a compliment to have been turned down! What will happen to me now I have no idea, I am thinking of chucking up the whole issue, have my papers destroyed & be posted as an ordinary A.T. The other alternative is to stay on here, & hope for promotion which is doubtful. They asked the damn silliest questions at the board, what I had done before the war, what since, & did I want a commission which was ridiculous because if I didn't I shouldn't have been there. They wavered a good deal before they decided, because you usually go in once & they ask you a few questions & then tell you to wait outside until they have decided, well they called me back three times questioning & re-questioning before they eventually told me I was no good. Mrs Gilmour the president of the board said I was to develop my powers of leadership! well how can I in this racket when all I do is to just obey the order of my Sgt or Cpl, I'm not even allowed to think for myself, if I do I'm told not to interfere in something which is not my job. As to leadership – well I know without blowing my own trumpet that my girls would follow me anywhere even if I was a private. I think Anne will have to get me [a] job, because I joined the A.T.S. to help win the war maybe only a day sooner but sooner anyway & bring Bill back to Anne & pray God David back to me, well I'm not doing that, I'm not helping to end the war I'm just waiting for it to end – dressed up in a uniform & masquerading as a soldier. If I can't fight physically at least I can to some small degree mentally, I *can't* think here I'm not allowed to, someone does it for me, & soon I shall loose the power to do so. Do you think someone can find me a real job, I'm sure Anne could, & I must do something more useful, but please not in Northumberland or else I would go mental if I couldn't get home to you & let off steam. Which is what I fear this is but I do mean it.

Yesterday anyway was a nice day off in London, & I got hold of Tim Atkinson & we had dinner together & saw a film.

While I remember, Mummy Darling, I don't think you ever paid for my bridesmaid dress. I gave you the bill & no doubt you put it in [a] ''funny place''!

I enclose the photographs which I don't think are too bad considering. I should like what I have put on the card & I will pay you for them.

Tell Anne that I think the only thing for me to do is to see her, but I don't know how because I am sure she is too busy to get away, & I can't get to her, but what I want is for her to find me any sort of job not too far removed from civilisation.

My love to Hughie & May,

Love & kisses

Lucia

P.S. I thought I had time to write Daddy today but I haven't please tell him the news gently because I'm afraid I've been rather a disappointment to him, & it was only for him.

W/219676 Sgt Lawson
A.T.S. Signals
Coles Dane Camp,
Harrietsham
Nr Maidstone
Kent.

May 31st '43.

Darling Mummy,

Never in "all my life" did I believe there could be a place so isolated as this is. It is ten miles from a town, two miles from a village half the size of Kintbury & on the top of a hill in a wood. Campaigning is not in it, I feel like an explorer of far distant climes!! We live in half built nissen huts, with outdoor sanitation & work places. I must be getting terribly tough though because it is far worse than Guildford & I don't somehow mind very much.

I'm sorry I haven't written before but I am senior N.C.O in charge of 40 girls except for one officer, & so I have been working terribly hard & have never been so tired in my life.

I can't say when at the moment I shall get home, but I hope soon at least before I get back to being a cave woman!

Please can you send me my dark glasses & any hay fever stuff because this place is having an awful effect on me & do write so as I know there are still human beings in this universe!

Will write again soon,
Love & kisses
Lucia

Public Relations Division,
SHAEF.,
No.1 A.P.D.C. London W.1.

13.9.44

1944

Mummy darling,

Here is a sort of diary of events up to the present time, it is not very well written, but it will give you an idea of what has been happening to me, and I am going to try and keep it up. So will you please guard them as I have no other copies, and one day in the dim and distant future of peace, I may get around to writing a book – always allowing for the fact that I am capable – show it to Daddy and anyone else who it may interest but don't broadcast it, as I shall be arrested and right at the moment that wouldn't suit as I am enjoying myself.

The Brig. is taking this back with him, and so it should reach you fairly soon. Also I have sent a little something else by devious routes, and I hope it will get to you sometime soon.

No time to write anymore now I will try and write you a long letter tonight before I go to bed.

Love and kisses,

Lucia

Sept. 11th. Left Hendon Airport at 9.30 on a Dacota named Hayride. Perfect weather, England looked wonderful, vast expanses of corn and green fields. Route took us via Guildford, Chichester and left U.K. east of Portsmouth. Channel crossing took about half an hour. We watched our journey over France closely, and noticed the terrific bombing that it had taken, craters in batches of anything from 10 to 100, chiefly on woods and railways. Arrived ORLY airfield at 11.20. Airfield terribly broken up, skeletons of hangers, and runways smashed to bits. Left airfield with all baggage by commandeered taxi. Paris hung with flags and huge posters welcoming the Allies. People on the streets in hundreds, bicycles predominating, no cars at all, except military transportation and old cars staped [stamped?] with F.F.I. all over them. Reached the Hotel Scribe and with great difficulty we managed to get all the baggage up to the Brigadier's suite. Taken down to the Officers and Correspondents Mess by Col. Dupuy, and had very good lunch with one of the correspondents who I knew from London. After lunch I succeeded in getting a room from a W.A.C. Captain on the Information Desk number 401. Got my baggage up to it with the help of Sgt. McDonald, who I should mention here had been of the greatest assistance and comfort for the whole journey. Unpacked in a lovely room with a balcony overlooking the interior courtyard of the Hotel, a huge bathroom, but *no* hot water. Went down to what was destined to be our office for the next few days, a wonderful room with big french windows overlooking the Boulevard des Capucins – sun streaming in, people hurrying past in the street with lovely colourful clothes, and huge smiles all over their faces, and in between these masses of french the G.I.s of the U.S. Army in steel helmets and boots covered with the dust of France. At 17.50 the Brigadier came in, and told me to go out and look for a bottle of Graves – I walked up the Boulevard amidst a battery of the most penetrating stares that I have ever had to encounter, I think that the people of France had never seen a woman in Uniform much less one in the A.T.S., the women especially seemed to find me somewhat of an oddity, and several of them who I asked directions from, enquired what I was and why! Mac and I walked the length of the Boulevard des Capucins to the Place des Etoiles and turned into the Rue St. Denis where I was informed there was a shop where I could buy some Graves, but we found the place shut, and so returned stopping at a cafe on the main Boulevard where I had my first drink in France – iced Cassis, and pretty good at that. Found on returning to the Hotel that I was so tired I could willingly have laid down and slept right there in the hall, but reported to the Brig. and he invited me to have dinner with him in his suite. We had a cocktail made of gin from London and a bottle of Graves obtained from the Hotel (which is still staffed by the French and well staffed at that hundreds of maids and porters etc.) and then dinner from American rations, with a bottle of Champagne. Went up to bed at about 20.30, undressed and lay on my bed for a few seconds to gain strength to go and wash, and fell fast asleep waking up rather cold at 23.00, finished my "toilet" and got to bed. Slept wonderfully and woke up at 0.7.30 to start my first whole day in one of the loveliest towns in the world PARIS.

Sept. 12th. Had breakfast in the Mess, but was not hungry and so just had a cup of coffee and a glass of fruit juice. Reported to the office at 09.00 and found as I expected that there was nothing to do. Spend most of the morning gazing out of the window, lovely day with a brilliant sun streaming in through the window. Went out to the A.P.O. at about 12.00 to post a couple of letters, still flabbergasted at the way we are stared at, passing three British soldiers the first I had seen in Paris, they seemed delighted to see me, and I stopped to talk to them for a few minutes, they had been over here some little while and were delighted to see an A.T.S. who they said was the first in Paris (have discovered that that is so – quite a distinction) in spite of this they remarked "well, now the A.T.S. are here, we can go to the Front!!!" Got back to the Hotel and went down to lunch, eat sausages, tomatoes and mixed salad all out of tins, should mention here that all our food comes out of tins, except the extraordinary sight of real live WHITE bread which we get all the time. Went up to the office, and typed a few letters and cables and tried to put a phone call through for the Brig. found this to be absolutely hopeless as all lines are delayed for a minimum of three hours! the Brig. went off to Versailles with Col. Chappell, and so I went down to see Col. Redding who I knew well from M.o.I. days, and had not seen for about three months. He was overjoyed – it really is wonderful to be welcomed with open arms wherever you go – and immediately produced a bottle of Cointreau which I liked strange to say. Sat and talked over old times and new ones for about half an hour, during the conversation it emerged that he was leaving for England the next day and would be delighted to take back anything I wanted to send. Left him and went out to do a little very important shopping, bought two lots of scent from a shop on the Boulevard des Capucins, one for myself and one for Col. Chappell to take back to Rhoda. Went on down to the Rue de la Paix to Pacquin and bought a bottle of Goya for Col. Redding to take back to Mummy, also a picture postcard from a little man on the street to send to mummy by the same route to remind her that Paris is FREE again. Returned to the Hotel and packed the scent up and took it down to Col. Redding, found them having their afternoon bottle of Champagne which I was invited to partake in. It occured to me at this point that really we are fighting the strangest war! gave Col. Redding the scent and he promised to take it back and give it to Ginny for onward transmission. Checked back to the office, found nothing to do and so hung around for a while during which time the Brig. came in, and told me to go. Went out for a walk for a little while, and then came in to dinner, which I had with Ned Buddy one of the newsreel men. He offered during the course of dinner to drive me on a tour round Paris, which I jumped at. We had a lovely drive round Paris – Arc de Triomphe, Place des Invalides etc. etc. Got back to the Hotel at 20.15 and went up to bed. With great courage I partook of a cold bath, and crawled into bed tired but on the happy.

Supreme Headquarters
ALLIED EXPEDITIONARY FORCE
Public Relations Division
F.P.O. C/o B.L.A.

15th November, 1944

Darling Mummy,

I think it is really your turn to write but I know you are very busy and my office is empty at the moment, Ginny is writing to her Mother, it is about seven days since I last wrote to you, all of which sum up the fact that I should write to you. So here we are KINCAID and LAWSON both writing to their MUMS.

I got the sheets safely, but probably by now you have heard that from Daddy as I sent a letter back to him via one of our officers going back. I have been in bed for a half day with a sort of bilious attack which everyone has had here, I think caused either by the bread or the water

I don't know which, anyway a couple of the girls have gone to the hospital, but I have now almost completely recovered.

My typewriter is not feeling very healthy though it has just lost its ashe and so I will have to write them in afterwards. As long as nothing else drops off it is all right and I can manage, but in this town anything is liable to happen and I wouldn't be a bit surprised if the whole thing threw itself into the Opera House across the way – come to think of it it is pretty musical – well anyway it makes a lot of noise.

Saturday we all had great fun especially me. At 10.30 the Brigadier left in his car to go up to his stand in the Champs Elysees and he took me along riding in front with the driver. We dropped him at the bottom of the Avenue George V, and he told us to wait – well I didn't think this was good enough, and so I said to the driver, I think we could get a little nearer if we tried. And so with my finger on the horn, and she with her foot on the accelerator, flying Brigadier's stars and plastered all over with notices saying M. Churchill en France – Service de Presse – Laissez Passer etc. etc. we proceeded rapidly in the direction of the Arc de triomphe, and were stopped about fifteen times whereupon I in my best french gave the old "Generals orders" routine, saying "Monsieur le General doit aller a l'Arc" and quickly drove on, before they had time to see that I had no General in the car. We eventually arrived up by the Arc and parked the car amongst all those belonging to the Powers that be and all carrying at least four stars each, and our one star looked a little meagre, but anyway we had made it, and what did we care. We really had a grandstand view, probably better than the Brigadier. I saw everyone arrive and heard the bands playing the National anthems, and saluted during the one minutes silence while they played the last post. I am going to try in my spare time to write a really short description of it, and when I do I will sent it to you.

Have at last succeeded in finding a typewriter with an h it took a bit of doing and entailed climbing from the bottom of the building to the top crying my wares. All I got from them was "you're British what do you want an h for". I took a very dim view.

I have been invited to tea with Mde. Debray on Sunday week, and I hope that I will be able to get away in time to go. I have also been having a little trouble with a woman who insists that I am a nice English girl and that I can teacher her daughter English, I have tried to persuade her otherwise, but so far without success, and so I look like getting tangled up with her, if I thought she was nice I wouldn't mind, but I don't think she is and yet I don't want to be rude to her.

I meant to tell you that on Saturday afternoon, we all went to the

Opera House, where there was a band concert, and it really was lovely. The bands of the Royal Artillery, the U.S. Army and the Garde Republique played, although it was a little long and rather cold I enjoyed it. Also on Friday evening they floodlit the Arc de Triomphe and had a band playing up there, with everyone singing tipperary, Le Madelon, Over there, Keep the home fires burning and so on and so forth, it was a very moving spectacle, in the cold starlit night with the huge floodlights and the people singing and crying all at the same time – you would have loved it.

On Sunday we watched the French parading all day, the funny thing was they seemed to have got started on parades and they couldn't stop, I don't think there can have been a single man or woman over the Armistice week end who had not taken part in some parade or other. As a matter of fact I didn't get up until about eleven o'clock as we had hot coffee and hot buttered toast in bed for breakfast all made on my little boilly pot. Pretty good, don't you think. In the afternoon Ginny and I were going to the races, but it was so cold and I had a cold that we decided not to go, and so we went to the cinema instead, we saw Lady in the Dark.

I don't think that there is anymore news for now, and so I will write again when some more has happened, anyway I will do my best to remain a better correspondent than the rest of your family.

Bless you Mummy darling and take care of yourself and give my love to Mrs. B and the Doc.

Love and kisses,
Lucia

1945   Supreme Headquarters
ALLIED EXPEDITIONARY FORCE
Public Relations Division

27th March, 1945

Darling Mummy,

This is the first moment I have had in which to write to you since I got back. As you can well imagine with the war going as it is we have been somewhat busy.

I had a lovely flight back, and when I got into the waiting room at Bovingdon who should walk in for a cup of coffee but the two boys who flew me over on Saturday, I went over and spoke to them, and found that completely by accident they were piloting my flight back to France. I went up forward again, and really had a wonderful last look at England for a while, you have no idea how beautifully green and tidy it looked, in contrast to France that looked brown and messy. Everybody seemed pleased to see me back for some unknown reason, and I had dinner with Ginny then went home and unpacked my orchids, which have travelled wonderfully. They are now sitting on my desk, and cause a terrific sensation. The "on dit" now, is that you can only enter the Kincaid–Lawson office if you bring orchids, or carnations as a poor second!!

I went out to the races at Auteuil on Sunday and with the help of some pretty good tips, won myself 400 francs. We are all going out on Easter afternoon as it is a big day out there.

The news is wonderful of course, and the end of the war seems pretty near. After so many years of saying "when the war is over" it seems almost unbelievable and somehow I have a feeling of anti-climax, I don't know how I expected it to end, but I don't think like this, and already I am scared – what's going to happen afterwards, what is it like when there isn't a war, what is going to happen to us in the A.T.S., where will I be sent to, what will I do when I don't have to get up in the morning, don't have to dress the way I'm told, all these questions to which I can find no answer, and questions which people like me are asking all over the world? it's strange to feel lost when I know I have a home to go to, but I can't just sit at home and do nothing at least not after about a month of it, I suppose I could take up some good "works", or travel but neither of them appeal to me, I could get married, but I suppose I'd better find someone I love before I do that.

As to my future in the army before I am demobilised, I have a feeling I would like to go to Washington, and work with BIS there, I seem to get on with Americans and the job would [be] somewhat like what I am doing here, Col. Scott-Bailey is going, and I wouldn't mind being his P.A., but I hate to leave the Brigadier, but I have no desire to be Army of Occupation.

This is an awful letter but I will write again within the next few days this was just really a note to let you know that I arrived safely and am back "on the job".

Darling Mummy, take care of yourself,

Lucia

BEATRICE CARTER

Beatrice Carter's husband was a Bombardier with the 152nd Field Regiment, RA, in North Africa. She was living at Benthill, Manchester.

30/3/43

My Darling Les,

Isnt the news wonderful this week from your side, I feel quite excited & I hope you will all be able to move the Jerry out of Africa neck & crop very shortly, I know it will be a hard struggle but I hope, trust & pray you will be alright, & the whole campaign can be done with as little loss as possible. According to the news, Berlin is certainly getting the works & everywhere else, I only hope it will finish the war quicker, & if it will, I say give it them heavier than ever, because the suffering, misery & loneliness they have caused, besides other things is enormous & they deserve everything that is coming to them, the only thing is the innocent have to suffer with the guilty but as far as I can see, the innocent must be a very small minority, otherwise there would have been a big rising by now.

I told you yesterday that I had completely finished decorating the back bedroom & how nice it looks & so the next job this week is the living room, & so I will let you know how I progress with it, but I think it will look nice, well, one thing, it will be clean, & it certainly has got very grubby looking.

I have practically finished everything for the new arrival now & by the time I have finished all the Spring cleaning, it won't be too far off, I am feeling a bit better this week, although yesterday I felt tired & sickly, but it is just the time & one cannot avoid all these things, but it is certainly a restless little thing. I told you about writing for Freda's Pram, & of hearing she isnt selling it now, perhaps she needs it eh Leslie, anyway don't worry I will manage to get hold of one, I am still waiting to hear if Edna Dodds is for sale.

Well darling enough of all that, how are you faring & looking, are you getting brown & healthy looking & is your hair coming off or is it just the same & is the weather hot there now, because the last letter I had, you said if the weather kept on you would be issued with tropical kit, anyway I hope that business out there will soon be finished & you will be able to look around you as I think it must be worth seeing the sights around those spots. Colin is a lovely little boy now, & for Easter I shall take him to have his photo taken in his new Coat & Beret, that Daddy bought, so that you will have a good idea how he has grown, I only hope he smiles, as his dimples are more pronounced than ever, he is really to nice looking & dainty for a boy, but I expect he will alter eh Les & get like all the rest of the lads. Cheerio now darling, I will write you tomorrow. Yours ever. Beatrice & Colin.

NANCY ISOBEL BUCHANAN

Captain Peter Buchanan served in the 6th Grenadier Guards (22nd Guards Brigade) in North Africa and Italy between March 1943 and June 1944. These letters were written to him by his mother, who was living in Wing, Leighton Buzzard.

1943
A.C. Easter Sunday Letter No 7.
April 25. 1943

My dearest Peter. We've had this week Letter No.2. from you "at Sea" – & a lovely letter it was too – Also received this week J.D's letter. "A.L.C." enclosed, *and* a telegram which read "Peter very well" Buchanan – We presume this to be from Uncle Douglas? & wonder if you have been at his home, or only telephoned, or what. No date on it of course, like your letter. How fussy everyone is! really I can never be scolded for fussing again – but perhaps its a different sort of fussing. To return to your letter. That you have become a good sailor was indeed good news – & lovely weather, of the Pink Gin kind! About getting the dog on board in a Mail Bag! & Audrey B-N. being on board too. All *most* interesting. Also full marks for telling me how long you were laid up, with flu – & your temp – & how you were treated, (a dose, that made me smile) & that you were quite all right again. And I hope you are now "in the Pink" after pink gins etc – Very good getting a larger cabin, only two of you – & I can see you enjoying being unable to do anything more than a little PT each day. It will be very different when you join the Br. Glad the food was so good – *Very* sorry the beard had to come off! I expect it was a lovely golden one? Well I think thats all about your letter. It was lovely getting one at last. Re J.D's letter. On page 2 you will see re the bit about Americans – These 2 words were censored by the blue pencil! *Most* disappointing. Long to know what the 2 words were! Interesting his meeting the Sergent of Exmouth days, you remember him – We are now sending out J.D. a Country Life

286

each week. Is there anything you would like?

Now for home news. Father is losing weight! under 16 stone, & so am I! we have been putting our weights in the book – Am I right in saying that you were 11 stone when you last weighed? *Please let me know this,* then I can book it as March 1943 – Father has had a quiet Easter. HG have had a holiday! and the Church Bells can now be rung, so its been quite like old days, very nice to hear – Mary, who has leave till next Wed – is quite O.K. – & very much impressed at Father's handyness! Quite Mother's little Right Hand Man! Makes the toast, & even sometimes the tea – Takes up the Hot Water Bottles, blackout etc! Really he is coming on fast – The latest local news is that Lady Henry got stuck in a lift alone *a whole hour,* in a Block of flats in London – We have enjoyed that a lot!

No special news of Yvonne. She turns out for the Home G with the van, & salutes Morton! Father always gets out of driving with her, & either I or Mary or someone takes him. Mary & Father have weeded all the thistles on the lawn tennis court – Archer has managed to mow lawn & paths – & the lower lawn is ploughed but not very successfully – still we hope to grow greens on it. I tether the pony about the garden, & 3 hutches keep Rose garden & odd bits down – I am selling bluebells now – & hope to do well with all sorts of flowers later. The field of wheat below Ascott is a glorious green.

I wonder if you will get more details of the attack in which Arthur was killed – We so far have had only the one letter from Gordon. Was he A's C. Coy? And the letter from Gordon tells us *so* little. We hope you may be able to find out more from some of the men. We still hope May will write, or some one from his Coy. I suppose accounts are always confused on such an occasion – but surely someone could tell us more. And about his things, personal – will you find out about this –? Its sad you 3 won't meet in N.A., but it was not to be. I am hoping you & J.D. will. In J.D's letter enclosed, he'd not heard the sad news – & I feel so sorry that you may be away from all family (unless Uncle Douglas told you) & you too will be wanting to know all about it, just as we do – 14 officers missing seems so enormous, & I don't know now how many it is killed – 8 to 10 I should think. I feel sure you will be very welcome in the 6th, & that you will hear more than we are ever likely to. They did not say if he was buried or a mark put, or if any others near him. Naturally I long to hear something. His dear Joanna that he played & so loved, has May kept them – Perhaps we may hear from May soon, as the O.R says he is not amongst the wounded or missing – There is a Gdsman, Doyle by name, Mother at Bletchley, & he is a prisoner – So there may be others – I've been to see her, as she wrote to me – Well, this must be all for to-day, & I must now get down to J.D's letter. Very much love my dearest, & how I do wonder where you will be when this letter reaches you – would I could pop over with it. The swallows & cuckoo are here, & have come from you to us – Bless you. Your loving

Mother

Ascott Cottage. May 2, 1943
LETTER NO. 8

My dearest Peter –

This week we have had your telegram saying "All well, safe, all my love" – & right glad we were to get it – I am to-morrow posting a A. Letter – addressed to 6th. Br. 8th. Army Tripoli – I am doing this on the chance that you may get it quickly if you go on soon to the 6th. Its how Arthur told me to address him on A.L.C's only – But the copy of J.D's letter to Granny about Arthur goes in this envelope – & address as ordered by you.

Well the chief event of note is that the cat I borrowed to keep in the stables to keep the rats away, was discovered by Father, returning from H.G practise, having a kitten in *my* armchair in the sitting room!! Most unpleasant!! & I need hardly say, all Father did was to make awful faces & go away – while I acted quickly – with help of duster, removed the kitten, cat etc: to her box in the stables – Odd only having one – but lucky, as the damage was less! Perhaps there will be more by the morning!!! We believe J.D is commanding H.Q Coy now, & I address him as Major – I'm longing to hear that you two have met. I know he is longing for that day. It was such a cruel disappointment that Arthur & his long waited for meeting was not to be. He has written me such a wonderful letter, a copy of which you will get next week. Meanwhile Granny got this one enclosed, & was deeply touched by his understanding & thought for her. She is I am glad to say much better, & getting out in the garden. But alas the Land Army have taken Rowney – so the sale is off – She wants to live in a cottage there – but we don't think this is possible, owing to light, telephone & bath etc. not being possible to put in. I go there on Tues: 4th for the day, & stay the night at the Ritz, as Mary is to be in London for a 5 day course – She & I were in London on Wed, the day she returned to Purbright, & we & Father & Arthur Penn attended a short service at the Guards Chapel, when Arthur's name &

many others were read out. We were glad we went, & felt Arthur would have liked us to have been with the other relations of the men who fell with him. In the afternoon Mary & I went to the film "The Gentle Sex" all about the A.T.S. It is "FIRST RATE" Leslie Howard speaks or is what is called the commentator – I enjoyed it hugely – & we are going to take Father. Mary & I have strawed & netted the strawberries – & I am now busy picking bluebells – & selling them at the Post Office. We took over £8 worth of daffodils! Im now thinking of all we can sell, such as lavender etc – & shall grow stuff that sells well. There is *such* a demand. Lettuce & radishes I should think would sell. Wish I could have a shop – The war is going along nicely. Will you have a "pot at em" before they are pushed out of N. Africa? Father has got to learn to use a Sten gun one evening this week!! & he has got to carry it on the Parade on May 16th! as he hasn't got a revolver – !! Father thinks you will enjoy this picture of him. Well my dear, thats all for to-day. All our best love

Your loving Mother.

Sunday May 23rd. *Ascott Cottage.*

My dearest Peter. We have had your letter "At Sea" No. 3 when you were looking forward to seeing Uncle Douglas. You see we've had A.L.C. from you since you arrived at No. 2. I.T.D. [Infantry Training Depot] so this "at sea" letter was of a much earlier date. We are hugely amused with your future plan for running an hotel & dance band, & getting married etc. after the war. It made us laugh a lot! I'm glad Willson is not so bad a Grenadier as J.D took him to be. No doubt your influence has improved him. Fancy pink gins at 4d each!! & all the nicknames of all the travelling companions are very apt Im sure. Glad you made money over the Backgammon. It was a great rage at one time. We are longing to get your account of your time with the Buchanans.

Ive got one good bit of news. We need not demobilize our cars anymore! Such a blessing, & how Ive escaped being fined I can't think. Also its lovely to hear church bells every Sunday – & with sign posts up again we are getting almost pre War. Very encouraging getting things back, instead of having to do without. Still our rationing is just the same as when you were here, which I think remarkably good.

I went to Granny for 1 night, & we went over to Rowney to mark the furniture she wants at Ponters – She enjoyed the drive – as she has so little petrol, so gets very few drives. She has more difficulty in walking: getting in & out of the car – But in herself is much the same. She so enjoyed hearing about your Lido – & Wop band & waiters – Father is left for 1 month in command of the Coy. While Maj Morton has a holiday. So Father has fixed it up for the HG to have 2 weeks holiday! So he won't be over worked! We had "Wings for Victory Parade" in L.B. yesterday. Just the same manoeuvre as last year which you watched. Only this year we were a Red X Coy of 26 of our own – so I led it, & we fairly put out our chests & swung along when they clapped us! Unluckily it poured in the middle of the speech part. All our nurses in Caps & Aprons – so the police lent their capes – & very smart they looked. We had been drilled by a Sergent, & did better than I expected. I had words with the St John's man who insisted on going in front going. This is incorrect *"in War Time"* so I got in front for the march past!!! Well that is all I can get in – the letter & enclosures will go either Mon: or Tues: These Parades have put me behind. Very best love my darling Peter. Your lvg Mother.

Ascott Cottage. June 6 1943.

My dearest Peter. You will I hope get this by the same post as my letter answering your questions. Now here are my questions that I want answered! They are chiefly about Arthur –

(1) How soon was he found (date) & on what *date* were he & the others buried.

(2) How many of his Platoon were killed, or which of his special men are alive? We have a P.C of him taken with a football group. You may see a copy? Its very good. (I realize some questions may not be answerable!)

(3) There were 2 with him when the shell fell between them. Are either of these 2 who bound him up safe?

(4) Which Coy are you in, & is it the same as Arthur's – can read *your* A G's *easily* without Magnifying Glass.

You will I am sure pick up from time to time little bits about Arthur, & you will realize how interested we shall be. At first we were very upset only hearing from S. Gordon (hush, a *very* poor letter!) & then a very nice one from the C.O. but he was in Hospital out of touch. It was 6 weeks before the Adj. wrote. Naughty this – and Pat B has never written. May wrote after John had seen him (I sent you a copy – & a very nice letter it was) I am hoping that some of the men will tell you small details all of which we shall love to hear – We shall miss Arthur more & more as time goes on. Its difficult to realize that we shall never see him again. But some day Father & I hope to visit all N. Africa where our 3 G.G's have fought – N. Forbes says they were all buried in sight of their objective. I shall hope to go there some day. I'm glad they are all to-gether.

Thank you for remembering my birthday. The A.G. has come a few days early, well timed!

Now a few questions about yourself. Hope gippy tummy has settled down? Do you wear sun glasses? Are you brown? Hear the P.M. was out at Carthage – so hope you & J.D cheered him?? Is Handcock attentive? Do you want anything sent out? About on an average, how long do these A.L.C's take? I see Real Air Mail is now open to all N.A. so my Sunday ones with enclosures ought to be speeded up – I still do the regular Sunday one – tho' a shorter letter part. Its useful to send the copies, & reminds me how many weeks you've been away – Don't feel you can't write classics like J.D! nor can I!!! my telegraphic style is awful – but we can't all be so gifted. His letters are outstandingly good – But you are a *splendid* letter writer, & write such a lovely *lot* – & so often. So amused at your ride! & weekend in Cairo, & sailing – All sounded lovely – We wanted to go away for a week soon – but couldn't find rooms – Dont want to go where we've been all together, reminds one too much – But we hear Tenby, S. Wales is lovely – so Father & I may go for a week in latter July. May's leave is 16th. this month – we can't get rooms then – strawberries swelling! Very best love your lvg Mother.

Ascott Cottage. June 18 1943.

My dearest Peter. I am writing you two letters to-day, one to 6th, one the 3rd. For its been a most exciting 2 days. Yesterday a letter from J.D to say he'd tracked you down – & then one from you to-day (an ordinary letter, No. 7. Dated June 8th) which came in 10 days. *Wonderful.* You really are a most magnificent letter writer. We just live for the post – & you give us the greatest joy & pleasure writing so often, & such lovely long letters. I shall comment on the rest of your letter in my Sunday edition – but will send this off to-morrow so as to say thank you quickly – You have no idea how hugely it has helped that you have passed through the battlefield where Arthur did so grandly – & that you have seen his grave. Its given me untold comfort – & J.D feels the same. The fact that one of our happy family has "been that way" is very comforting – And you told me what I wanted to know – I can now picture it. Some day, if we & you are spared, we must visit the country our wonderful family has fought over – We do feel proud, very very proud – & I won't let you down by going around with a long face. No, we must hold our heads high – & I don't worry. You tell me not to. Well – this is how it is. I just put everything in Gods hands & mean to accept with courage whatever He plans for our future – And darling I thank God for all our blessings which are *many*, & thank for each day that passes without bad news – I don't look ahead too far – & go cheerfully about my work. I wouldn't let the side down by going around with a long face. But you can understand that here, so often, at every turn in fact, our tragic loss is brought home to us. This has its advantages & disadvantages. One sees the motor bike, the music room, the tree in which he shot a pigeon, everywhere in fact. Time will help – but one has got to face it that life can never be the same without Arthur. But how grateful we are that you & John have met, & I feel sure its been a comfort to you both. It must have been sad for you seeing Arthur's grave all alone – But I am sure you were glad to have been able to pay tribute to the memory of all those splendid heroes who gave their lives in such a gallant attack. All my love dearest Peter, you are a very dear helpful son, & I do thank you for your dear self so much. Bless you. Your lvng Mother.

Ascott Cottage. July 1st. 1943

My dearest Peter

Many Many Happy Returns of July 15th. To think that you will be 21! As these letters take 10 to 15 days it seems – I am writing you a birthday letter daily for a week, in the hopes that one of them will reach you on about the date! And it will tell you how MUCH you are in our thoughts – *What* a celebration we shall have, please God, when this job is done, & we can meet & drink to your coming of age – I suppose as we are all seperated for the 15th this year we must each do the best we can where ever we are. We shall get out a ½ Pt. Champagne & as its on a Thursday – doubtful if Mary can be with us – You will I hope have a special party amongst your brother officers. This very day we got your ALC of June 23rd. Quick isn't it – And your excellent suggestion that I send you some ALC's – This I will do, via Miss Cleaver at once – & put them in an envelope. I also hope to send off the stockings in a day or two. Uncle Johnny has offered to try & get them to you, so I may accept this offer – We've had photographs of the graves of Arthur's comrades – sent us by Lord Trenchard, & he's marked Arthur's grave –

Kind of him wasn't it? Also J.D has sent us a long letter describing it all, as he's been there & had it explained like you did. So we are very lucky to have had all this information – The only letter missing still is your one of all your time at the Cape. It may still turn up – I will go and see about the torch. When I am in London to-morrow – Bless you my darling. What wouldnt I give to have a sight of you – but we must not grumble. We must finish off this job first. All our love & blessings & *thank* you for such splendid & such frequent letters. Love from Mother.

Ascott Cottage. July 11 – 1943. Letter 17.

My dearest Peter,

Last weeks letter was so short, so I must do better this week, & will comment on all the information you gave me about Arthur – I am very glad to know the answers you sent. I had imagined it was about a fortnight before he was found. I am only *so very thankful* that he was found. There are 2 officers I believe who are still missing. Evelyn Major – & he has such a nice wife & 2 little girls. I believe a baby. I wonder if there has ever been any news of him? I am glad you are with Pat B – its a very good Coy – Arthur was always most enthusiastic about him. But did Arthur leave that Coy? & why did Sandy Gordon write, & not Pat. A does not appear to have been with his Platoon? This part Father & I have never got quite clear. One letter says he went back for the guns, & it was bringing them up when the shell fell that wounded him – After that we know all there is to know, & accept it – But we don't understand how it was that Pat. B. never wrote, & only Sandy G – No doubt you will be able to explain this – No hurry! but you can understand how every little scrap of detail is interesting – You will probably hear a little more when the two that tied him up return to the Br. You know, I don't say, if only so & so had happened – because I believe all is arranged, & not for us to question. I was upset to think he was left – alone, but *fully* realize that this has to be in war – I regret that I have not answered all the many lovely letters I've had. Over 100 still to be answered. I suppose I shall do it some day – but in the summer, there is so much to be done out of doors, that I have entirely failed to tackle it – Father says I need not answer them, but I feel very much that I want to. We have got rooms at Tenby, S. Wales for Aug. 10 for a week. It will be a great effort going away, but we must, so that Mrs Farrar gets a change – But we have heard that some Hotels have lately been taken by the Gov: so perhaps ours will be! How lovely your bathing sounds – I only hope you stayed there over your 21st so that you had the Omlettes & Wine feast! So the 2nd front & Invasion has begun – & so far so good. It is all very exciting. Father had to go & be "shot over" to-day, over at Mursley! You can imagine how agitated I was hearing Machine gun fire from here! & wondering if I should see him alive again!!! Great relief when he turned up with a good appetite for Lunch – You sound most content – You are a splendid calm & peaceful temperament, just like Father – don't fuss! But we were *very* interested on your views of Huns & Wops – & that you feel as I do that the best German is a dead one. I wish I could feel otherwise, but after all they started both the wars. Perhaps we deserve both, owing to our lack of moral courage. But its hard to understand. Anyway its clear now that we've got to smash all Nazi & Facist machinery & then try & build all Europe up on sound foundations – Well I think I have rambled on enough – Arthur Penn has said a letter can go more quickly if we give it to him next Tues. (13th) so we shall do this, & may be you'll get quite late news & perhaps I might put in a few A.L's – Very much love. Your loving, I mean Nancy & Mother!!

Ascott Cottage. July 15. 1943.

My darling Peter. 21 to-day! & its not rained yet – We've drunk your health in sherry for Luncheon, & are opening something for dinner. Father has taken the day off & has *alas*, smoked 4 cigarettes – Pity as he had entirely lost his cough – To return to drink – ! Father has bought a Magnum of Brandy! money went to Red X. Hush Hush as to what he paid for it! But it stands in the corner cupboard in the dining room, ready for celebrating (2) peace (1) victory – & I hope it won't have to stand there too many years – I'm hoping you are able to have your party to-day, & celebrate properly such an important day. We have not decided what to drink to-night yet. We shall also drink to "the Major" as Mary has had a letter from J.D saying he is a Major, but I'm not addressing him as such until I hear it from him, himself. Arthur Penn told us that the King was furious at being flashed past his Grenadiers at such a pace. *Too* bad.

I went to see the room in the Nursing Home for Granny before she went in. Asked for the Matron, who took me up, showed me the room, we discussed prices, etc. I then admired the colour of the rooms etc. "Yes," she said. "its my home, Im the Matron, Princess Arthur of Connaught, you know –" Democratic? We shall not be able to make a row if Mother isn't comfortable!! We go up for day to-morrow, & Mary meets us at Wilton's for Luncheon, where we shall again drink to ''Pete, bless him'' Its been good having all this excuse for drinking! We general[ly] have Lobster or Crab at Wilton's, sherry & lots of brown bread & butter, then very good biscuits & cheese. One of the best Luncheons in London I think – none of your starvation meals like at the Ritz, when we had to go on to the Savoy to satisfy our hunger. Well, well, I must rush to put this in the box by 4.30 PM. All our love & blessings. Your loving Mother.

NOTES

MARGARET PASTON

1. Margaret of Anjou, Queen of Henry VI, alarmed at the report of the approach of Edward Earl of March (son to the Duke of York) towards London with a great power, endeavoured to make what friends she could; and amongst other places, on her journey for that purpose, visited Norwich.
2. Windlasses, for drawing the bow-string home.
3. An arrow with a square head.
4. This letter has no direction, and lest it should be opened, the paper which fastens the seal is, along the edge, marked with lines by a pen which communicates with the latter, so the reader might easily discern any attempts to open it, as the lines would then not exactly coincide again. On the back of it, but in a later hand, is written, 'A lre, to J. Paston, ar. from his wife.'

HONOR LISLE

1. boisterous.
2. i.e. the Earls of Hertford and Bridgewater.
3. An estate in Gloucestershire, inherited by Lord Lisle through his first wife.

BRILLIANA HARLEY

1. Scholastic exercises at Oxford.
2. Early in May the Commons issued their ordinance for raising the militia, which the King commanded his subjects not to obey.
3. The House of Commons had recently made an order for the bringing in of money, horses and plate. Sir Robert later responded to the order by bringing in 350 pounds in plate, with a promise of 150 pounds more, and two horses.
4. Dr Wright had been actively engaged in trying to get Edward Harley made a burgess for the city of Hereford.
5. This letter was written on cloth for easier concealment about the messenger's person. Later letters in this last series to her son are coded.
6. William Marquis of Hertford had been appointed Lord Lieutenant-General for the King's troops for much of the West Country, from Oxford to Cornwall.
7. In the propositions for peace presented from the Parliament to the King at Oxford in January 1642–3, and in those sent back by the Commissioners to the Parliament, one was, that there be a cessation of arms during the treaty. The treaty was still in debate. The Commissioners were eventually recalled to London in April 1643.

QUEEN HENRIETTA MARIA

1. This is a pseudonym, and not necessarily for a woman.
2. Sir John Hotham, Governor of Hull.
3. The Earl of Northumberland, Lord High Admiral, had appointed the Earl of Warwick as his Deputy, in opposition to Charles, who wished the royalist Sir John Pennington to be appointed.
4. Will Murray came over to Holland in May, and was entrusted with confidential business between the King and Queen.
5. Parliament's envoy Walter Strickland made constant trouble for the Royalists and annoyed old Sir William Boswell, who had represented King Charles in Holland for fifteen years.
6. Alluding to the liberation of the Dutch from Spanish rule, with the assistance of Queen Elizabeth.
7. Charles Louis, Elector Palatine, then at the Hague.
8. Sir Hugh Cholmley, governor of Scarborough, gave up the fortress to the Royalists. He had been appointed by Parliament, and his defection came after some months of heart-searching and doubt.
9. A pardon was offered in it to all who would put themselves under the royal protection at Oxford. – Perfect Diurnal, 3 July.
10. Probably William Cavendish, Marquis of Newcastle, trying to defend the North against the Scottish army of Covenanters, and unable to get as much military assistance from the King as he asked for.

FRANCES NELSON

1. Sir Andrew Hammond was Comptroller of the Navy, 1794–1806.
2. Admiral Viscount Samuel Hood.
3. Nelson's sister Catherine, married to George Matcham.
4. Nelson's servant and coxswain, Frank Lepee.
5. Captain Molloy, of the *Glory*, was dismissed from his ship for not taking up proper station in the battle of June 1.
6. Daughter of the President of Nevis, and Fanny's cousin.
7. John Stanley, Attorney General of Nevis.
8. Captain Andrew Sutherland, who had served in the West Indies with Nelson, was appointed Commissioner at Gibraltar in 1794.
9. Lady Northesk, the niece of Sir John Jervis, married William Carnegie, later Admiral Lord Northesk.
10. Nelson's sister Susannah.
11. Sister of Sir John Jervis and mother of Lady Northesk.
12. Lady Bickerton was Miss Ann Athill.
13. The account by Colonel John Drinkwater, who had been deputy judge-advocate in Corsica. In his *Narrative of the Battle of St. Vincent*, Drinkwater praised Nelson's services, which he considered had been underestimated.
14. Lady Elliot.
15. The Duke of Hamilton, brother of Lady Derby.
16. Mr. William Bolton.
17. Lady Spenser.
18. Nelson's niece, twin sister to Catherine Bolton.
19. A sailor from the *Agamemnon* whose conduct was specially mentioned by Nelson on February 14, 1797.
20. Wrongly dated for 1800.
21. Sir John Orde challenged Lord St. Vincent to a duel, which was refused.
22. Lieutenant Edward Parker, one of Nelson's protégés, had been sent to Vienna

with dispatches from the King of Naples and thence to England. He was promoted captain and died of wounds after the attack on the French flotilla at Boulogne in September 1801.

23. Captain James Oswald, sent to England with Nelson's dispatches after the liberation of Naples; died 1822.

24. This letter, addressed to Nelson at Alexander Davison's house, was returned to Lady Nelson with a note by Davison, a friend of Nelson's: 'Opened by mistake by Lord Nelson, but not read. A. Davison.'

FANNY BURNEY

1. James Burney's son Martin was Fanny's solicitor.
2. The d'Arblays' housekeeper.
3. Her father, Dr. Charles Burney, had died in April 1814.
4. Probably because Fanny Burney had heard rumours that the King would leave Bruges for Ghent on the following day.
5. A reference to Belgians who had armed themselves on first hearing of Napoleon's return & his apparently imminent attack on Belgium. They were mobilized on 22 March but the rapid concentration of allied forces made it possible for the Belgian Guard to be disarmed.
6. The princess d'Hénin, with whom Fanny Burney had fled Paris.
7. Refers to a letter from the princess dated 13 March.
8. To less sympathetic observers the serenity of Louix XVIII seemed more like inertia or incapacity.
9. On their arrival in Bordeaux on 5 March the duc and duchesse d'Angoulême were greeted with the news of Napoleon's landing and of the duc's appointment to command the right wing of the royal army under his father. The duchesse remained in Bordeaux whilst the duc went to Nîmes on 10 March in an attempt to raise an army to hold Provence and Languedoc for the King.
10. Before Napoleon's appearance the companies of the Gardes du Corps were in turn posted inside the rooms of the Palace of the Tuileries, which during the Restoration was known always to the courtiers by the name Fanny Burney uses here, the 'Château'.
11. Many others declined. We know from another participant that very few of the troops in the 'compagnies rouges' assembled as ordered for the march. Even among the Gardes du Corps only a little over half left Paris during the night of 19–20 March.
12. On the journey from England to France in December 1814, M. d'Arblay had been run down by a cart and struck in the chest.
13. This was William I, King of the Netherlands. Forced to take refuge in England in 1794, he became Sovereign Prince of the United Provinces in 1813. Crowned King on 18 March 1815, he had first to assure himself of the loyalty of his people, especially the Belgians, who little welcomed the forced unification with Holland.
14. After Napoleon's return to the Tuileries the troopers of his cavalry escort were forced by a shortage of barracks to hitch their horses in the Place de Carrousel and sleep there under their cloaks. This gave that part of Paris the look of a bivouac in a city taken by assault. During the following days many more troops who had marched to the capital and could not find space in barracks were assigned temporary billets in the prosperous neighbourhoods near the Tuileries.
15. Wellington accepted the offered command of the allied army on 25 March 1815. Fanny Burney hoped that he would lead his army immediately into France, thereby provoking Napoleon's overthrow at the hands of his own subjects.

Wellington was less sanguine, however, judging it impossible to take the offensive before 10 or 15 May.

16. To forestall Fanny Burney's uneasiness in writing, Princess Elizabeth had directed in her letter of 13 March that a reply could be sent in the care of Stephen Rolleston, chief clerk, office of the Secretary of State, Foreign Affairs, Downing Street.

17. The 'English Minister' was Sir Charles Stuart, diplomat, at that time British Minister at The Hague.

18. A false report – in fact Napoleon reached the palace at Fontainebleau on the morning of 20 March.

19. Marie-Victor-Nicolas de Fay Latour-Maubourg formed a detachment of mounted volunteers while the octogenarian Marshal Vioménil raised infantry volunteers in the last days before the King's flight from Paris. Both detachments were meant to hold the Château of Vincennes for the King. The Governor of the Château found Vioménil's two battalions, most of them students, a pathetic force, *'marmots incapable de tenir un fusil'*.

20. Joseph-Hyacinth-Charles du Houx, marquis de Vioménil, who had been one of the great nobles and leading generals of the *ancien régime*, was notable even in the Restoration for the rigidity and arrogance of his views. Even though his service after he emigrated in 1791 had been chiefly in the Russian and Portuguese armies and although he had not served at all while in England from 1802 until 1814, he insisted on his return to France in 1814 that he should not only be made a marshal at the age of 80 but also that his promotion should be pre-dated to give him seniority over all of Napoleon's marshals.

21. This refers literally to the constant rain that turned the roads to the north into quagmires and figuratively to the swamps of confusion and frustration that trapped so many members of the *Maison du Roi*.

22. Fanny Burney is here translating the French military term for the discharge or disbanding of troops.

23. Esther Burney's daughters.

24. Matthew Gregory Lewis, author of *The Monk,* owed money to Dr. Charles Burney at the time of his death.

25. This was the first sounding of the alarm at Brussels.

26. Departure to Antwerp was also the safest course in Wellington's eyes, and he proposed it to an English lady in a note written just before Waterloo.

27. Actually Sunday 18 June, the day of Waterloo.

28. Fanny Burney's change of name and omission of her address were intended to conceal her identity as the wife of an active royalist.

29. A further step to avoid detection in the event of a French victory.

30. The napoleon was a gold coin worth 20 francs, which at the exchange rates of the time equalled 16 shillings. Fanny Burney had therefore only £8 with which to make her escape from Brussels, where all the banks had closed and where widespread panic and requisitioning had made horses, carriages and boats both scarce and expensive.

31. Burney means that M. d'Arblay will be able to get money by drawing on their bankers in England if Brussels falls and Louix XVIII's court leaves Ghent.

32. Apart from the noise, shock waves from the Waterloo cannonade were strong enough to break window-panes in some Brussels houses.

33. Frederick William, Duke of Brunswick and kinsman of the British royal family, had been shot in the chest and killed at the Battle of Quatre Bras on 16 June.

34. Wellington's medical officers were forced by the heavy casualties at Quatre Bras and Waterloo to start at once to evacuate wounded by barge to Antwerp. The Brussels hospitals were inadequate and the roads were clogged by refugees, deserters, and advancing troops.

35.   There were in fact roughly 8,000 French prisoners captured at Waterloo, but Burney is probably right about the number who reached Brussels on the night of the battle.

36.   This was a false report, though it was, according to Wellington's later comments on Waterloo, the manoeuvre that Napoleon should have attempted.

37.   'Unravelled linen' or lint used in making bandages, a task that many ladies in Brussels took on themselves. Burney's old friend Mme de Tessé had prepared charpie for use in Fanny Burney's mastectomy in 1811.

38.   These trophies, which on 19 June Wellington promised to send to the Prince Regent, were among the first to be displayed after Waterloo.

39.   This was a see-saw battle between the French and the Prussians that lasted throughout 18 and 19 June, when the news of disaster at Waterloo forced Grouchy to retreat through Gembloux to Namur while the remnants of Napoleon's main force retreated through Genappe to Charleroi.

40.   Only Blücher and the Prussians continued the pursuit during the night of 18–19 June. Wellington's army was exhausted and his cavalry had been virtually destroyed by repeated charges.

41.   Kleist von Nollendorf, whose civilized views were, as Fanny Burney suggests, a contrast to more vengeful Prussians, who regarded the war as against France itself rather than to depose Napoleon, and wanted to divide the country into the regional kingdoms that resulted from the collapse of the Carolingian empire.

42.   The duc de Feltre.

43.   In a General Order of 20 June, Wellington, after briefly thanking his troops for their service at Waterloo, reverted to his more usual stern tones to provide for the wounded, order the return of all absentees and deserters, reminding his soldiers that 'their Sovereigns are in alliance with the King of France and that France therefore must be considered as a friendly country'.

44.   Burney means that she has managed to send a letter to Princess Elizabeth at Frogmore, despite the departure of Sir Charles Stuart.

45.   Lille was famous during this period for its strong royalist leanings, but in the event Louis XVIII bypassed Lille and entered France by way of Bavay and Cambrai.

46.   Until lately the Belgian regiments were in fact part of the French army, and the change of government had not yet been followed by a change of uniform.

47.   This is only a slight overstatement. The Imperial Guard suffered heavy casualties.

48.   This bulletin, dated 15 June from Charleroi and published in the *Moniteur* on the 18th, was, given its date and place, a fairly accurate statement of Napoleon's position and opening success.

49.   M. d'Arblay's earlier and ambitious notion was that Fanny Burney would maintain contact with the courtiers in Brussels and Ghent, thereby encouraging his advancement. Burney's exposure to the malicious intrigues around Louis XVIII had convinced her that she would be better off at Trèves.

50.   *L'Oracle,* the Brussels daily newspaper.

51.   Although Napoleon had abdicated in favour of his son on 22 June and the French provisional government wrote to Wellington three days later to ask that he be allowed to go into exile in the United States, there had been no surrender and no direct communication between Napoleon and Wellington.

52.   Eugène-Rose de Beauharnais, son of the Empress Josephine.

53.   Fanny Burney here compresses Bourzac's report, itself pieced together from the *Moniteur* and the *Journal d'Empire,* on the stormy sessions in both Chambers (of deputies and peers) of 21–24 June.

54.   Louis XVIII's proclamation of 25 June, a paternal announcement of his return

that included promises of rewards for the good and punishment for the guilty.

55. The household troops, together with the units of royal volunteers, had in fact followed the King.

56. In a letter written by Fanny Burney to her husband on 29 May she reported: 'M. de Lally is here. I saw him this morning. Some of his Manifestos were sent to Lille, & received with applause: – but the bearer was discovered – & shot!' It was a manifesto in favour of Louis XVIII.

57. The conflicting factions within France and around Louis XVIII.

58. Louis XVIII's Proclamation from Cambrai of 28 June, drafted and countersigned by Tallyrand, repudiated his earlier unforgiving manifesto and outraged the *ultras* by admitting past mistakes.

59. Accompanied by a small staff, Napoleon left Malmaison for Rochefort at nine o'clock on the morning of 29 June.

60. Most of the Belgian and Dutch troops fought bravely at both Quatre Bras and Waterloo, and those regiments that collapsed were more victims of the Prince of Orange's tactical stupidity than cowards or traitors.

61. Fanny Burney here adapts the line 'Teach me to feel another's Woe' from Pope's 'Universal Prayer'.

62. Fervently royalist, but with overtones of delirium.

63. Mme de Maisonneuve, sister of César de Latour-Maubourg, who had been named as one of Napoleon's pairs des Cent-Jours, and Victor, who remained staunchly royalist.

64. Scott's successful first novel was published anonymously in 1814.

65. The 'Cabinet Littéraire' in the Marché au bois.

66. Mrs Waddington had three surviving daughters. Emelie was in poor health. Augusta, the youngest, was at this time only 13 years old.

67. Napoleon reached Rochefort on 3 July, but took no part in the retreat of his former troops, who were regrouped as the Army of the Loire by 10 July and ordered by the terms of the military armistice of 3 July to remain south of the river. Louis XVIII had already dismissed from his service *'tous officiers et soldats passés sous le commandement de Napoléon Bonaparte et de ses adherents'*. The decree disbanding the old army (and creating a new one loyal to the Bourbons) was not signed until 16 July and not made public until 12 August.

FLORENCE NIGHTINGALE

1. Lady Maria Forester (d. 1894) was an Evangelical widow who devoted herself to philanthropy.

2. Lord Clarendon, George William Frederick Villiers (1800–70), was Secretary of Foreign Affairs in Lord Aberdeen's government.

3. Lord Palmerston, Henry John Temple (1784–1865), was Home Secretary in Lord Aberdeen's government; he became Prime Minister in January 1855 when Aberdeen's government fell.

4. Lord Stratford (1786–1880) was the British Ambassador to Turkey.

5. Dr Andrew Smith (1797–1872) was Director-General, Army and Ordnance Medical Departments (1853–58). He was a frequent opponent of many of Florence Nightingale's reforms, but he had warned the Horse Guards early on about the unhealthy conditions in the Crimea. When they failed to take his advice, he was left to deal with the consequences.

6. Sidney Herbert (1810–61), Lord Herbert of Lea, was Secretary-at-War under Aberdeen. He was Honorary Secretary of the Nightingale Fund, Chair of the Royal Commission on the Health of the Army, the Indian Sanitary Commission, and of the four sub-commissions on army sanitary matters. He asked his friend Florence Nightingale to lead a group of nurses to serve officially

in army hospitals in the Crimea.

7.   Angela Burdett-Coutts (1814–1906) was one of the wealthiest women in England. She was a distinguished philanthropist who promoted education, housing and improved sanitation for the working class, as well as the reform of prostitutes.

8.   The Duke of Newcastle, Henry Pelham F.P. Clinton (1811–64), Secretary for War in Aberdeen's government. When out of office in 1855 he visited the Crimea to investigate conditions.

9.   William Bowman (1816–92) was a distinguished opthalmic surgeon at King's College Hospital. From 1848, he was professor of physiology and general and morbid anatomy. He was knighted in 1884. He had attended the patients at the Harley Street hospital. He was also a leader in the founding of the High Church St John's House, which had supplied several nurses.

10.   Henry Bence Jones, MD (1814–73), was a physician and chemist at St. George's Hospital, a specialist in urine, kidney and diabetic diseases.

11.   The God of Thunder.

12.   Blind strike.

13.   Dr. Thomas Spence, Deputy Inspector General of Army Hospitals, drowned aboard the *Prince,* Balaclava Bay, 14 November 1854.

14.   Dr. Alexander Cumming was appointed Inspector-General of Army Hospitals in the East, 27 October 1854.

15.   Lord Napier, Robert Cornelis Napier (1819–98), was Secretary at the British Embassy in Constantinople. Later, as Governor of Madras (1866–72), he corresponded with Florence Nightingale about sanitation, irrigation and public works.

16.   Her pet owl, who had died from neglect during her preparation for the East.

17.   When the Sultan of Turkey granted permission for a British military cemetery at Scutari, Nightingale was asked to recommend a suitable memorial.

18.   Nicholas 1 of Russia died 2 March 1855. The British hoped that his successor, Alexander II, would be more willing to negotiate peace on their terms.

19.   Not in Florence Nightingale's handwriting; the letter was probably copied and circulated among friends.

20.   Pastor Fliedner ran a school for nurses in Kaiserswerth, Germany, and Florence Nightingale had received a brief training there less than two years before going to the Crimea.

21.   Alexis Soyer, a French chef.

22.   Sir John McNeill (1795–1883) was a diplomat and doctor. In 1855 he was sent to the Crimea with Colonel Alexander Tulloch to report on the management of the commissariat and its methods of keeping accounts, and delays in distribution.

23.   Florence Nightingale used a long dash for the sergeant's name.

24.   The letter breaks off here.

25.   Written by Miss Nightingale's aunt Mrs Smith, signed by Florence Nightingale.

26.   Taken the advantage.

27.   Sir Richard Airey (1803–81) was Quartermaster-General to the Crimean Army until November 1855.

28.   Filder was Commissary-General at Scutari. He defended himself against the allegations of incompetence put forward by McNeill and Tulloch in *The Commissariat in the Crimea* (1856) in which he claimed that the only major difficulty was a lack of hay for the horses.

29.   Lord Cardigan, James Thomas Brudenel (1797–1868), notorious for his quick temper, led the disastrous 'Charge of the Light Brigade'.

30.   Dr. John Hall: Inspector-General of the Hospitals in the Crimea, with whom Florence Nightingale was constantly at odds.

31. We have forgotten nothing and learned nothing.
32. Bishop Southwark, Thomas Grant (1816–70), the first Roman Catholic Bishop of Southwark, was known for his learning and zeal on behalf of the poor.
33. It is good that this is so.
34. Sir James Graham (1792–1861), as First Lord of the Admiralty, was blamed by Admiral Sir Charles Napier (1786–1860) for not supplying him with sufficient gunboats after he had boasted of what the navy could accomplish in the Baltic. Napier, in turn, was accused of poor leadership, due to a capricious humour and intemperance.
35. Lord Henry Hardinge (1785–1856) was widely blamed for the lack of preparation on the part of the military in the Crimean War. Lord Panmure had taken over from Sidney Herbert early in 1855.
36. Kars was one of the two main Ottoman army bases. It fell to the Russians on 25 November 1855 when the Allies failed to supply military assistance.

QUEEN VICTORIA

1. Feodore, Princess of Hohenlohe-Langenburg, Queen Victoria's half-sister.
2. There had been an assassination attempt on Napoleon's life on the 7th.
3. Only son of the Prince of Prussia, afterwards Emperor.

CHARLOTTE CANNING

1. The Princess Royal married Frederick of Prussia in January 1858.

MARIA (MINNIE) WOOD

1. A screen or mat, usually made of the roots of the fragrant cuscus grass, placed in door and window frames, and kept wet, in order to keep rooms cool.

ISABEL GORE

1. General Piet Cronje and his troops surrendered to Lord Roberts on 27 February 1900. Ladysmith was relieved by Buller's troops on 28 February.
2. The sister to whom Isabel Gore was writing was the wife of James Heath, who was elected Conservative member for North-West Staffordshire in the autumn election of 1900.
3. The enclosed newspaper cutting reads: 'Great and wanton destruction is reported done to English property round Kuruman by rebels under Fieldcornet Van der Byl. Even fruit trees have been destroyed in the gardens. All English residents have been heavily commandeered in the shape of stock.'
4. For the recovery of unpaid rents.
5. A reference to the Boxer Rebellion.
6. General Sir Redvers Buller sailed for England on 24 October, and was sacked from the army at the request of Lord Roberts. There had been a running feud between the two generals throughout the war.
7. Queen Victoria's soldier grandson Prince Christian Victor died of typhoid in Pretoria.
8. Lord Roberts' daughter Aileen, who nearly died of typhoid.
9. General Christiaan De Wet.
10. Presumably a reference to the concentration camps set up by the British. The scandal of the appalling conditions in the camps was to be exposed by Emily Hobhouse, and her findings confirmed by Millicent Fawcett's Commission.

BABBS VAN DER BYL

1. Sir Alfred, later Lord Milner, High Commissioner for South Africa (1897–1905) and Governor of Cape Colony (1897–1901).
2. Her husband had been badly wounded, and his condition is frequently mentioned by both Babbs and her sister Isabel.
3. Col. R.S.S. Baden-Powell, hero of Mafeking, later to become founder of the Boy Scout movement. He was always referred to by his initials, B.P.